Genre Analysis

THE CAMBRIDGE APPLIED LINGUISTICS SERIES

Series editors

2007–present: Carol A. Chapelle and Susan Hunston

1988–2007: Michael H. Long and Jack C. Richards

Publications in this series:

Cognition and Second Language Instruction *edited by Peter Robinson*
Computer Applications in Second Language Acquisition *by Carol A. Chapelle*
Contrastive Rhetoric *by Ulla Connor*
Corpora in Applied Linguistics *by Susan Hunston*
Criterion-referenced Language Testing *by James Dean Brown and Thom Hudson*
Critical Pedagogies in Language Learning *by Bonny Norton and Kelleen Toohey*
Culture in Second Language Teaching and Learning *edited by Eli Hinkel*
Exploring the Dynamics of Second Language Writing *edited by Barbara Kroll*
Exploring the Second Language Mental Lexicon *by David Singleton*
Feedback in Second Language Writing *edited by Ken Hyland and Fiona Hyland*
Focus on Form in Classroom Second Language Acquisition *edited by Catherine Doughty and Jessica Williams*
Immersion Education: International Perspectives *edited by Robert Keith Johnson and Merrill Swain*
Insights into Second Language Reading: A Cross-Linguistic Approach *by Keiko Koda*
Interfaces Between Second Language Acquisition and Language Testing Research *edited by Lyle F. Bachman and Andrew D. Cohen*
Learning Vocabulary in Another Language *by I.S.P. Nation*
Network-based Language Teaching *edited by Mark Warschauer and Richard Kern*
Pragmatics in Language Teaching *edited by Kenneth R. Rose and Gabriele Kasper*
Research Genres: Explorations and Applications *by John M. Swales*
Research Perspectives on English for Academic Purposes *edited by John Flowerdew and Matthew Peacock*
Researching and Applying Metaphor *edited by Lynne Cameron and Graham Low*
Second Language Vocabulary Acquisition *edited by James Coady and Thomas Huckin*
Sociolinguistics and Language Teaching *edited by Sandra Lee McKay and Nancy H. Hornberger*
Task-Based Language: From Theory to Practice *edited by Susan Hunston*
Teacher Cognition in Language Teaching: Beliefs, Decision-Making, and Classroom Practice *by Devon Woods*
Text, Role, and Context *by Ann M. Johns*
Understanding, Expertise in Teaching: Case Studies of Language Teacher Development *by Amy B. M. Tsui*

Genre Analysis

English in academic and research settings

John M. Swales
The University of Michigan, Ann Arbor

This title was published under the series editorship
of Michael H. Long and Jack C. Richards

CAMBRIDGE UNIVERSITY PRESS
Cambridge, New York, Melbourne, Madrid, Cape Town, Singapore, São Paulo, Delhi

Cambridge University Press
The Edinburgh Building, Cambridge CB2 8RU, UK

www.cambridge.org
Information on this title: www.cambridge.org/9780521338134

First published 1990
13th printing 2008

Printed in the United Kingdom at the University Press, Cambridge

A catalogue record for this publication is available from the British Library

Library of Congress Cataloguing in Publication data
Swales, John.
Genre analysis.

(Cambridge applied linguistics series).
1. English language – Study and teaching (Higher) –
Foreign speaker. 2. Interdisciplinary approach in
education. I. Title. II. Series.
PE1128.A2S93 1990   428'.0071'1   90-2464

British Library Cataloguing in Publication data
Swales, John M. (John Malcolm), 1938–

Genre analysis: English in academic and research settings. –
(The Cambridge applied linguistics series).
1. English language. Analysis
I. Title
428

ISBN 978-0-521-33813-4 paperback

Contents

Series Editors' Preface   vii
Thanks   ix
Acknowledgements   xi

PART I   PRELIMINARIES   1

1   *Genre analysis – setting the scene*   1
    1.1   Aims and purposes   1
    1.2   Outline of the book   8
    1.3   Origins and influences   13

PART II   KEY CONCEPTS   21

2   *The concept of discourse community*   21
    2.1   A need for clarification   21
    2.2   Speech communities and discourse communities   23
    2.3   A conceptualization of discourse community   24
    2.4   An example of a discourse community   27
    2.5   Remaining issues   29

3   *The concept of genre*   33
    3.1   Genre in folklore studies   34
    3.2   Genre in literary studies   36
    3.3   Genre in linguistics   38
    3.4   Genre in rhetoric   42
    3.5   A working definition of genre   45
    3.6   Pre-genres   58
    3.7   Differences among genres   61

4   *The concept of task*   68
    4.1   Task and academic English programs   68
    4.2   Towards a concept of task   73
    4.3   A pedagogical illustration   77

5   *Genres, schemata and acquisition*   83

PART III RESEARCH-PROCESS GENRES   93

6   *The role of English in research*   96
   6.1   General perspectives   96
   6.2   Individual perspectives   102

7   *Research articles in English*   110
   7.1   Episodes in the history of the research article   110
   7.2   The constructing of research articles   117
   7.3   Textual overview of the research article   127
   7.4   Introductions   137
   7.5   Methods   166
   7.6   Results, Discussions and Conclusions   170
   7.7   Review   174

8   *Observations on other research-process genres*   177
   8.1   Abstracts   179
   8.2   Research presentations   182
   8.3   Grant proposals   186
   8.4   Theses and dissertations   187
   8.5   Reprint requests   189

PART IV APPLICATIONS   202

9   *Orientations*   203
   9.1   Individual case work   203
   9.2   Rhetorical consciousness – course content   213
   9.3   Alternative uses of discourse community   217
   9.4   Reflections on the 'process' approach to writing   220

10   *Exhibits*   222

11   *Epilogue*   232

References   235
Index   255
Author index   255
Subject index   259

Series Editors' Preface

The role of language in academic settings is of vital interest to all those concerned with tertiary education, including students, teachers, researchers, employers, and publishers. Recurring concerns focus on such issues as the rhetorical styles and discourse types employed in such settings – whether these are unique to a given language or culture or reflect universal modes of academic discourse – and how such norms can be effectively taught, both to native and non-native language users.

In order to investigate these and related issues, however, a theoretical framework is required which defines the scope and nature of academic discourse and which offers an approach to how it can be described and investigated. This is the goal of the present book, in which John Swales provides an approach to the understanding of academic discourse. Central to his book are the concepts of discourse community, genre, and language-learning task. Discourse communities, such as academic groupings of various kinds, are recognized by the specific genres that they employ, which include both speech events and written text types. The work that members of the discourse community are engaged in involves the processing of tasks which reflect specific linguistic, discoursal and rhetoric skills.

With this framework, Swales is able to offer a model which is both descriptively powerful but, at the same time, applicable to practical situations, such as the teaching of advanced composition and the teaching of English for Academic Purposes. Swales selects for particular analysis, a number of text types which are problematic in tertiary education, namely the academic research paper and other research related genres. He notes that since English is the world's major language for the communication of research findings, the ability to write research papers is a major goal of tertiary education. He describes a number of options for addressing the pedagogic issues involved, and sets his discussion against a description of how the field of genre analysis has evolved, drawing on work from several different disciplines.

Genre Analysis thus adds to our understanding of how language is used within an important discourse community, and is a model of applied linguistics in its best sense – it draws on linguistic and sociolinguistic theory to clarify the nature of language use and language learning in an educational setting.

Michael H. Long
Jack C. Richards

Thanks

During the slow and often interrupted evolution of this book I have accumulated many debts, only a proportion of which I have space to acknowledge here. Via conversation or correspondence or both, I am particularly indebted to the following: Patricia Bizzell, Eleanor McKenna and Patricia Rounds for discussions of discourse community; Charles Bazerman, Tony Becher, Vijay Bhatia, Catharine Cooper, Betty Lou Dubois, Tony Dudley-Evans, Daniel Horowitz, Carolyn Miller, Leslie Olsen, Patricia Radecki and Larry Selinker for adding to my notion of genre; Graham Crookes, Carolyn Madden and Dermot Murphy for their critiques of the section on task; Ann Johns, Ulla Connor and Liz Hamp-Lyons for valuable assistance with schema theory; and Richard Baldauf and Bjorn Jernudd for the generous way in which they have shared their ongoing work on the role of English as an international research language.

I would also like here to acknowledge the valuable commentaries provided by the two anonymous reviewers of Cambridge University Press and to thank the series co-editor Jack Richards for his forbearance and counsel. I owe the greatest debt, however, to Liz Hamp-Lyons, Ann Johns and Dennis Preston, who each took the considerable trouble to give the draft manuscript a very close and very educated reading.

While I believe that all of those mentioned have contributed to an improved final manuscript, none is, of course, responsible for remaining weaknesses.

I also owe much to my students. A first debt is to those on the M.Sc in Teaching English for Specific Purposes at the University of Aston, UK, with whom I first began working out my ideas on applied genre analysis in 1983–4. Since then I have gained much from the observations, comments and papers of students on both undergraduate and graduate courses in discourse analysis at The University of Michigan. Of at least equal importance has been the willing participation over many years of students taking experimental courses in English for Academic Purposes. Among these shaping experiences a particularly significant one has been the recent opportunity to teach a course in dissertation and proposal writing for non-native speakers.

I am also very grateful to Patricia Aldridge and Eva Stahlheber of the English Language Institute Library for their help in tracking down references, and to my secretary, Rosemary Tackabery, for her patience and her professionalism in the long process of creating the final manuscript.

Finally, I am deeply beholden to Vi Benner – for her encouragement, especially in times of uncertainty, for her continued belief in the value of the enterprise, and for her acceptance of the disruptions and distractions that writing a book in a small house has entailed.

John Swales
Ann Arbor, June 1989.

Acknowledgements

The author and publishers would like to thank the following for permission to reproduce copyright material:

Basic Books, Inc., *Local Knowledge* by Clifford Geertz (1983: pp. 7 and 155) on p. 19; Utah State University Press, *Folk Groups and Folklore Genres: An Introduction* edited by Elliott Oring (1986: pp. 134–5) on p. 35; Michael Swan and Catherine Walter, 'The Use of Sensory Deprivation in Foreign Language Teaching' in *ELT Journal* Vol. 36 (1982: p. 183) on p. 48; Basil Blackwell, *Philosophical Investigations* by Ludwig Wittgenstein (1958: p. 31–2) on p. 50; David Edge, Roy McLeod and Sage Publications, 'National scientific strategies in tropical soil sciences' by Rigas Arvanitis and Yvon Chatelin in *Social Studies of Science* Vol. 18, Number 1 (1988: pp. 118–19) on p. 108; Cambridge University Press, *Opening Pandora's Box* by G. N. Gilbert and M. Mulkay (1984: p. 56) on p. 123; Baywood Publishing Company, Inc., 'A rhetoric for research in sciences and technologies' by J. P. Zappen in *New Essays in Technical and Scientific Communication* edited by P. V. Anderson, R. J. Brockman and C. R. Miller (1983: Figure 7, p. 210) on p. 139; American Institute of Aeronautics and Astronautics, 'High Angle-of-Attack Calculations of the Subsonic Vortex Flow in Slender Bodies' by D. Almosino in *AIAA Journal* Vol. 23, Number 8 (1985: p. 1150) reprinted with permission on p. 143; Gregory West and TESOL: for the extract from 'That-Nominal Constructions in Traditional Rhetorical Divisions of Scientific Research Papers' by Gregory West, 1980, *TESOL Quarterly*, 14, p. 484. Copyright 1980 by TESOL. Reprinted with permission on p. 169; Institute of Physics Publishing Ltd, *J. Phys. C: Solid State Physics* Vol. 14, Number 12 by S. Kelham and H. H. Rosenburgh (1981: p. 1737) on p. 214; The British Council, for the extract adapted from 'Seminar Overview' by Kenneth James in *ELT Documents 109* edited by G. M. Greenall and J. E. Price (1980: p. 7) on pp. 223–4.

PART I PRELIMINARIES

1 Genre analysis – setting the scene

1.1 Aims and purposes

The main aim of this book is to offer an approach to the teaching of academic and research English. The approach develops and makes use of three key concepts: discourse community, genre and language-learning task. While all three terms have extensive contemporary currency, all three suffer from variable and uncertain usage. One of the book's purposes therefore is to discuss these concepts in sufficient detail to reach a clearer understanding of how they have been and may be employed. Additionally, the book attempts to demonstrate the general value of genre analysis as a means of studying spoken and written discourse for applied ends. In particular, it tries to show that a genre-centered approach offers a workable way of making sense of the myriad communicative events that occur in the contemporary English-speaking academy – a sense-making directly relevant to those concerned with devising English courses and, by extension, to those participating in such courses.

I have, for the most part, restricted both discussion and illustration to post-secondary academic English. The rapid growth of discoursal studies on the English language makes wider coverage impossible in a book of this length. For example, the literature in areas such as international business communication and the processing and production of technical manuals has rapidly become so large as to require, for adequate treatment, volumes of their own. Meanwhile there have appeared a number of major surveys of key professional areas such as those by Maher (1986) on medical English and Bhatia (1987) on legal English.

There are, in fact, good reasons for this particular restriction. First, the training of people to process and produce academic and research English remains a major international endeavor, whether in contexts where English is a first language, a second language (as in much of the 'new' Commonwealth) or a foreign language (as in Europe or Latin America). Secondly, this endeavor tends to be an institutionalized public-sector responsibility. It thus interfaces with national language planning and manpower training policies in ways that are much less obviously true of company training programs or private sector initiatives. Thirdly, even within this limited scope, the number and variety of unanswered research questions is dauntingly large, while issues of curriculum and pedagogy remain bafflingly complex. Finally, academic English training has typically had to compete for resources – and typically unsuccessfully – against other interest groups which usually have more campus prestige and power. Whatever the language policy, and whether the endeavor is categorized as Composition, Study Skills, Writing Across the Curriculum, or English for Academic Purposes, contact hours rarely seem enough and are often only available at the wrong times in the educational development of the students. Further, instructor conditions of service are typically below the institutional norm, and the viability of the operation itself is characteristically subject to recurring institutional scrutiny. Given all these circumstances, there is arguably something to be said for a book that concentrates on academic English, perhaps particularly for one that emphasizes the *seriousness* of the challenge imposed upon us if we are to understand the forces which variously shape the language of the academy, and for one which stands against the view that our teaching of academic English is at bottom nothing more than remedial. For if there is one factor that has debilitated academic English programs more than any other around the world, it has been the concept of *remediation* – that we have nothing to teach but that which should have been learnt before.

The foregoing paragraphs have already hinted at a further aim. I have taken the opportunity to try and build a bridge between English for Specific Purposes / Applied Discourse Analysis on the one side and L1 writing/composition on the other. However, in order to see why taking up this challenge may be both timely and useful, it is first necessary to review briefly developments in these two areas.

Historically, language analyses for specific purposes began in quantitative studies of the linguistic properties of functional varieties or *registers* of a language (Barber, 1962; Halliday, McIntosh and Strevens, 1964). A prototypical study of this kind would involve investigating the occurrence of verb forms in scientific English, such as in Huddleston (1971). The motivations for such studies were respectable enough in the sense that they were designed to provide (within their limitations) a descriptively-adequate account of distributional frequencies in the target language variety and thus offer a basis for prioritizing teaching items in specialized ESL* materials. Barber (1962), for instance, was able to show that continuous tenses were so rare in scientific prose that they could be virtually discounted. Whatever the value of these ground-breaking

---

* I have in this book adopted the standard American usage of using ESL to cover situations that may elsewhere be divided into English as a *Second* Language and English as a *Foreign* Language.

investigations into sentence length, voice, vocabulary and so on, such discrete-item surface feature assemblies of data were not likely to be of much interest to those concerned with L1 composition.

While ESP-type analyses have developed in various directions since those early days, they can generally be characterized by saying that they have concomitantly become narrower and deeper. Even if there remains some shorthand convenience attached to retaining registral labels such as scientific, medical, legal or even newspaper English, in reality such terms can now be seen to be systematically misleading. They overprivilege a homogeneity of content at the expense of variation in communicative purpose, addresser–addressee relationships and genre conventions. In fact, mainly due to the influence of the register concept, recognition of differences between, say, medical journal editorials and articles (Adams Smith, 1984) or between legislative prose, legal textbooks and legal case reports (Bhatia, 1983) has developed rather slowly in the English for Specific Purposes field, especially in comparison with such areas as Rhetoric and Technical Communication. Even so, ESP researchers have also been able to show how differentiating influences such as changing communicative purpose can operate within a single spoken or written discourse of a particular type. To take an obvious case, there are discernible differences between sections of research articles (Heslot, 1982; Hopkins and Dudley-Evans, 1988) or, less obviously, between paragraphs in newspaper editorials (de Bolivar, 1985).

This narrowing of textual scope has been compensated for by an interest in providing a deeper or multi-layered textual account. As a result, there is growing interest in assessing rhetorical purposes, in unpacking information structures and in accounting for syntactic and lexical choices. Moreover, the resulting findings are no longer viewed simply in terms of stylistic appropriacy but, increasingly, in terms of the contributions they may or may not make to communicative effectiveness. An important early example of a narrow and deep study is the account by Tarone et al. (1981) of the rhetorical choices that may affect the choice of *we + active verb* as opposed to its passive alternate in two astrophysics papers. Such developments go most of the way towards answering Widdowson's (1979) criticism:

> The fact that scientific English exhibits a relatively high proportion of certain syntactic features and a relatively low proportion of others may be useful for identifying scientific English texts should we ever wish to do such a thing. In fact this approach has proved useful for establishing authorship; it can reveal, with the help of the computer, who wrote what. But it cannot reveal the communicative character of what was written. It cannot of its nature deal with discourse.

(Widdowson, 1979: 55–6)

Work in ESP was, by the middle eighties, not merely interested in characterizing linguistic *effects*; it was also concerned to seek out the *determinants* of those effects. It thus, of its nature, deals with the 'communicative character' of discourse.

And yet these recent contributions to our understanding of discourse in educational and functional settings have largely remained, despite their increasing 'thickness' (Geertz, 1973), faithful to their primary motivation and disciplinary tradition. An orientation towards providing assistance for non-native speakers has preserved a strong interest in the linguistic manifestation of rhetorical and organizational features. Whatever else EAP practitioners may be legitimately involved in, they can hardly avoid such matters as phraseology, syntactic choice and pronunciation. Secondly, most EAP professionals have received training in linguistics and applied linguistics and so place value on establishing appropriate corpora of material, giving criteria for categories, providing evidence for claims and for bringing anomalies and exceptions out into the open. Therefore, while current aims in EAP-driven discourse analysis have moved closer to those found in Composition or Business and Technical Communication, both the methods of proceeding and the selection of cited works retain a distinctly linguistic flavor that can make its own distinctive contribution to inter- or cross-disciplinary enterprises.

In the meantime, influential groups of people in the composition field in the United States have been moving in a direction that brings them closer to the contemporary world of English for Academic Purposes. Potential rapprochement is most obviously manifest in the area of writing, but in so far as the study of writing may also include the study of texts and of conversations about writing, linkage can expand into other skill areas of particular relevance to non-native speakers. One relevant development has been a growing sense that cognitive models of the writing process, such as the influential Carnegie Mellon model (e.g. Flower and Hayes, 1981) lack a crucial social dimension. Bizzell (1982) in a watershed paper argued that writing, especially student writing in colleges and universities, should not be viewed solely as an individually-oriented, inner-directed cognitive process, but as much as an acquired response to the discourse conventions which arise from preferred ways of creating and communicating knowledge within particular communities. The view that writing is typically a socially-situated act has been reinforced by the aims and experiences of the recent Writing Across the Curriculum (WAC) movement (Young and Fulwiler, 1986). A primary research agenda for WAC has been firmly laid out by Faigley and Hansen:

> If teachers of English are to offer courses that truly prepare
> students to write in other disciplines, they will have to explore why
> those disciplines study certain subjects, why certain methods of

enquiry are sanctioned, how the conventions of a discipline shape a text in that discipline, how individual writers represent themselves in the text, how a text is read and disseminated, and how one text influences subsequent texts. In short, teachers of English will have to adopt a rhetorical approach to the study of writing in the disciplines, an approach that examines the negotiation of meaning among writers, readers and subject matters.

(Faigley and Hansen, 1985: 149)

The above agenda outlines a vast territory to be explored – and presumably one so prone to environmental and ecological change that the geographer's work will never be done. Nevertheless, US studies linking textual content and context have already produced some fascinating descriptions of particular locales. These include Bazerman's (1981) discussion of the differences between three papers representing the natural sciences, the social sciences and the humanities; Peck MacDonald's (1987) study of disciplinary variation in problem statements; Herrington's (1985) investigation into writing processes and products in two advanced Chemical Engineering courses; and Myer's (forthcoming) narrative of the transmogrification of a paper from its original journal into a *Scientific American* format.

One strength of this emerging work is its successful adaptation of a rhetorical approach originally used for highly-valued literary, political or religious discourse to more mundane academic writing – and one reason for its success has been a built-in assumption that discourse is indeed both socially situated and designed to achieve rhetorical goals. Its weakness also lies in its rhetorical and literary origins. While Becher (1987) in a critique of studies of disciplinary discourse can rightly observe that Bazerman (1981) has the most interesting story to tell, that story depends crucially (as in literary criticism) on the 'pointedness' of the examples and the persuasiveness of the commentator. Issues of representativeness of sample, validation of claims, and possible alternative explanations of phenomena are rarely raised or discussed.

As EAP and WAC have considerable areas of overlap in their exploratory agendas, an opportunity arises, as I said earlier, to bring the two movements together. The opportunity is not lightly declined, because the strength of each side is rather precisely – or so I have argued – the weakness of the other. Further, at present the two movements are really quite far apart. As far as I can see, relevant linguistic work is somewhat selectively cited in composition studies; Halliday's work, especially *Cohesion in English* by Halliday and Hasan (1976), is clearly well known, but that of others much less so. Conversely, only Bazerman and Myers seem known to EAP practitioners.

Another motive for proposing cross-fertilization is that the two movements share a number of professional concerns such as methods of student assessment and training instructors in discourse analysis, ethnography and methodology. Additionally, they face comparable practical problems. For instance, at the time of writing, *College English* has been running a debate on whether a WAC program should be housed in an English Department or should be organized independently (e.g. Blair, 1988; Smith, 1988). As it turns out, the proper location of English language service units in post-secondary institutions is a controversy that has had a long and turbulent history in English for Academic Purposes (Swales, 1984a).

In spite of the fact that much is shared at certain levels, it of course remains the case that WAC and EAP serve different populations: in the former case mostly native-speaker (NS) undergraduates concentrated in a single, extremely large college and university system (with some work also in countries like Australia and Canada); in the latter, predominantly non-native speakers (NNS) in a wide range of educational institutions spread across the world and varying in status from pre-college students to senior professors. It follows that different populations require different applications, which in turn presents a problem for the bridge-building aspect of this book. I have sometimes tried to minimize the problem by looking for pedagogical applications that might serve both populations; at other times I have concentrated on a non-native speaker perspective. It is reasonable to believe that NNS academic English tasks typically require more structure and input, and it is presumably easier to see how an elaborately structured task might be simplified for native speakers than to see how a simple task assignment could be elaborated for non-native speakers.

It may be recalled that my second aim is to try and demonstrate the general value of a genre-based approach to the teaching of academic communicative competence. Since genre study is commonly identified with the analysis of texts, it would be useful, at an early juncture, to clarify that I propose to view genres as rather more than texts. While it remains necessary to use texts in order to understand how texts organize themselves informationally, rhetorically and stylistically, textual knowledge remains generally insufficient for a full account of genre.

Textual analysis does not of itself provide a *rationale* of why genre texts have acquired certain features. Consider, for example, the well-known phenomenon of citing the work of others in academic papers. (Citations in textbooks probably have other motivations, as do, alas, citations of the author's own previous work.) What is the rationale for this practice? Do we simply say that it is conventionally expected? That without a certain number of citations per paper, other things being equal, is not acceptable? A kind of style sheet requirement? Or is citation best viewed as a matter of ethics – of acknowledgement of the intellectual property rights of others? Or is it homage, a kind of 'nods all round to previous researchers'? Or is citation, as Ravetz (1971) has argued, a kind of co-operative reward system, payments (rather precisely) *in kind*? Or do we follow Gilbert (1977) in believing that citation is a tool of persuasion, a device that makes statements containing citations more authoritative? Or are they better seen as documentary evidence that the writer qualifies for membership in the target discourse community by demonstrating his or her familiarity with the field (Bavelas, 1978)? Or are citations, as I shall be inclined to argue in Part III, a means of creating a personal research space? Or more than one, or all of these?

As Cronin (1981) has argued, citing the work of others is a private process but with a public face. We can go behind the public document by interviewing academic writers and asking them to retrospect and introspect about their citation practices. We can use protocol analysis and ask writers to vocalize their thoughts as they are in the process of writing and so attempt to capture the moment of a citation's conception. These then are ways of taking us beyond the text.

Another approach, illustrated in the two previous paragraphs, is to seek out the explanations of those who are interested in the phenomenon from different perspectives; in fact, none of the people I have cited has anything to do with linguistics or English, for Ravetz and Gilbert appear to be sociologists, Bavelas a psychologist, and Cronin an information scientist. Admittedly, searching for the rationale behind particular genre features may prove elusive, but the process of seeking for it can be enlightening for the investigator – as indeed for the instructor and student. In my own experience, raising the issue of how we are to account for citations has a valuable consciousness-raising effect on my students, both NS and NNS, and starts them towards developing a high-level sense of where and why citational support for their statements may be advisable.

If these first two kinds of extra-textual territory I wish to draw into genre analysis lie somewhere in the field of psychology, the next and last belongs to ethnography. In particular, I am now interested in those situations in which it is appropriate to consider the *roles* that texts play in particular environments (Doheny-Farina, 1986). Elsewhere (Swales, 1985a) I have tried to illustrate the significance of text-role by discussing possible relationships between lecture courses and their assigned textbooks. As that relationship is variable, an analysis of the textbook alone – for, say, the development of reading materials – runs the risk of being over-restrictive. It may be relevant to know in addition how the instructor utilizes the textbook. Is it replete with central truths to be laboriously assimilated and acquired by the class? Or is it a tired straw man to be challenged, updated or modified in the lecture material? Or is it sometimes one, and sometimes the other? The kinds of answers we reach will doubtless affect, among other things, the amount of time and attention we might give to critical reading as opposed to reading for information.

There is nothing particularly new or surprising about advocating moves beyond the analysis of discourse for interpretive purposes. Participation, observation and interview have long been part of the 'team-teaching' school in ESP (i.e. collaborative ventures between subject and language teachers), as perhaps best represented in the seminal paper by Johns and Dudley-Evans (1980). Back in 1977, Douglas paid students at the University of Khartoum in Sudan to keep diaries of their study habits which revealed, at least to western eyes, the powerful organizing effects of the five daily Muslim prayer sessions. More recently in composition research impressive ethnographies of academic writing contexts have been carried out by Herrington (1985), McCarthy (1987), and Berkenkotter et al. (1988), while North (1986) has recently explored the distinctive qualities of a 'hermeneutical' approach to writing in a philosophy class.

In this opening section I have tried to explain why the book's illustrative material has been limited to that of academic and research English. I have also given reasons for my hope that this volume may hold some interest for those who are professionally concerned with academic English in first as well as second language contexts. In so doing I have taken the opportunity of making some preliminary remarks about investigative developments in both the composition and EAP fields. One particular motive was to establish that a number of appropriate areas for investigation in each field currently overlap. A second was to disassociate early the concept of a genre-based approach from an exclusive concern with the spoken and written substance of discourse. As the following section outlines the organization of the book, it will, I trust, clarify what is understood by a genre-based approach and further illustrate how that approach can be usefully applied.

1.2   Outline of the book

The book has four parts. As has been seen, Part I, entitled Preliminaries, opened with an exploration of its aims and purposes framed against a number of recent developments. This first section proposed the advantages of – but did not define – a genre-based approach, the goal of which is to arrive at sufficient understanding of academic discourse outside FL/ESL/L1 classrooms so that language learning and development activities within them can have appropriate shape and purpose. The final section in Part I will briefly discuss elements in ESL work (and some from elsewhere) that have contributed to the formulation of the approach.

Part II provides the intellectual and schematic foundations. In order to handle the additional dimensions created by text-role and text-environment, I shall adopt the concept of *discourse community* as the first of three key elements. The other two are *genre* itself and (language-learning) *task*. As all three terms have wide but variable currency in contemporary L1/ESL writing, one of the main purposes of Part II is to offer sufficient discussion for their use in this book to be (relatively) unambiguous. I do not intend that the criteria proposed in Part II be considered definitive. Indeed rather the opposite, for I have deliberately opted for criteria that are tight and narrow and so will inevitably exclude parameters that are known to exist. In the case of *discourse community* and *genre*, for instance, I shall not consider differences that arise as a result of differing ideological perspectives (Bizzell, 1986b), such as those found in the work of neo-Marxist and capitalist economists (Tinberg, 1988). A specific reason for this exclusion is that the proposed approach is not activated by a wish to make a contribution to intellectual history or to construct a schematic vision of disciplinary cultures, but rests on a pragmatic concern to help people, both non-native and native speakers, to develop their academic communicative competence. In the case of *task*, I have similarly opted for a narrow definition, particularly in order to distinguish *task* from the looser term *activity*. Narrow definitions have the advantages of being manageable and of creating possibilities for useful dialogue. The fact that I propose, for example, that one of the key elements requires features A, B and C, allows others to challenge the criteria themselves, or to argue, usefully, that other definitions are more appropriate for other circumstances.

The way the three key elements are seen to interlock can be summarized in the following way. Discourse communities are sociorhetorical networks that form in order to work towards sets of common goals. One of the characteristics that established members of these discourse communities possess is familiarity with the particular genres that are used in the communicative furtherance of those sets of goals. In consequence, genres are the properties of discourse communities; that is to say, genres belong to discourse communities, not to individuals, other kinds of grouping or to wider speech communities. Genres themselves are classes of communicative events which typically possess features of stability, name recognition and so on. Genre-type communicative events (and perhaps others) consist of texts themselves (spoken, written, or a combination) plus encoding and decoding procedures as moderated by genre-related aspects of text-role and text-environment.* These processing procedures can be viewed as *tasks*. The acquisition of genre skills depends on previous knowledge of the world, giving rise to *content*

---

* Although genres are not to be equated with texts, I shall often use textual genre-names such as *textbook* or *lecture* as a matter of short hand convenience.

schemata, knowledge of prior texts, giving rise to *formal schemata*, and experience with appropriate tasks. Thus, the teaching of genre skills essentially involves the development of acquisition-promoting text-task activities.

A strong thread that binds the three key elements together is that of communicative purpose. It is communicative purpose that drives the *language* activities of the discourse community; it is communicative purpose that is the prototypical criterion for genre identity, and it is communicative purpose that operates as the primary determinant of task.

Chapter 4 (The concept of task) ends by illustrating how the general discussion might translate into a set of pedagogic activities. For this purpose I have chosen the area of academic correspondence – an area of concern to graduate students as they begin to establish their major research interests (Cukor-Avila and Swales, 1989). The final chapter in Part II is a somewhat condensed look at the relationships between genres and schemata. In essence, the chapter argues that an individual's development of genre-specific schemata has a number of generative and empowering consequences.

Part III contains the bulk of the descriptive material, occasionally interspersed with illustrations and examples of possible pedagogical activities. The discussion of research-process genres has been given clear prominence. This decision is sufficiently at odds with standard expectations to require some justification. The central genre of Part III is the research paper, partly because it is in this area that there lies the best hope of integrating studies that have no direct pedagogical motivation, such as those in the sociology of knowledge, with those of pedagogical inspiration. It is in this genre also that the complementary strengths of linguistic and rhetorical analysis can be shown to best advantage. Moreover, the fact that English now occupies an overwhelmingly predominant role in the international world of scholarship and research (Jernudd and Baldauf, 1987) entails that the coming generation of the world's researchers and scholars need – with relatively few exceptions in the arts and humanities – to have more than adequate professional skills in the English language if that generation is to make its way without linguistic disadvantage in its chosen world.

In this context, it is worth remembering that in the average world of English as a Second Language, the highest expectation of an instructional program is to raise the level of the students' language proficiency to somewhere fairly close to that of an average native speaker, however we might attempt to define such a person. Native-speaker competence is a point of arrival. In the research world, the aim is to help people achieve a level of competence that, in career-related genres at least, surpasses that of the average native speaker. And that competence is not necessarily manifest in quality textual products, for a paper may have received

comprehensive outside editing or a presentation may have been meticu-
lously rehearsed. Rather it is achieved when non-native speakers can
operate as members of the anglophone discourse communities that most
likely dominate their research areas.

And it is also worth remembering that for WAC and for Business and
Technical Communication, average native-speaker competence is also a
point of departure, not arrival, for the acquisition of career-relatable
communicative skills (Coupland, 1984). Thus, this volume's concern
with advanced English is also shared with these fields, especially in a
general academic climate that gives much evaluative weight to publication and presentation, and increasingly at the graduate student level.
Nor do I think that there is merit in the charge that attention to research
English is somehow elitist; partly for the reasons already given, partly
because the geopolitical world is increasingly divided between, broadly
speaking, an advantaged northern hemisphere and a disadvantaged
southern one, and partly because the academic world is itself divided into
privileged researchers and unprivileged instructors.

My final reason for giving priority to research-process genres is
possibly as important as any of the others. At least in research institutions, efforts to provide instruction in 'senior' genres (to go up the
academic ladder) are important for the upward mobility itself of the units
that provide that instruction, for those efforts can provide an escape
route from the ivory ghetto of remediation. Therefore, if the longest
chapter in the book has been allotted to the research article, it is in some
small part because my own experience suggests that being able to provide
assistance with this genre is one of the more rewarding ways of winning
friends and having influence in higher places.

Part III opens with some general comments on the research article, its
rapid growth in terms of numbers, and its consolidation as the standard
product of the knowledge-manufacturing industry (Knorr-Cetina, 1981).
Chapter 6 then addresses the role of English in this global research
activity. In so doing, it explores issues of (potential) disadvantage for
non-native speakers of English, particularly those in peripheral non-
anglophone locations. The section closes with a discussion of the types of
inequity that may result and how they might be reduced.

Chapter 7 concentrates on the English-language research article (RA)
itself. It opens with a highly selective review of its development since the
latter half of the seventeenth century. 7.2 recounts and critiques some of
the major studies investigating how researchers go about publishing their
findings. The next four sections deal with the textual analysis of the
RA as a whole and of its constituent parts (Introduction, Method, Results
and Discussion). The chapter closes with a brief review.

Chapter 8 in Part III examines more expeditiously other research-
process genres. It treats in turn abstracts, research presentations, grant

proposals, theses and dissertations, and reprint requests. In many respects, most of these are little-explored genres and would, I am sure, repay the kind of time and attention that has been extended to the research article itself.

The aim of Part IV is to offer a selection of genre-driven pedagogical activities. Some of these are primarily concerned with getting student-apprentices to explore, reflect upon and better articulate the ethos of their particular discourse communities, for there is evidence that such students, especially if they are minority or non-native speakers, see those communities as dangerously monodimensional (Johns, 1988a). Other activities are primarily concerned with genre skills themselves. In the latter context I have on occasion proposed that students utilize models in their writing. I have done so only in those situations where I feel that research into the genre has reached a level of credibility to permit some generalization. Additionally, the use of models is here assumed to be *temporary*; the approach is to say to the students something like the following:

> Look, this appears to be the standard way of doing this in your area. Will you please practice doing it the standard way for me as an exercise. Once you can show me that you both understand and can operate the standard (and safe) way, you are free to carry on in another way if you like, especially if the other ways suit your individual intellectual character or your perceptions of your particular writing situation.

I have drawn the activities mainly from three of my current teaching situations: an upper-level writing-intensive class entitled 'Discourse and Discipline', which is built around extracts from the work of many of the people who have figured most prominently in this volume; classes for entering NNS graduate students in paragraph writing and academic grammar; and an NNS class currently called 'Proposal, Thesis and Dissertation Writing'. The range of genres and subgeneric elements used in the illustrative fragments is quite varied. At one end, there are activities related to the construction of titles; at the other, activities concerned with the rhetoric of suggestions for further research.

The short final chapter reviews the general orientation of the book and then singles out one area of crucial importance for future research and development.

As this volume represents a long-standing interest in educational linguistics, it is not surprising that preliminary versions of certain sections have already been published elsewhere. My first pass at *discourse community* (Chapter 2) was a paper entitled 'Communication in the public sector : a discourse community approach to skills' (Swales, 1987a). An earlier exploration of a genre-based approach appeared in a RELC Anthology (Swales, 1986a). The *TESOL Quarterly* article, 'Utilizing the literatures in teaching the research paper', represents a first iteration of Chapters 6 and 7 and Part IV (Swales, 1987b), while a paper in *Scientometrics* (Swales, 1988a) has provided the basis for the shorter discussion of reprint requests in 8.5.

1.3   Origins and influences

The genre-based approach as proposed here owes a substantial debt to previous work in both applied and non-applied fields. Indeed, whatever small measure of originality the approach may possess probably lies as much in integrating the work of several different traditions as in new thinking *per se*. It thus attempts to make a virtue of eclecticism for, in terms of one of this book's major metaphors, to be eclectic is to be able to borrow profitably from the activities of several distinct discourse communities. These influences are summarized in Figure 1.

Variety studies

One tradition, already discussed at some length in 1.1, is that of enquiry into the properties of functional varieties of English. The fact that this tradition continues, both in the broader field of ESP and in the more localized one of genre analysis, reflects a valuable kind of linguistic responsibility in an era which quite appropriately stresses the devising of communicative methodologies and gives much attention to understanding the processes of language learning (e.g. Chaudron, 1988). However, these educational concerns need not and should not be at the expense of ignoring the actual properties of communicative events in the real world. Scotton and Bernsten (1988), to cite one example of several possible, have revealed a surprising disparity between how ESL textbooks characterize the procedures of 'asking the way' and what actually happened in their on-campus corpus.

Skill and strategy studies

A second influence has its point of departure in the traditional categorization of language-learning activities into the four skills of reading, writing, listening and speaking. The influence is somewhat indirect in that it is not the primary four-way classification which is of interest; it lies rather in the distinctions that have been established by specialists within a particular skill area. In the case of reading, for example, explorations of differences between intensive and extensive reading, reading for gist and detailed information, and reading for action and for content are all valuable in the construction of the text-task sequences central to a

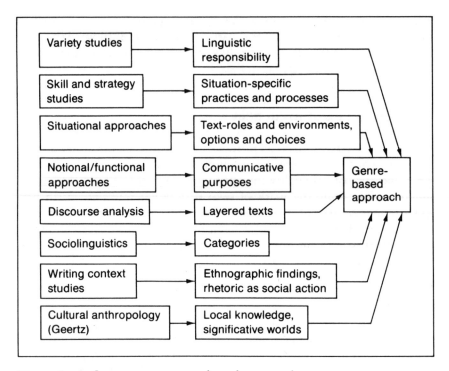

Figure 1   Influences on a genre-based approach

genre-based approach. Studies of student reading strategies are also directly relevant such as Sarig's taxonomy of four major reading move types: technical-aid moves (e.g. marking the text); clarification moves such as paraphrase; coherence-detecting moves; and monitoring moves (Sarig, 1987). Of comparable interest are discussions of the threats and opportunities provided by individual cognitive differences (Hudson, 1967) and how these interface with disciplinary differences in the relative values assigned to particular processing strategies (Widdowson, 1981; Flowerdew, 1986).

One specific area of investigation which holds particular promise is the tapping into the processing strategies of experts in a specific genre. Such studies can reveal target-like behaviors which may be very different from those we might anticipate, and additionally may be able to throw light on how, why and to what extent genre-texts evolve in response to processing strategy. A particularly interesting case is that of expert strategies for processing research articles. Bazerman (1985:11) studied, through observation and interview, the processes used by seven research physicists and found that his subjects rarely read sequentially, but tended to look 'at the introduction and conclusions, perhaps scanning figures, to get a general idea of what the writer was trying to do'. According to Bazerman, most of the interviewees used selective reading strategies in order to concentrate on what they considered to be 'news' for their own particular visions of their research fields.

Nigel Bruce (personal communication) has unveiled even more marked strategies among a group of medical doctors working in Kuwait. This group tended to start with the Discussion section. If that caught their interest they would move forward to the Results. If the Results were sufficiently intriguing they would jump ahead to Method; only then might they read all of the Introduction. Although academics often report that they write their introductions last, they might be somewhat surprised to find that their introductions can be read last as well.

Huckin's (1987) study of six senior US scientists unearths a comparable general strategy but somewhat different specifics:

> When I asked them to demonstrate how they customarily read a newly-published article in the field, they all displayed a reading pattern dominated by the search for new information. First they read the title, then the abstract, then they looked for the most important data, usually in graphs, tables, drawings and other visual aids. Next, they typically read the Results section. At this point, their reading patterns varied, depending on how well they knew the topic and how confident they were of the scientific methods used.
>
> (Huckin, 1987:4)

Huckin makes a number of interesting claims in consequence of his investigation. First, and like Bazerman, he suggests that scientists read journal articles in their specialty in such a way as to identify the most newsworthy information; however, he goes on to suggest that the scientists' strategy is actually quite comparable to the way people read the front pages of newspapers. He notes the parallelism between headline and title, lead and abstract, main event and major findings, and so on. He is further able to show that while newspaper reports are structured so as to assist the reader in the search for newsworthiness (Van Dijk, 1986), scientific articles have a traditional organization that 'reflects the chronology of idealized scientific procedure, not necessarily the chronology of reading' (1987:5). This disjunction, he claims, is beginning to have certain effects on genre texts in fields such as molecular biology: titles are becoming more informative, abstracts more prevalent and prominent (even in 'letters'), sectioning and subsectioning more marked, and non-verbal material more *visual*, tables being replaced by graphs, schematic diagrams and the like.

Situational approaches

This use of research into situation-specific skills and strategies (as well as the incorporation of composition research into writing contexts) shows a general affinity with a situational approach to language learning. The situational approach was very much a product of the 1960s, one of its pioneering achievements being Neile Osman's work with Australian immigrants (Osman, 1959). As a movement, however, it did not really survive the attack made upon it by Wilkins in the early 1970s (e.g. Wilkins, 1973). In particular, Wilkins noted that there is likely to be diversity of linguistic forms in any one situational setting (say, At the Butcher's), which will, in consequence, make the task of generalizing grammatical learning difficult. As a further consequence, learners will, by dialogue practice and so on, achieve overly restricted sets of repertoires, so that they will be learning not language but, in Spolsky's phrase, 'language-like behavior' (Spolsky, 1966). Wilkins' main objection therefore is that the situational approach is superficial:

> The grammatical and situational approaches are essentially
> answers to different questions. The former is an answer to the
> question *how*? How do speakers of language X express them-
> selves? The latter is a response to the questions *when*? *where*?
> When and where will the learner need the target language? There
> is, however, a more fundamental question to be asked, the answer
> to which may provide an alternative to grammatical or situational
> organizations of language teaching, while allowing important
> grammatical and situational considerations to operate. The
> question is the question *what*? What are the notions that the
> learner will expect to be able to express through the target
> language?
>
> (Wilkins, 1973: 3–4)

We shall discuss the impact of the alternative shortly; first we need to review, many years later, whether the 'language-like behavior' charge is warranted. Accusations of formulaic parroting are certainly frequent enough in discussion of genre analysis and its uses and abuses. Widdow-son, for instance, observes that 'The danger of such analysis is that in revealing typical textualizations, it might lead us to suppose that form–function correlations are fixed and can be learnt as formulae, and so to minimize the importance of the procedural aspect of language use and learning' (1983:102). There is certainly danger, and possibility of abuse. I am dismayed, for instance, when I ask my senior NS undergraduates how they write their résumés and they reply 'out of a book'. But there is equally certainly protection too. One way is to stress, as I have tried to do in 1.2, the importance of understanding the *rationale* of a genre. Another is to emphasize the process aspect of genre instantiation. For instance, recent sophisticated work on Service Encounters (which, incidentally, shows how much further on we are now in understanding 'At the Butcher's' types of situation than we were in the 1960s) by Ventola (1983; 1984), Martin (1985), Coupland (1983) and others opts for flexible flow-chart depictions of their general structure rather than any type of rigid linear sequencing. And even in the analysis of written texts, which have often been assumed – as by Ventola (1984) – to be more open to linear sequencing, current trends are towards constructing accounts that include recursion and the condition-specific recycling of elements (Dudley-Evans, 1987). A third kind of protection lies precisely in viewing the communicative world in situation-specific terms, because in so doing – to return to a previous example – my American undergraduates can see that 'the same facts' in a résumé can be highlighted or downgraded in certain ways so as to improve their chances of success with particular audiences.

Notional/functional approaches

The notional and functional approaches have had considerable influence on the development of my thinking, principally because of their inbuilt commitment to communicative purpose and learner need. They have, however, for my purposes a number of disadvantages. The tendency to see functions as realized by individual sentences or utterances leads to an excessive atomism which does not easily countenance the broader rhetorical purposes of larger sections of discourse. A further disadvantage has been another tendency to assume that sentences or utterances are monofunctional. However, monofunctionality can be a dangerous simplification, especially in professional settings. For example, Candlin et al. (1976) have revealed that the following type of utterance, 'I'm just going to pop a couple of little stitches in', made in the setting of a hospital Casualty Department, can have three functions. Obviously enough, it functions as a piece of news for the patient. Secondly, the form of words chosen reflects the doctor's desire to reassure the patient that what is to come is relatively non-serious and non-painful. (Compare 'You are going to need some sutures'.) However, Candlin and his colleagues were also able to show that the third function of the utterance was an indirect instruction (as an overheard remark) to the nurse to prepare the suture-set. It is clear that communicating on those three levels *simultaneously* requires a very considerable degree of communicative skill and, not surprisingly, working in Casualty emerged as one of the key situations in which foreign doctors required screening and support.

A final difficulty with notional/functional approaches lies in the tendency of their advocates to be satisfied with *identifying* functions. In fact, to be able to label a statement as, say, 'a definition' is not of itself to have achieved very much. More to the point would be insight into why a definition had been introduced at that particular juncture – a sense of its rationale (Swales, 1981a).

Discourse analysis

Another strong influence on my thinking has been that of discourse analysis, but once again with some reservation. I personally have benefited from studies of such discoursal topics as given/new, theme/rheme, cohesion/coherence and background/foreground information and from the establishment of 'macro-patterns' in English such as Problem–Solution (Hoey, 1983) or Topic–Restriction–Illustration (Crombie, 1985). However, as a teacher of English, my own experience leads me to suppose that students can get a better handle on communicative affairs by concentrating, at least initially, on the *sui generis* features of particular genre texts. This particular–general direction is the opposite of that advocated by Crombie (1985) among others, (even though it does have affinities with the orientation of the 'conversation analysts' such as Schegloff (1979). Overall, I see no good reason for believing that the kind of analysis that may best advance our understanding of discourse in general is necessarily the kind of analysis that will best advance the communicative competence of groups of learners whose main interests lie outside the linguistic sciences.

Sociolinguistics

The approach I am proposing has long been influenced by some of the major sociolinguists of the last two decades such as Halliday (e.g. 1978), Hymes (e.g. 1974) and Gumperz (e.g. 1962). These scholars offer frameworks and categorizations within which I have been able to place my more local and practical interests. Their contribution is explored in more detail in Chapter 3.

Writing context studies

Another and more recent influence derives from studies in the social contexts of academic writing as an outgrowth of a tradition of rhetorical scholarship (Bazerman, 1989). Slightly differently, my thinking has been affected by those rhetoricians who see genre as a vehicle of social action, particularly Miller (1984). Again these influences are discussed at greater length in Chapter 3.

Cultural anthropology

I have also profited from the work of numerous people engaged in fields completely unrelated to language teaching. Of these, one individual stands out above all the others – the cultural anthropologist, Clifford Geertz. The later Geertz, particularly his second collection of essays .entitled *Local Knowledge* (1983), has a well-nigh irresistible appeal to lesser and more mundane observers of the academic scenery.

To begin with, Geertz sets his face against simple classification:

> Grand rubrics like 'Natural Science', 'Biological Science', 'Social Science' and 'The Humanities' have their uses in organizing curricula, in sorting scholars into cliques and professional communities, and in distinguishing broad traditions of intellectual style. And, of course, the sorts of work conducted under any one of them do show some general resemblances to one another and some genuine differences from the sorts that are conducted under the others. There is, so far anyway, no historiography of motion; and inertia in a novel means something else. But when these rubrics are taken to be a borders-and-territories map of modern intellectual life, or, worse, a Linnaean Catalogue into which to classify scholarly species, they merely block from view what is really going on out there where men and women are thinking about things and writing down what it is they think.

(Geertz, 1983:7)

For Geertz, an assumption crucial to unblocking from view the significative worlds of others is to see that they are:

> ... more than just intellectual coigns of vantage but are ways of being in the world, to invoke a Heideggerian formula, forms of life, to use a Wittgensteinian, or varieties of noetic experience, to adapt a Jamesian. In the way that Papuans or Amazons inhabit the world they imagine, so do high energy physicists or historians of the Mediterranean in the age of Phillip II – or so, at least, an anthropologist imagines. It is when we begin to see this, to see that to set out to deconstruct Yeats' imagery, absorb oneself in black holes, or measure the effect of schooling on economic achievement is not just to take up a technical task but to take on a cultural frame that defines a great part of one's life, that an ethnography of modern thought begins to seem an imperative project. Those roles we think to occupy turn out to be minds we find ourselves to have.

(Geertz, 1983:155)

And thus it comes about that for Geertz *local knowledge* is both emblem and key, for 'to an ethnographer, sorting through the machinery of distant ideas, the shapes of knowledge are always ineluctably local, indivisible from their instruments and their encasements' (1983:4). As those distant ideas are not merely distant in space and time, but equally likely to be occurring in the department next door, and as the *encasements* are presumably realized in preferred rhetorical and linguistic choices, the genre-based approach proposed in this volume can hope, at least, for some enlightenment from the world's most charismatic cultural anthropologist.

2 *The concept of discourse community*

2.1   A need for clarification

Discourse community, the first of three terms to be examined in Part II, has so far been principally appropriated by instructors and researchers adopting a 'Social View' (Faigley, 1986) of the writing process. Although I am not aware of the original provenance of the term itself, formative influences can be traced to several of the leading 'relativist' or 'social constructionist' thinkers of our time. Herzberg (1986) instances Perelman and Olbrechts-Tyteca's *The New Rhetoric* (1969), Kuhn's *The Structure of Scientific Revolutions* (1970) and Fish's *Is There a Text in this Class?* (1980). Porter (1988) discusses the significance of Foucault's analysis of 'discursive formations' in *The Archaeology of Knowledge* (1972); other contributors are Rorty (*Philosophy and the Mirror of Nature*, 1979) and Geertz (*Local Knowledge*, 1983), with Wittgenstein's *Philosophical Investigations* (1958) as an earlier antecedent (Bruffee, 1986), particularly perhaps for the commentary therein on 'language games' (3.5).

Whatever the genealogy of the term discourse community, the relevant point in the present context is that it has been appropriated by the 'social perspectivists' for their variously applied purposes in writing research. It is this use that I wish to explore and in turn appropriate. Herzberg (1986) sets the scene as follows:

> Use of the term 'discourse community' testifies to the increasingly common assumption that discourse operates within conventions defined by communities, be they academic disciplines or social groups. The pedagogies associated with writing across the curriculum and academic English now use the notion of 'discourse communities' to signify a cluster of ideas: that language use in a group is a form of social behavior, that discourse is a means of maintaining and extending the group's knowledge and of initiating new members into the group, and that discourse is epistemic or constitutive of the group's knowledge.
>
> (Herzberg, 1986:1)

Irrespective of the merits of this 'cluster of ideas', the cluster is, I suggest, *consequential* of the assumption that there are indeed entities identifiable as discourse communities, not *criterial* for establishing or identifying them. They point us towards asking *how* a particular discourse community uses its discoursal conventions to initiate new members or *how* the discourse of another reifies particular values or beliefs. While such questions are well worth asking, they do not directly assist with the logically prior ones of how we recognize such communities in the first place.

Herzberg in fact concedes that there may be a definitional problem: 'The idea of "discourse community" is not well defined as yet, but like many imperfectly defined terms, it is suggestive, the center of a set of ideas rather than the sign of a settled notion' (1986:1). However, if discourse community is to be 'the center of a set of ideas' – as it is in this book – then it becomes reasonable to expect it to be, if not a settled notion, at least one that is sufficiently explicit for others to be able to accept, modify or reject on the basis of the criteria proposed.

Several other proponents of the 'social view', while believing that discourse community is a powerful and useful concept, recognize it currently raises as many questions as it answers. Porter (1988:2), for instance, puts one set of problems with exemplary conciseness: 'Should discourse communities be determined by shared objects of study, by common research methodology, by opportunity and frequency of communication, or by genre and stylistic conventions?' Fennell et al. (1987) note that current definitions have considerable vagueness and in consequence offer little guidance in identifying discourse communities. They further point out that definitions which emphasize the reciprocity of 'discourse' and 'community' (community involves discourse and discourse involves community) suffer the uncomfortable fate of ending up circular.

We need then to clarify, for procedural purposes, what is to be understood by discourse community and, perhaps in the present circumstances, it is better to offer a set of criteria sufficiently narrow that it will eliminate many of the marginal, blurred and controversial contenders. A 'strong' list of criteria will also avoid the circularity problem, because in consequence it will certainly follow that not all communities – as defined on other criteria – will be discourse communities, just as it will follow that not all discourse activity is relevant to discourse community consolidation. An exclusionary list will also presumably show that the kind of disjunctive question raised by Porter is misplaced. It is likely to show that neither shared object of study nor common procedure nor interaction nor agreed discoursal convention will themselves individually be necessary and sufficient conditions for the emergence of a discourse community, although a combination of some or all might. Conversely, the absence of any one (different subject areas, conflicting procedures, no interaction, and multiple discourse conventions) may be enough to prevent discourse community formation – as international politics frequently reminds us.

It is possible, of course, that there is no pressing need to clarify the concept of *discourse community* because, at the end of the account, it will turn out to be nothing more than composition specialists' convenient translation of the long-established concept of *speech community* common to sociolinguistics and central to the ethnography of communication. This view, for example, would seem to be the position of Freed and Broadhead (1987). After a couple of opening paragraphs on *speech community* in linguistics and on audience analysis, they observe, 'only recently have compositional studies begun to investigate communities of writers and readers, though the terminology seems to be changing to "discourse communities" in order to signal the focus on the written rather than the spoken' (1987:154). Whether it is appropriate to identify *discourse community* with a subset of *speech community* is the topic of the next section.

2.2 Speech communities and discourse communities

Speech community has been an evolving concept in sociolinguistics and the consequent variety of definitional criteria has been discussed – among others – by Hudson (1980), Saville-Troike (1982) and especially by Braithwaite (1984). At the outset, a speech community was seen as being composed of those who share similar *linguistic rules* (Bloomfield, 1933), and in those terms we could legitimately refer to, say, the speech community of the English-speaking world. Later, Labov will emphasize 'shared norms' rather than shared performance characteristics but still conclude that 'New York City is a single speech community, and not a collection of speakers living side by side, borrowing occasionally from each other's dialects' (Labov, 1966:7). Others, such as Fishman (1971), have taken as criterial patterned regularities in the *use* of language. In consequence, a speech community is seen as being composed of those who share functional rules that determine the appropriacy of utterances. Finally, there are those such as Hymes who argue for multiple criteria:

> A speech community is defined, then, tautologically but radically, as a community sharing knowledge of rules for the conduct and interpretation of speech. Such sharing comprises knowledge of at least one form of speech, and knowledge also of its patterns of use. Both conditions are necessary.

(Hymes, 1974:51)

There are a number of reasons why I believe even a tight definition of speech community (shared linguistic forms, shared regulative rules and shared cultural concepts) will not result in making an alternative definition of discourse community unnecessary. The first is concerned with medium; not so much in the trivial sense that 'speech' just will not do as an exclusive modifier of communities that are often heavily engaged in writing, but rather in terms of what that literary activity implies. Literacy takes away locality and parochiality, for members are more likely to communicate with other members in distant places, and are more likely to react and respond to writings rather than speech from the past.

A second reason for separating the two concepts derives from the need to distinguish a *sociolinguistic* grouping from a *sociorhetorical* one. In a sociolinguistic speech community, the communicative needs of the *group*, such as socialization or group solidarity, tend to predominate in the development and maintenance of its discoursal characteristics. The primary determinants of linguistic behavior are social. However, in a sociorhetorical discourse community, the primary determinants of linguistic behavior are functional, since a discourse community consists of a group of people who link up in order to pursue objectives that are prior to those of socialization and solidarity, even if these latter should consequently occur. In a discourse community, the communicative needs of the *goals* tend to predominate in the development and maintenance of its discoursal characteristics.

Thirdly, in terms of the fabric of society, speech communities are centripetal (they tend to absorb people into that general fabric), whereas discourse communities are centrifugal (they tend to separate people into occupational or speciality-interest groups). A speech community typically inherits its membership by birth, accident or adoption; a discourse community recruits its members by persuasion, training or relevant qualification. To borrow a term from the kind of association readers of this book are likely to belong to, an archetypal discourse community tends to be a *Specific Interest Group*.

2.3   A conceptualization of discourse community

I would now like to propose six defining characteristics that will be necessary and sufficient for identifying a group of individuals as a discourse community.

1. *A discourse community has a broadly agreed set of common public goals.*
These public goals may be formally inscribed in documents (as is often the case with associations and clubs), or they may be more tacit. The

goals are *public*, because spies may join speech and discourse communities for hidden purposes of subversion, while more ordinary people may join organizations with private hopes of commercial or romantic advancement. In some instances, but not in many, the goals may be high level or abstract. In a Senate or Parliament there may well exist overtly adversarial groups of members, but these adversaries may broadly share some common objective as striving for improved government. In the much more typical non-adversarial discourse communities, reduction in the broad level of agreement may fall to a point where communication breaks down and the discourse community splits. It is commonality of goal, not shared object of study that is criterial, even if the former often subsumes the latter. But not always. The fact that the shared object of study is, say, the Vatican, does not imply that students of the Vatican in history departments, the Kremlin, dioceses, birth control agencies and liberation theology seminaries form a discourse community.

2. A discourse community has mechanisms of intercommunication among its members.

The participatory mechanisms will vary according to the community: meetings, telecommunications, correspondence, newsletters, conversations and so forth. This criterion is quite stringent because it produces a negative answer to the case of 'The Café Owner Problem' (Najjar, personal communication). In generalized form, the problem goes as follows: individuals A, B, C and so on occupy the same professional roles in life. They interact (in speech and writing) with the same clienteles; they originate, receive and respond to the same kind of messages for the same purposes; they have an approximately similar range of genre skills. And yet, as café owners working long hours in their own establishments, and not being members of the Local Chamber of Commerce, A, B and C never interact with one another. Do they form a discourse community? We can notice first that 'The Café Owner Problem' is not quite like those situations where A, B and C operate as 'point'. A, B and C may be lighthouse keepers on their lonely rocks, or missionaries in their separate jungles, or neglected consular officials in their rotting outposts. In all these cases, although A, B and C may never interact, they all have lines of communication back to base, and presumably acquired discourse community membership as a key element in their initial training.

Bizzell (1987) argues that the café owner kind of social group will be a discourse community because 'its members may share the social-class-based or ethnically-based discursive practices of people who are likely to become café owners in their neighborhood' (1987:5). However, even if this sharing of discursive practice occurs, it does not resolve the logical problem of assigning membership of a community to individuals who neither admit nor recognize that such a community exists.

3. A discourse community uses its participatory mechanisms primarily to provide information and feedback.

Thus, membership implies uptake of the informational opportunities. Individuals might pay an annual subscription to the *Acoustical Society of America* but if they never open any of its communications they cannot be said to belong to the discourse community, even though they are formally members of the society. The secondary purposes of the information exchange will vary according to the common goals: to improve performance in a football squad or in an orchestra, to make money in a brokerage house, to grow better roses in a gardening club, or to dent the research front in an academic department.

4. A discourse community utilizes and hence possesses one or more genres in the communicative furtherance of its aims.

A discourse community has developed and continues to develop discoursal expectations. These may involve appropriacy of topics, the form, function and positioning of discoursal elements, and the roles texts play in the operation of the discourse community. In so far as 'genres are how things get done, when language is used to accomplish them' (Martin, 1985:250), these discoursal expectations are created by the *genres* that articulate the operations of the discourse community. One of the purposes of this criterion is to question discourse community status for new or newly-emergent groupings. Such groupings need, as it were, to settle down and work out their communicative proceedings and practices before they can be recognized as discourse communities. If a new grouping 'borrows' genres from other discourse communities, such borrowings have to be assimilated.

5. In addition to owning genres, a discourse community has acquired some specific lexis.

This specialization may involve using lexical items known to the wider speech communities in special and technical ways, as in information technology discourse communities, or using highly technical terminology as in medical communities. Most commonly, however, the inbuilt dynamic towards an increasingly shared and specialized terminology is realized through the development of community-specific abbreviations and acronyms. The use of these (ESL, EAP, WAC, NCTE, TOEFL, etc.) is, of course, driven by the requirements for efficient communication exchange between experts. It is hard to conceive, at least in the contemporary English-speaking world, of a group of well-established members of a discourse community communicating among themselves on topics relevant to the goals of the community and not using lexical items puzzling to outsiders. It is hard to imagine attending perchance the convention of some group of which one is an outsider and understanding every word. If it were to happen – as might occur in the inaugural meeting of some quite new grouping – then that grouping would not yet constitute a discourse community.

6. *A discourse community has a threshold level of members with a suitable degree of relevant content and discoursal expertise.*
Discourse communities have changing memberships; individuals enter as apprentices and leave by death or in other less involuntary ways. However, survival of the community depends on a reasonable ratio between novices and experts.

2.4   An example of a discourse community

As we have seen, those interested in discourse communities have typically sited their discussions within academic contexts, thus possibly creating a false impression that such communities are only to be associated with intellectual paradigms or scholarly cliques. Therefore, for my principal example of a discourse community, I have deliberately chosen one that is not academic, but which nevertheless is probably typical enough of many others. The discourse community is a hobby group and has an 'umbrella organization' called the Hong Kong Study Circle, of which I happen to be a member. The aims of the HKSC (note the abbreviation) are to foster interest in and knowledge of the stamps of Hong Kong (the various printings, etc.) and of their uses (postal rates, cancellations, etc.). Currently there are about 320 members scattered across the world, but with major concentrations in Great Britain, the USA and Hong Kong itself and minor ones in Holland and Japan. Based on the membership list, my guess is that about a third of the members are non-native speakers of English and about a fifth women. The membership varies in other ways: a few are rich and have acquired world-class collections of classic rarities, but many are not and pursue their hobby interest with material that costs very little to acquire. Some are full-time specialist dealers, auctioneers and catalogue publishers, but most are collectors. From what little I know, the collectors vary greatly in occupation. One standard reference work was co-authored by a stamp dealer and a Dean at Yale; another was written by a retired Lieutenant-Colonel. The greatest authority on the nineteenth century carriage of Hong Kong mail, with three books to his credit, has recently retired from a lifetime of service as a signalman with British Rail. I mention these brief facts to show that the members of the discourse community have, superficially at least, nothing in common except their shared hobby interest, although Bizzell (forthcoming) is probably correct in pointing out that there may be psychological predispositions that attract particular people to collecting and make them 'kindred spirits'.

The main mechanism, or 'forum' (Herrington, 1985) for inter-communication is a bi-monthly Journal and Newsletter, the latest to arrive being No. 265. There are scheduled meetings, including an Annual General Meeting, that takes place in London, but rarely more than a dozen members attend. There is a certain amount of correspondence and some phoning, but without the Journal/Newsletter I doubt the discourse community would survive. The combined periodical often has a highly interactive content as the following extracts show:

> 2. Hong Kong, Type 12, with Index
> No one has yet produced another example of this c.d.s. that I
> mentioned on J.256/7 as having been found with an index letter
> 'C' with its opening facing downwards, but Mr. Scamp reports
> that he has seen one illustrated in an auction catalogue having a
> normal 'C' and dated MY 9/59 (Type 12 is the 20 mm single-circle
> broken in upper half by HONG KONG). It must be in someone's
> collection!
>
> 3. The B.P.O.'s in Kobe and Nagasaki
> Mr. Pullan disputes the statement at the top of J.257/3 that 'If the
> postal clerk had not violated regulations by affixing the MR 17/79
> (HIOGO) datestamp on the front, we might have no example of
> this c.d.s. at all.' He states that 'By 1879 it was normal practice for
> the sorter's datestamp to be struck on the front, the change from
> the back of the cover occurring generally in 1877, though there are
> isolated earlier examples'; thus there was no violation of
> regulations.

My own early attempts to be a full member of the community were not marked by success. Early on I published an article in the journal which used a fairly complex frequency analysis of occurrence – derived from Applied Linguistics – in order to offer an alternative explanation of a puzzle well known to members of the HKSC. The only comments that this effort to establish credibility elicited were 'too clever by half' and 'Mr Swales, we won't change our minds without a chemical analysis'. I have also had to learn over time the particular terms of approval and disapproval for a philatelic item (cf. Becher, 1981) such as 'significant', 'useful', 'normal', and not to comment directly on the monetary value of such items.

Apart from the conventions governing articles, queries and replies in the Journal/Newsletter, the discourse community has developed a genre-specific set of conventions for describing items of Hong Kong postal history. These occur in members' collections, whether for display or not, and are found in somewhat more abbreviated forms in specialized auction catalogues, as in the following example:

> 1176   1899 Combination PPC to Europe franked CIP 4 C canc
>   large CANTON dollar chop, pair HK 2 C carmine added
>   & Hong Kong index B cds. Arr cds. (1) (Photo) HK $1500.

Even if luck and skill were to combine to interpret PPC as 'picture postcard', CIP as 'Chinese Imperial Post', a 'combination' as a postal item legitimately combining the stamps of two or more nations and so on, an outsider would still not be in a position to estimate whether 1500 Hong Kong dollars would be an appropriate sum to bid. However, the distinction between insider and outsider is not absolute but consists of gradations. A professional stamp dealer not dealing in Hong Kong material would have a useful general schema, while a member of a very similar discourse community, say the China Postal History Society, may do as well as a member of the HKSC because of overlapping goals.

The discourse community I have discussed meets all six of the proposed defining criteria: there are common goals, participatory mechanisms, information exchange, community specific genres, a highly specialized terminology and a high general level of expertise. On the other hand, distance between members geographically, ethnically and socially presumably means that they do not form a speech community.

2.5   Remaining issues

If we now return to Herzberg's 'cluster of ideas' quoted near the beginning of this section, we can see that the first two (language use is a form of social behaviour, and discourse maintains and extends a group's knowledge) accord with the conceptualization of discourse community proposed here. The third is the claim that 'discourse is epistemic or constitutive of the group's knowledge' (Herzberg, 1986:1). This claim is also advanced, although in slightly different form, in a forthcoming paper by Bizzell:

> In the absence of consensus, let me offer a tentative definition: a 'discourse community' is a group of people who share certain language-using practices. These practices can be seen as conventionalized in two ways. Stylistic conventions regulate social interactions both within the group and in its dealings with outsiders: to this extent 'discourse community' borrows from the sociolinguistic concept of 'speech community'. Also, canonical knowledge regulates the world-views of group members, how they interpret experience; to this extent 'discourse community' borrows from the literary-critical concept of 'interpretive community'.
>
> (Bizzell, forthcoming: 1)

The issue of whether a community's discourse and its discoursal expectations are constitutive or regulative of world-view is a contemporary reworking of the Whorfian hypothesis that each language possesses a structure which must at some level influence the way its users view the world (Carroll, 1956). The issue is an important one, because as Bizzell later observes 'If we acknowledge that participating in a discourse community entails some assimilation of its world view, then it becomes difficult to maintain the position that discourse conventions can be employed in a detached, instrumental way' (Bizzell, forthcoming: 9).

However, this is precisely the position I wish to maintain, especially if *can be employed* is interpreted as *may sometimes be employed*. There are several reasons for this. First, it is possible to deny the premise that participation entails assimilation. There are enough spies, undercover agents and fifth columnists in the world to suggest that non-assimilation is at least possible. Spies are only successful if they participate successfully in the relevant speech and discourse communities of the domain which they have infiltrated; however, if they also *assimilate* they cease to be single spies but become double agents. On a less dramatic level, there is enough pretense, deception and face-work around to suggest that the acting out of roles is not that uncommon; and to take a relatively innocuous context, a prospective son-in-law may pretend to be an active and participating member of a bridge-playing community in order to make a favorable impression on his prospective parents-in-law.

Secondly, sketching the boundaries of discourse communities in ways that I have attempted implies (a) that individuals may belong to several discourse communities and (b) that individuals will vary in the number of discourse communities they belong to and hence in the number of genres they command. At one extreme there may be a sense of discourse community deprivation – 'Cooped up in the house with the children all day'. At the other extreme, there stand the skilled professional journalists with their chameleon-like ability to assume temporary membership of a wide range of discourse communities. These observations suggest discourse communities will vary, both intrinsically and in terms of the member's perspective, in the degree to which they impose a world-view. Belonging to the Hong Kong Study Circle is not likely to be as constitutive as abandoning the world for the seclusion of a closed religious order.

Thirdly, to deny the instrumental employment of discourse conventions is to threaten one common type of apprenticeship and to cast a hegemonical shadow over international education. Students taking a range of different courses often operate successfully as 'ethnographers' of these various academic milieux (Johns, 1988a) and do so with sufficient detachment and instrumentality to avoid developing multiple personalities, even if, with more senior and specialized students, the epistemic nature of the discourse may be more apparent, as the interesting case study by Berkenkotter et al. (1988) shows. I would also like to avoid taking a position whereby a foreign student is seen, via participation, to assimilate inevitably the world-view of the host discourse community. While this may happen, I would not want to accept that discourse conventions cannot be successfully deployed in an instrumental manner (see James, 1980 for further discussion of variability in foreign student roles). Overall, the extent to which discourse is constitutive of world-view would seem to be a matter of investigation rather than assumption.

Just as, for my applied purposes, I do not want to accept assimilation of world-view as criterial, so neither do I want to accept a threshold level of personal involvement as criterial. While it may be high in a small business, a class or a department, and may be notoriously high among members of amateur dramatic discourse communities, the fact remains that the active members of the Hong Kong Study Circle – to use an example already discussed – form a successful discourse community despite a very low level of personal involvement. Nor is centrality to the main affairs of life, family, work, money, education, and so on, criterial. Memberships of hobby groups may be quite peripheral, while memberships of professional associations may be closely connected to the business of a career (shockingly so as when a member is *debarred*), but both may equally constitute discourse communities. Finally, discourse communities will vary in the extent to which they are norm-developed, or have their set and settled ways. Some, at a particular moment in time, will be highly conservative ('these are things that have been and remain'), while others may be norm-developing and in a state of flux (Kuhn, 1970; Huckin, 1987).

The delineation of these variable features throws interesting light on the fine study of contexts for writing in two senior college Chemical Engineering classes by Herrington (1985). Herrington concluded the Lab course and Design Process course 'represented distinct communities where different issues were addressed, different lines of reasoning used, different writer and audience roles assumed, and different social purposes served by writing' (1985:331). (If we also note that the two courses were taught in the same department at the same institution by the same staff to largely the same students, then the Herrington study suggests additionally that there may be more of invention than we would like to see in our models of disciplinary culture.) The disparities between the two courses can be interpreted in the following way. Writing in the Lab course was central to the 'display familiarity' macro-act of college assignments (Horowitz, 1986a) – which the students were accustomed to. Writing in the Design course was central to the persuasive reporting macro-act of the looming professional world, which the students were not accustomed to. The Lab course was *norm-developed*, while the Design course was *norm-developing*. As Herrington observes, in Lab both students and faculty were all too aware that the conceptual issue in the assignments was *not* an issue for the audience – the professor knew the answers. But it was an issue in Design. As a part consequence, the level of *personal involvement* was much higher in the Design course where professor and student interacted together in a joint problem-solving environment.

The next issue to be addressed in this section is whether certain groupings, including academic classes, constitute *discourse* communities. Given the six criteria, it would seem clear that shareholders of General Motors, members of the Book of the Month Club, voters for a particular political party, clienteles of restaurants and bars (except perhaps in soap-operas), employees of a university, and inhabitants of an apartment block all fail to qualify. But what about academic classes? Except in exceptional cases of well-knit groups of advanced students already familiar with much of the material, an academic class is unlikely to be a discourse community at the outset. However, the hoped-for outcome is that it will form a discourse community (McKenna, 1987). Somewhere down the line, broad agreement on goals will be established, a full range of participatory mechanisms will be created, information exchange and feedback will flourish by peer-review and instructor commentary, understanding the rationale of and facility with appropriate genres will develop, control of the technical vocabulary in both oral and written contexts will emerge, and a level of expertise that permits critical thinking be made manifest. Thus it turns out that providing a relatively constrained operational set of criteria for defining discourse communities also provides a coign of vantage, if from the applied linguist's corner, for assessing educational processes and for reviewing what needs to be done to assist non-native speakers and others to engage fully in them.

Finally, it is necessary to concede that the account I have provided of discourse community, for all its attempts to offer a set of pragmatic and operational criteria, remains in at least one sense somewhat removed from reality. It is utopian and 'oddly free of many of the tensions, discontinuities and conflicts in the sorts of talk and writing that go on everyday in the classrooms and departments of an actual university' (Harris, 1989:14). Bizzell (1987) too has claimed that discourse communities can be healthy and yet contain contradictions; and Herrington (1989) continues to describe composition researchers as a 'community' while unveiling the tensions and divisions within the group. The precise status of conflictive discourse communities is doubtless a matter for future study, but here it can at least be accepted that discourse communities can, over a period of time, lose as well as gain consensus, and at some critical juncture, be so divided as to be on the point of splintering.

3 The concept of genre

Genre is a term which, as Preston says, one approaches with some trepidation (Preston, 1986). The word is highly attractive – even to the Parisian timbre of its normal pronunciation – but extremely slippery. As a first step in the arduous process of pinning it down, I shall discount all uses of the term to refer to non-verbal objects. These include the original meaning of the term (in English) to refer to a type of small picture representing a scene from everyday domestic life and its growing employment as a fancy way of referring to classes of real world entities. The latter is illustrated in *Webster's Third New International Dictionary* by 'large floppy rag dolls, a *genre* favored by two-year olds'.

The use of *genre* relevant to this study is glossed by *Webster's Third* as 'a distinctive type or category of literary composition'; however, the dictionary's citation – from *The New Yorker* – usefully expands the context of literary to include 'such unpromising *genres* as Indian Treaties, colonial promotional tracts and theological works'. Indeed today, *genre* is quite easily used to refer to a distinctive category of discourse of any type, spoken or written, with or without literary aspirations. So when we now hear or read of 'the genre of the Presidential Press Conference', 'the new genre of the music video' or 'the survival of game-show genres', we do so, I believe, without feeling that a term proper to rhetorical or literary studies has been maladroitly usurped.

Even so, genre remains a fuzzy concept, a somewhat loose term of art. Worse, especially in the US, genre has in recent years become associated with a disreputably formulaic way of constructing (or aiding the construction of) particular texts – a kind of writing or speaking by numbers. This association characterizes genre as mere mechanism, and hence is inimical to the enlightened and enlightening concept that language is ultimately a matter of *choice*. The issue then is whether genre as a structuring device for language teaching is doomed to encourage the unthinking application of formulas, or whether such an outcome is rather an oversimplification brought about by pedagogical convenience. An initial way of tackling the issue is to examine what scholars have actually said about genres in a number of fields. For this purpose, the following four sections briefly consider uses of the term in folklore, literary studies, linguistics and rhetoric. (Another possible area would have been film studies, e.g. Neale, 1980.)

3.1   Genre in folklore studies

The concept of genre has maintained a central position in folklore studies ever since the pioneering work in the early nineteenth century on German myths, legends and folktales by the Brothers Grimm. And yet as a major figure in folklore studies has remarked, 'thus far in the illustrious history of the discipline, not so much as one genre has been completely defined' (Dundes, 1980:21). Ben-Amos (1976), whose valuable survey I have relied on, comments that this failure is partly ascribable to high standards of rigor and clarity expected in scientific definitions, and partly to continuous changes in theoretical perspective. As he pertinently observes 'the adequacy of generic descriptions depends entirely on the theoretical view they are designed to satisfy' (1976:xiii).

Ben-Amos goes on to consider a number of these perspectives. One is to consider genre, following Linnaeus, as a classificatory category; for example, a story may be classified as a myth, legend or tale. The value of classification is seen to lie in its use as a research tool for categorizing and filing individual texts, that is, as an effective storage and retrieval system. This, in turn, can lead, as might be expected, to the devising of the genre maps that place particular genres along various kinds of planes such as the prosaic/poetic and the secular/religious. However, it is apparently common in this classificatory work to consider genres as 'ideal types' rather than as actual entities. Actual texts will deviate from the ideal in various kinds of ways.

Another major group of approaches sees genres as *forms*, one established tradition taking these forms as permanent. Thus, legends and proverbs have not changed their character over recorded history: 'they have an independent literary integrity, which withstands social variations and technological developments' (1976:xx). They thus have kinds of cognitive deep structure preserved by the relations among the discoursal components of the texts themselves. What does change, of course, is the role of such texts in society: vicious political satires become innocuous nursery rhymes; incantations to prevent the soul from leaving the body reduce to formulaic 'God Bless You' responses to a sneeze; and proverbs no longer play as central a role in popular education as they once used to. A strong motive for the concept of an underlying permanent form apparently derives from the long-standing interest among folklorists in using the classic exemplars of myth and legend to trace beliefs back into *pre-history*. For that motive, the assumption of an enduring substrate is clearly useful, perhaps even necessary, but closely tied to a field-specific research agenda.

The functionalists in folklore would rather stress sociocultural value. For Malinowski (1960), for example, folklore genres contribute to the maintenance and survival of social groups because they serve social and spiritual needs. Perhaps inevitably, to assign cultural value also requires the investigator to pay attention to how a community views and itself classifies genres. Thus, for many folklorists major narrative genres such as myth, legend and tale are not so labeled according to the *form* of the narrative itself but according to how the narrative is received by the community.

> Do the people regard the narrative as sacred? If so, then it would seem a myth. Do they entertain the narrative as a potentially accurate recounting of actual events? Then it is a legend. Do they regard the narrative as a total fiction with a requisite suspension of belief? Then it is one form of tale. The central point is that the folklorist is primarily concerned with the folk narrative in some larger context of belief and behavior. The folklorist recognizes that folk narratives are the production of individuals, produced during social interactions and informed by surrounding cultural traditions. The entire sense of folktale is not sandwiched in between 'Once upon a time' and 'they lived happily ever after'. A tale is much larger than that. The folklorist must attempt to understand why people tell stories in the first place, why listeners appreciate them, and why they favor some stories over others. The problem is not only to understand how a text 'hangs together', but also to understand why a particular individual or group of people would find such a text meaningful, worthy of attention, and deserving of repetition.

> (Oring, 1986:134–5)

A final observation in this brief survey is that not all folklorists accept the *permanence of form* concept. Some are more interested in the *evolution* of the genres themselves as a necessary response to a changing world. This is particularly true of those who study relatively recent genres in developed countries, such as 'The Blues' in the USA, or have watched the evolution (and atrophy) of folklorist genres in traditional communities affected by modernizing influences.

The lessons from the folklorists for a genre-based approach to academic English are, I believe, several. First, the classifying of genres is seen as having some limited use, but as an archival or typological convenience rather than as a discovery procedure (a point we have already seen Geertz make at the end of Part I). Second, a community, whether social or discoursal, will often view genres as means to ends.

Third, a community's perceptions of how a text is generically interpreted is of considerable importance to the analyst.

3.2   Genre in literary studies

We have already seen that folklorists may have special historicist reasons for holding onto the permanence of form. In contrast, literary critics and theorists may have special reasons for de-emphasizing stability, since *their* scholarly activity is typically designed to show how the chosen author breaks the mould of convention and so establishes significance and originality. Moreover, actual literary practice in this century would seem, on the surface, to have so thrown away convention – in form, in content and in authorial role – as to render obsolete the very term *genre* itself. As Todorov remarks:

> To persist in discussing genres today might seem like an idle if not obviously anachronistic pastime. Everybody knows that they existed in the good old days of the classics – ballads, odes, sonnets, tragedies, and comedies – but today?

(Todorov, 1976:159)

However, the above quotation comprises the opening sentences of Todorov's paper and our genre knowledge of such papers leads us to expect, in this case quite correctly, that the author is indeed about to persist. He argues that the fact that works 'disobey' their genres does not mean that those genres necessarily disappear. For one thing, transgression, in order to exist, requires regulations to be transgressed. For another, the norms only retain visibility and vitality by being transgressed. This is the process, according to Todorov, of genre generation. 'A new genre is always the transformation of one or several old genres: by inversion, by displacement, by combination' (1976:161). He then turns to the issue of what genres are, and rejects a widely-held view, especially common in literary circles, that genres are classes of texts. He prefers instead to argue:

> In a society, the recurrence of certain discursive properties is institutionalized, and individual texts are produced and perceived in relation to the norm constituted by that codification. A genre, literary or otherwise, is nothing but this codification of discursive properties.

(Todorov, 1976:162)

Further, since ideological changes affect what a society chooses to codify, so change may come about from institutional sources as well as from individual experimentation with discursive (or discoursal) properties.

These processes make it possible to claim that the whole issue of genre conventions and their realignment is central to the evolution of the creative arts – in film, in music, in art and in literature. On the last, Hepburn (1983) has this to say:

> How a competent reader approaches a work of literature, his attitudes and expectations, depend importantly upon the genre he sees it as exemplifying. A work that rebels against genre-conventions equally relies on the reader's recognition of the conventions being rejected. Aesthetically relevant features of a work may stand out only if its reader has a background awareness of the historical development of the genre, or of the style, that the work is transforming in its distinctive way and perhaps without direct allusion within the text itself. The work may demand to be seen against the foil of the whole tradition from which it stems, and which it modifies by its very existence.
>
> (Hepburn, 1983:496)

Thus a claim is advanced that an appreciation of genre is a necessary if not sufficient condition for an appreciation of literature. It is necessary because it not only provides an interpretative and evaluative frame for a work of art but, more to the point, that frame is as much *textual* as it is cultural, historical, socioeconomic or political.

Fowler (1982), in the most exhaustive contemporary study known to me of literary genres, additionally stresses the value of genre to the *writer*:

> Far from inhibiting the author, genres are a positive support. They offer room, one might say, for him to write in – a habitation of mediated definiteness; a proportional neutral space; a literary matrix by which to order his experience during composition ... Instead of a daunting void, they extend a provocatively definite invitation. The writer is invited to match experience and form in a specific yet undetermined way. Accepting the invitation does not solve his problems of expression ... But it gives him access to formal ideas as to how a variety of constituents might suitably be combined. Genre also offers a challenge by provoking a free spirit to transcend the limitations of previous examples.
>
> (Fowler, 1982:31)

Although Fowler discusses genre classification with great erudition, he concludes that all such constructions have relatively little value when seen against the inescapable evidence of continuous genre evolution. At the end of the day, genre analysis is valuable because it is clarificatory, not because it is classificatory. It provides 'a communication system, for the use of writers in writing, and readers and critics in reading and interpreting' (1982:286). In taking this stance Fowler is able to lay at rest a number of 'ancient misapprehensions':

1. Genre theory is of little relevance because it corresponds ill with actual works of literature.
2. Genre theory leads to heavy prescription and slavish imitation.
3. It sets up highly conservative value hierarchies ('no great novels since Joyce or Lawrence').
4. It is inevitably obsolescent in its attempts to characterize a present period by then gone.

This very brief excursion into literary views of genres has singled out a few authors who have given *genre* particular attention. In consequence they may be atypical, but in fact none represents a view as extreme as that of Hawkes, who contends that 'a world without a theory of *genre* is unthinkable, and untrue to experience' (1977:101). Those few authors appear to concur that in living civilizations genres change as a result of internal pressure, and, in consequence, classificatory schemes are at best a secondary outcome of analysis. As Schauber and Spolsky (1986) observe, genres form an open-ended set. Neither Todorov nor Fowler accept that genres are simply assemblies of more-or-less similar textual objects but, instead, are coded and keyed events set within social communicative processes. Recognizing those codes and keys can be a powerful facilitator of both comprehension and composition.

3.3   Genre in linguistics

Linguists as a group have been more partial in the attention they have given to the term *genre*. This may be partly due to traditional tendencies to deal with aspects of language below the level of texts and partly due to a reluctance to employ a 'term of art' (Levinson, 1979) so closely associated with literary studies. In any event, the term is only found with any frequency among linguists of either ethnographic or systemic persuasions.

For the ethnographer Hymes:

> Genres often coincide with speech events, but must be treated as
> analytically independent of them. They may occur in (or as)
> different events. The sermon as a genre is typically identified with a
> certain place in a church service, but its properties may be invoked,
> for serious or humorous effect, in other situations.
>
> (Hymes, 1974:61)

As for *speech event* itself, it 'will be restricted to activities, or aspects of activities, that are directly governed by rules or norms for the use of speech' (1974:52). Leaving aside the restriction to only the oral mode, there is, I suggest, something a little unsatisfactory about Hymes' reasons for separating *genre* and *speech event* analytically. Invoking the properties of a sermon for humorous effect is clearly not the same thing as delivering a sermon, if only because they have very different communicative purposes. If, on the other hand, some of the sermon's properties are invoked for serious effect, then this may (or may not) strengthen the rhetorical effectiveness of *another* genre such as a political speech. It is still not a sermon, however 'sermonizing' it may be. Whereas if all the characteristics are transposed, then we can recognize the fact that we are listening to a sermon occurring in an atypical location. As Preston (1989) notes, it is not that *speech events* and *genres* need to be kept apart, but rather that *situations* and *genres* need to be.

A position much closer to that adopted in this book is that of Saville-Troike (1982). Like most other ethnographers, she takes *genre* to refer to the *type* of communicative event and offers the following as examples: jokes, stories, lectures, greetings and conversations. Like some of the folklorists, there is interest in discovering in a community which communications are generically typed and what labels are used, as these will reveal elements of verbal behavior which the community considers sociolinguistically salient. In addition, the ethnographers give considerable attention to how best to interpret and utilize the elicited metalanguage. Saville-Troike is quite clear on the matter:

> Since we cannot expect any language to have a perfect metalanguage, the elicitation of labels for categories of talk is clearly not adequate to assure a full inventory and must be supplemented by other discovery procedures, but it is basic to ethnography that the units used for segmenting, ordering and describing data should be those of the group, and not *a priori* categories of the investigator.
>
> (Saville-Troike, 1982:34)

It is not, of course, difficult to recognize the danger of basing units on the '*a priori* categories of the investigator', and indeed text-linguistics and certain text-typologies are somewhat prone to this very danger. In that respect, the ethnographic position as represented by Saville-Troike is both salutary and admirable. However, what we might call 'folk' categorization and the investigator's *a priori* categorization are not necessarily in exclusive opposition. Indeed, it can be argued that the investigator's role in genre analysis is neither to follow slavishly the nomenclatures of groups, nor is it to provide his or her own deductive and introspective categorial system. Rather, the procedure should be to develop sets of *a posteriori* categories, ones based on empirical investigation and observation, within which eliciting the community's category-labels plays a central role. Indeed, this seems to be what Saville-Troike is getting at when she observes that languages do not have 'perfect' metalanguages and so need supplementation and refinement.

The concept of *genre* has also in recent years been discussed by the systemic or 'Hallidayean' linguists (cf. Halliday, 1978). However, the relationship between *genre* and the longer established concept of *register* is not always very clear – see Ventola (1984) for a discussion of this uncertainty. Register, or functional language variation, is 'a contextual category correlating groupings of linguistic features with recurrent situational features' (Gregory and Carroll, 1978:4). This category has typically been analyzed in terms of three variables labeled *field, tenor* and *mode*. *Field* indicates the type of activity in which the discourse operates, its content, ideas and 'institutional focus' (Benson and Greaves, 1981). *Tenor* handles the status and role relationships of the participants, while *mode* is concerned with the channel of communication (prototypically speech or writing). 'The field, tenor and mode act collectively as determinants of the text through their specification of the register; at the same time they are systematically associated with the linguistic system through the functional components of the semantics' (Halliday, 1978: 122). Thus, field is associated with the management of the ideas, tenor with the management of personal relations, and mode with the management of discourse itself. The categories provide a conceptual framework for analysis; they are not themselves kinds of language use.

It is only comparatively recently in the systemic school that *genre* has become disentangled from *register*: Frow (1980:78), for instance, refers to 'discourse genre, or register'. On the other hand, Martin (1985) makes the following three-way distinction: genres are realized through registers, and registers in turn are realized through language. As for genres themselves:

> Genres are how things get done, when language is used to
> accomplish them. They range from literary to far from literary
> forms: poems, narratives, expositions, lectures, seminars, recipes,
> manuals, appointment making, service encounters, news
> broadcasts and so on. The term genre is used here to embrace each
> of the linguistically realized activity types which comprise so much
> of our culture.

(Martin, 1985:250)

Martin gives two kinds of reasons for establishing genre as a system underlying register. One revolves around the fact that genres constrain the ways in which register variables of field, tenor and mode can be combined in a particular society. Some topics will be more or less suitable for lectures than others; others will be more or less suitable for informal conversation between unequals. Recognizing the gaps is not only valuable in itself, but can have important consequences for cross-cultural awareness and training.

The second reason for recognizing that genres comprise a system for accomplishing social purposes by verbal means is that this recognition leads to an analysis of discourse structure. Genres have beginnings, middles and ends of various kinds. Verbal strategies 'can be thought of in terms of states through which one moves in order to realize a genre' (Martin, 1985:251). Genre 'refers to the staged purposeful social processes through which a culture is realized in a language' (Martin and Rothery, 1986:243).

Couture (1986) provides unusual clarification of the use of *register* and *genre* within systemic linguistics. Registers impose constraints at the linguistic levels of vocabulary and syntax, whereas genre constraints operate at the level of discourse structure. Further, 'Unlike register, genre can only be realized in completed texts or texts that can be projected as complete, for a genre does more than specify kinds of codes extant in a group of related texts; it specifies conditions for beginning, continuing and ending a text' (1986:82). For Couture then the two concepts need to be kept apart: genres (research report, explanation, business report) are completable structured texts, while registers (language of scientific reporting, language of newspaper reporting, bureaucratic language) represent more generalizable stylistic choices. Genres have 'complementary' registers, and communicative success with texts may require 'an appropriate relationship to systems of genre and register' (1986:86).

In a detailed application of how genres and registers could relate differentially to a scale which runs from the highly explicit to the highly elliptical, Couture gives the following illustration:

> Since the two sides of the scale are independent, a writer could select a genre that implies a high level of explicitness (like a business report) and at the same time select a register that demands less explicitness (such as bureaucratic language). In doing so, the writer must decide which critera for explicitness he or she wishes to dictate linguistic choice (clear hierarchical development of message and support demanded by the *report* genre or implicit expression of the cultural values of impartiality, power and prestige associated with *bureaucratic* style).

> (Couture, 1986:87)

Aside from scholars such as Martin, Rothery and Couture, linguistics as a whole has tended to find genre indigestible. The difficulty seems to derive from the fact that *register* is a well-established and central concept in linguistics, while *genre* is a recent appendage found to be necessary as a result of important studies of text structure. Although *genre* is now seen as valuably fundamental to the realization of goals, and thus acts as a determinant of linguistic choices, there has been an understandable unwillingness to demote *register* to a secondary position, an unwillingness strengthened, on the one hand, by large-scale investment in analysis of language varieties (for lexicographic among other purposes) and underpinned, on the other, by relatively little interest in seeing how texts are perceived, categorized and used by members of a community.

Despite these equivocations, linguistic contributions to the evolving study of genre lie in the emphasis given to: (a) genres as types of goal-directed communicative events; (b) genres as having schematic structures; and most strikingly (c) genres as disassociated from registers or styles.

3.4 Genre in rhetoric

Ever since Aristotle, rhetorical inquiry and criticism has been interested in classifying discourse. One common approach has been to proceed deductively, in a top-down manner, and construct a closed system of categories. A prominent modern example – and one of many – is Kinneavy's *A Theory of Discourse: The Aims of Discourse* (1971). Kinneavy classifies discourse into four main types: expressive, persuasive, literary and referential. A discourse will be classified into a particular type according to which component in the communication process receives the primary focus. If the focus or aim is on the sender, the discourse will be expressive; if on the receiver, persuasive; if on the linguistic form or code, it will be literary; and if the aim is to represent the realities of the world, it will be referential. Although such classifications have impressive intellectual credentials and considerable organizing power, the propensity for *early* categorization can lead to a failure to understand particular discourses in their own terms. For example, the scientific paper appears, in Kinneavy's system, to be a classic instance of referential discourse but, as we shall see in Part III, there may be very good reasons for not coming to quick conclusions about its predominantly referential nature.

In contrast, rhetorical scholars who have taken a more inductive approach have tended to take context more into account and to give genre a more central place. This is perhaps particularly so among those who study the historical development of discourses in recurrent settings, as has been done by Jamieson (1975). She outlines her position as follows:

> Three bodies of discourse may serve as evidence for the thesis that it is sometimes rhetorical genres and not rhetorical situations that are decisively formative. These bodies of discourse are the papal encyclical, the early state of the union addresses, and their

> congressional replies. I will argue that these discourses bear the
> chromosomal imprint of ancestral genres. Specifically, I propose to
> track essential elements of the contemporary papal encyclical to
> Roman imperial documents and the apostolic epistles, essential
> elements of the early state of the union addresses to the 'King's
> Speech' from the throne, and essential elements of the early
> congressional replies to the parliamentary replies to the king.

(Jamieson, 1975:406)

Jamieson is able to show, in these cases anyway, how antecedent genres
operate as powerful constraining models. As she observes, without such a
concept, it would be difficult to reconcile the fact, on the one hand, that
the first leaders of the United States incorporated monarchical forms into
key early public statements and the fact, on the other, that one of their
prime purposes was to reject the tyranny and trappings of a monarchical
system.

Jamieson is careful not to assert that established rhetoric will necessarily be a prevailing influence on a particular rhetorical response. Whether
it is situation, audience expectations or genre itself is, she advocates, a
matter of inquiry. Even so, it will come as little surprise to find that many
rhetorical scholars with an inductive and/or historical orientation stress
the recurrence of similar forms in genre creation:

> A genre is a group of acts unified by a constellation of forms that
> recurs in each of its members. These forms, *in isolation*, appear in
> other discourses. What is distinctive about the acts in a genre is a
> recurrence of the forms *together* in constellation.

(Campbell and Jamieson, 1978:20)

This kind of generic analysis, as in most others we have seen, aims to
illuminate rather than classify. It offers, amongst other things, a way of
studying discoursal development over time that is detachable from an
analysis of an individual event or an individual author; it also suggests,
by way of comparing rhetorical similarities and differences, a potential
method of establishing the genre-membership or otherwise of a particular
text.

Miller (1984), in a seminal paper, shares Campbell and Jamieson's
view that analysis of actual genres can clarify certain social and historical
aspects of rhetoric that might otherwise be missed. She is also like them
an anti-taxonomist, because genres are unstable entities: 'the number of
genres in any society is indeterminate and depends upon the complexity
and diversity of society' (1984:163).

However, Miller also advances the discussion in a number of important ways. First, she has principled reasons for extending the scope of
genre analysis to types of discourse usually disregarded by rhetorical
scholars:

> To consider as potential genres such homely discourse as the letter
> of recommendation, the user manual, the progress report, the
> ransom note, the lecture, and the white paper, as well as the
> eulogy, the apologia, the inaugural, the public proceeding, and the
> sermon, is not to trivialize the study of genres: it is to take
> seriously the rhetoric in which we are immersed and the situations
> in which we find ourselves.
>
> (Miller, 1984:155)

Secondly, she argues that 'a rhetorically sound definition of genre must be centered not on the substance or form of discourse but on the action it is used to accomplish' (1984:151).

Thirdly, Miller gives serious attention to how genres fit into the wider scale of human affairs. She suggests that:

> What we learn when we learn a genre is not just a pattern of forms
> or even a method of achieving our own ends. We learn, more
> importantly, what ends we may have ...
>
> (Miller, 1984:165)

As students and struggling scholars, we may learn that we may create a research space for ourselves, we may promote the interests of our discourse community, we may fight either for or against its expansion, we may uncouple the chronological order of research action from the spatial order of its description and justification, we may approach unexpected sources for funding, or we may negotiate academic or editorial decisions.

Genre analysts among the rhetoricians thus make a substantial contribution to an evolving concept of genre suitable for the applied purposes of this study. They provide a valuable historical context for the study of genre movements and they finally destroy the myth – or so I hope – that genre analysis *necessarily* has something to do with constructing a classification of genres. Miller's exceptional work reinforces the concept of genre as a means of social action, one situated in a wider sociorhetorical context and operating not only as a mechanism for reaching communicative goals but also of clarifying what those goals might be.

Overview

The foregoing brief survey of how genres are perceived in four different disciplines indicates something of a common stance. Its components can be summarized as follows:

1. a *distrust* of classification and of facile or premature prescriptivism;
2. a *sense* that genres are important for integrating past and present;
3. a *recognition* that genres are situated within discourse communi-

ties, wherein the beliefs and naming practices of members have relevance;

4. an *emphasis* on communicative purpose and social action;
5. an *interest* in generic structure (and its rationale);
6. an *understanding* of the double generative capacity of genres – to establish rhetorical goals and to further their accomplishment.

This stance suggests that it is indeed possible to use genres for teaching purposes without reducing courses to narrow prescriptivism or formalism and without denying students opportunities for reflecting upon rhetorical or linguistic choices.

3.5   A working definition of genre

This section offers a characterization of genres that I believe to be appropriate for the applied purposes that I have in mind, although detailed consideration of links to language-teaching activity and language-learning theory will be held over to Chapters 4 and 5 respectively. I shall proceed by making a series of short criterial observations, which will be followed in each case by commentary. Sometimes the commentaries are short and directly to the point; at other times they are more extensive as they explore wider discoursal or procedural issues. I hope in this way – as the section title indicates – to create a sufficiently adequate characterization for others to be able to use, modify or reject as they think fit.

1. *A genre is a class of communicative events.*
I will assume that a communicative event is one in which language (and/or paralanguage) plays both a significant and an indispensable role. Of course, there are a number of situations where it may be difficult to say whether verbal communication is an integral part of the activity or not. Levinson neatly illustrates the possibilities for speech contexts:

> On the one hand we have activities constituted entirely by talk (a telephone conversation, a lecture for example), on the other activities where talk is non-occuring or if it does occur is incidental (a game of football for instance). Somewhere in between we have the placing of bets, or a Bingo session, or a visit to the grocer's. And there are sometimes rather special relations between what is said and what is done, as in a sports commentary, a slide show, a cookery demonstration, a conjurer's show, and the like.
>
> (Levinson, 1979:368)

Activities in which talk is incidental, as in engaging in physical exercise, doing the household chores, or driving, will not be considered as communicative events; nor will activities that involve the eyes and ears in non-verbal ways such as looking at pictures or listening to music.

Secondly, communicative events of a particular class will vary in their occurrence from the extremely common (service encounters, news items in newspapers) to the relatively rare (Papal Encyclicals, Presidential Press Conferences). By and large, classes with few instances need to have prominence within the relevant culture to exist as a genre class. If a communicative event of a particular kind only occurs once a year it needs to be noteworthy for class formation: a TV advert using a talking dog will not do. Finally, and to repeat an earlier claim, a communicative event is here conceived of as comprising not only the discourse itself and its participants, but also the role of that discourse and the environment of its production and reception, including its historical and cultural associations.

2. *The principal criterial feature that turns a collection of communicative events into a genre is some shared set of communicative purposes.*
Placing the primary determinant of genre-membership on shared purpose rather than on similarities of form or some other criterion is to take a position that accords with that of Miller (1984) or Martin (1985). The decision is based on the assumption that, except for a few interesting and exceptional cases, genres are communicative vehicles for the achievement of goals. At this juncture, it may be objected that *purpose* is a somewhat less overt and demonstrable feature than, say, form and therefore serves less well as a primary criterion. However, the fact that purposes of some genres may be hard to get at is itself of considerable heuristic value. Stressing the primacy of purpose may require the analyst to undertake a fair amount of independent and open-minded investigation, thus offering protection against a facile classification based on stylistic features and inherited beliefs, such as typifying research articles as simple reports of experiments.

In some cases, of course, identifying purpose may be relatively easy. *Recipes*, for example, would appear to be straightforward instructional texts designed to ensure that if a series of activities is carried out according to the prescriptions offered, a successful gastronomic outcome will be achieved. In others it may not be so easy. For instance, we might suppose that the examination and cross-examination of witnesses and parties carried out by lawyers under an adversarial system of justice are designed and structured to elicit 'the facts of the case'. However, independent investigation shows this not to be so (Atkinson and Drew, 1979; Danet et al., 1980). The elaborate sequences of closed 'yes–no' questions are designed to control how much the hostile or friendly witnesses will be allowed to reveal of what, in fact, they do know.

Or, to take another example, we might suppose that the purposes of party political speeches are to present party policies in as convincing a way as possible, to ridicule the policies and personalities of opposition parties, and to rally the faithful. However, especially in these days of massive television coverage, party political speeches may now be being written, structured and delivered in order to generate the maximum amount of applause (Atkinson, 1984). And certainly there are signs in Britain that the 'applause factor' is becoming raised in consciousness, as it were, not only as a result of the interest in Atkinson's work, but also because of the recently established journalistic practice of measuring the length of ovations following major speeches at conventions.

The immediately preceding example suggests that it is not uncommon to find genres that have *sets* of communicative purposes. While news broadcasts are doubtless designed to keep their audiences up to date with events in the world (including verbal events), they may also have purposes of moulding public opinion, organizing public behavior (as in an emergency), or presenting the controllers and paymasters of the broadcasting organization in a favorable light. When purposive elements come into conflict with each other, as in the early Environmental Impact Statements studied by Miller (1984), the effectiveness of the genre as sociorhetorical action becomes questionable. In the academic context, a genre with high potential for conflicting purposes is that of the student written examination (Searle, 1969; Horowitz, 1986a).

There remain, of course, some genres for which purpose is unsuited as a primary criterion. Poetic genres are an obvious example. Although there may be overt political, religious or patriotic tracts put out in the form of verse, the poetry that is taught, remembered, known and loved is rarely of that kind and inevitably makes an appeal to the reader or listener so complex as to allow no easy or useful categorization of purpose. Poems, and other genres whose appeal may lie in the verbal pleasure they give, can thus be separately characterized by the fact that they defy ascription of communicative purpose.

The need, in all but exceptional cases, to ascribe privileged status to purpose derives not only from a general recognition of the power it has to shape our affairs, but also because it provides a way of separating 'the real thing' from parody. The *Oxford Dictionary* defines *parody* as 'A composition in which the characteristic turns of thought and phrase of an author are mimicked and made to appear ridiculous, especially by applying them to ludicrously inappropriate subjects'. However, Mac-Donald (1960:557) is surely right when he complains that the final clause does not sufficiently distinguish parody from its poor relations, *travesty* and *burlesque*. Good parody is often applied to subject matter that is only slightly or subtly inappropriate. As a result, *content* and *form* may not reveal the fact that parody is being attempted, as in Cyril Connolly's parody of Aldous Huxley in 'Told in Gath' or Henry Reed's celebrated

Eliot-esque 'Chard Whitlow'. Consider, for instance, the opening two paragraphs from a paper by Michael Swan and Catherine Walter published in the *English Language Teaching Journal* entitled 'The use of sensory deprivation in foreign language teaching':

視覚(視)

> The term 'sensory deprivation' is probably familiar to most of us from recent reports of interrogation procedures, but it may seem strange to find the expression used in a discussion of language teaching, especially since, at first sight, it is difficult to imagine how *deprivation* of sensory input could contribute to learning. However, recent experiments in this field (carried out principally by the Chilton Research Association at Didcot, near Oxford) have suggested that sensory deprivation (SD) could well become a powerful pedagogic tool in the not too distant future. The purpose of this article is simply to provide a résumé of current research in SD; readers who would like more complete information are referred to the very detailed account by Groboshenko and Rubashov (1980).
>
> Interest in the use of SD in language teaching arose initially as a natural extension of the work of such researchers as Gattegno, Rand Morton, Lozanov and Watanabe. Gattegno's refusal (in the 'Silent Way') to allow learners more than minimum access to the second language (L2) model; Rand Morton's insistence on eliminating meaning entirely from the early 'phonetic programming' stages of language learning; Lozanov's concern to purge the student of his former identity and to build a new, autonomous L2 personality through 'Suggestopaedia'; and finally Watanabe's controversial but impressive use of 'hostile environment' as a conditioning factor – all these elements are clearly recognizable in current SD practice. But SD goes a great deal further.
>
> (Swan and Walter, 1982:183)

Most of the regular readers of *ELTJ* with whom I have discussed this paper stated that they read it with increasing incredulity. However, they also admitted that they were by no means sure it was a 'spoof' until they reached the end and saw the words 'Received 1 April 1982'. After all, the content is conceivable (just), and certainly not 'ludicrously inappropriate'. Further, the Swan and Walter paper is of an appropriate length, uses standard style, has the expected information-structure and is appropriately referenced, some of the references being genuine. Although the publication of this fake paper may have been an exceptional event in the world of language teaching publications, other academic groups, particularly scientists, have an established tradition of parodying both their research methods and their publication formats. For instance, there exist 'specialized' periodicals like the *Journal of Irreproducible Results* and the *Journal of Insignificant Research* (see Gilbert and Mulkay, 1984, Chapter 8 for an excellent discussion). In the end, although we may well find contextual clues that help us to separate the spurious from the genuine, we need to rely on the privileged property of identifiable communicative purpose to disentangle the clever parody from 'the real thing'.

3. *Exemplars or instances of genres vary in their prototypicality.*

So far I have argued that genre membership is based on communicative purpose. What else is it based on? What additional features will be required to establish such membership? There are, as far as I can see, two possible ways of trying to find answers to such questions: the *definitional* approach and the *family resemblance* approach.

The definitional view is much the better established and, indeed, underpins the creation and worth of dictionaries, glossaries and specialized technologies. It asserts that, in theory at least, it is possible to produce a small set of simple properties that are individually necessary and cumulatively sufficient to identify all the members and only the members of a particular category from everything else in the world. Thus, a *bird* can be defined in terms of being an animal, having wings and feathers, and laying eggs, or some such list of properties. As long as the object has the stipulated features, it is a member of the category; it matters not whether the bird is a 'normal' one like a sparrow or a 'far-out' member of the category such as an ostrich or a penguin – they are all equally birds. The definitional view has had some success in certain areas. Kinship terms have been extensively analyzed in this way; a bachelor is 'an adult unmarried male' (Katz and Fodor, 1963); and other areas where it seems to work with relatively little problem are numbers (ordinal, cardinal, real, rational etc.) and physical and chemical elements. However, in practice, great difficulty has been experienced in drawing up lists or defining characteristics of such everyday categories as *fruit, vegetables, furniture* and *vehicles*. And if that is so, then there would appear little hope of identifying the all-or-none defining features of *lectures, staff meetings, research papers, jokes* or *consultations*. A further difficulty is created by the easily-attested phenomenon that we still recognize category membership even when many of the suggested defining characteristics are missing; the roast chicken emerging from the cooker is still identified as a *bird*. As Armstrong, Gleitman and Gleitman observe, 'It's not at all hard to convince the man in the street that there are three-legged, tame, toothless albino tigers, that are tigers all the same' (1983:296).

It might therefore be the case that what holds shared membership together is not a shared list of defining features, but inter-relationships of a somewhat looser kind. This indeed would seem to be the view taken by Wittgenstein in a justly famous passage in the *Philosophical Investigations* that is worth quoting in full:

66.   Consider for example the proceedings we call 'games'.
I mean board games, card games, ball games, Olympic games, and
so on. What is common to them all? – Don't say: 'There *must* be
something common, or they would not be called "games"' – but
look and see whether there is anything common to all. – For if you
look at them you will not see something that is common to *all*, but
similarities, relationships, and a whole series of them at that. To
repeat: don't think, but look! – Look for example at board games,
with their multifarious relationships. Now pass to card games;
here you find many correspondences with the first group, but many
common features drop out, and others appear. When we pass next
to ball games, much that is common is retained, but much is lost. –
Are they all 'amusing'? Compare chess with noughts and crosses.
Or is there always winning and losing, or competition between
players? Think of patience. In ball games there is winning and
losing; but when a child throws his ball at the wall and catches it
again, this feature has disappeared. Look at the parts played by
skill and luck; and at the difference between skill in chess and skill
in tennis. Think now of games like ring-a-ring-a-roses; here is the
element of amusement, but how many other characteristic features
have disappeared! And we can go through many, many other
groups of games in the same way; can see how similarities crop up
and disappear.
     And the result of this examination is; we see a complicated
network of similarities overlapping and criss-crossing: sometimes
overall similarities, sometimes similarities of detail.

67.   I can think of no better expression to characterize these
similarities than 'family resemblances'; for the various
resemblances between members of a family: build, features, colour
of eyes, gait, temperament, etc., etc. overlap and criss-cross in the
same way. – And I shall say: 'games' form a family.

(Wittgenstein, 1958:31–2)

Thus, we could perhaps argue that in, say, the case of lectures 'we see a
complicated network of similarities overlapping and criss-crossing:
sometimes overall similarities, somtimes similarities of detail'. Thus some
lectures may be like others in terms of some of the following: the
arrangement of speaking roles, seating arrangements, the level of formality in language, the use of visual support, the number and positioning of
examples, the employment of metadiscoursal features of recapitulation
and advanced signaling, and so on. Others will be like others in
equivalent but different ways.

     However, 'family resemblance' has not been without its critics. To
start with, we would do well to bear in mind Lodge's observation that 'no
choice of a text for illustrative purposes is innocent' (Lodge, 1981:23).
Just as kinship-terms suit Katz and Fodor, so games may particularly
favor Wittgenstein's observations. In fact, we can note that nearly all

games offer a contest or a challenge. The *Oxford Dictionary* proposes this definition of a game: 'A diversion of the nature of a contest, played according to rules, and decided by superior strength, skill or good fortune' – and, of course, this contest can be against the game itself as in patience, solitaire, or in a jig-saw puzzle. Admittedly, we are left with an unaccounted-for residue as represented by such children's games as 'ring-a-ring-a-roses'.

Rather more seriously, it can be objected that a family resemblance theory can make anything resemble anything. Consider, for instance, a set-up like that shown below.

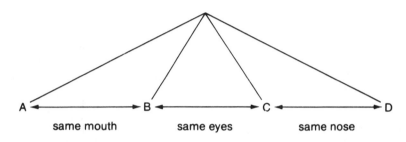

Thus whilst B and C share a common feature, A and D have nothing in common themselves except that they share a different feature with B and C. So a knife is like a spoon because they are both eating instruments, and a spoon is like a teapot because they are both used to contain liquids, and a teapot is like a suitcase because they both have handles, so a knife is like a suitcase. Indeed it was precisely this kind of undisciplined chaining that Vygotsky (1962) characterized as being typical of the young child, to be replaced in maturity by a more orderly system of categorization. However, as Bloor (1983) has argued, we need to remember that Wittgenstein was concerned with *family* resemblances and that families cohere by reason of other things beside physical characteristics such as blood-ties and shared experiences; therefore it would be inappropriate to leave the domain of eating activities (knives and spoons) for that of traveling activities (suitcases).

Wittgenstein's discussion of family resemblances and subsequent comment have given rise to a 'prototype' or cluster theory designed to account for our capacity to recognize instances of categories.

The *prototype* approach to categories is particularly associated with the work of Eleanor Rosch (Rosch, 1975; 1978; Mervis and Rosch, 1981; Armstrong, Gleitman and Gleitman, 1983; for a useful introduction see Clark and Clark, 1977: 464–8; for a full discussion of the issues see Smith and Medin, 1981). Rosch and her co-workers begin with the observation that although by definition robins, eagles, swallows, ostriches and penguins are all birds, we somehow feel that they do not all have the same status. Some are 'birdier' than others. Rosch then conducted a number of experiments to establish this; she was able to show, for example, that the time subjects took to verify the correctness of a statement depended on whether the subject was a 'typical' member of its class or not. Hence, in the United States, verification times for 'a robin is a bird' were faster than for 'an ostrich is a bird'. Further, Rosch (1975) was able to establish that when subjects were asked to rank examples in order from most typical to least typical they did so with a large degree of agreement. Thus, in US culture chairs and tables were the most typical members of items of furniture and lamps and ashtrays least typical; similarly, apples and plums were typical fruits and olives and coconuts atypical.

The most typical category members are *prototypes*; a *chair* is what is likely to come to mind when we think of an item of furniture and an *apple* similarly comes to mind in the case of fruit. A *robin* is a prototype bird within US culture because its body and legs are average size, and it flies, perches in trees and sings. According to Rosch (1975) a category has its own internal structure, which will assign features or properties a certain probability for being included in category membership. An ostrich is a marginal member because it fails to meet the high probability expectations of flight and relatively small size. Organisms like bats and whales are problematic because they carry properties that meet high probability expectations of categories to which they do not technically belong.

Armstrong et al. bring the definitional and cluster approaches together in the following generalized way:

> There are privileged properties, manifest in most or even all
> examples of the category; these could even be necessary properties.
> Even so, these privileged properties are insufficient for picking out
> all and only the class members, and hence a family resemblance
> description is still required.
>
> (Armstrong et al., 1983:270)

This integration has considerable appeal. It allows the genre analyst to find a course between trying to produce unassailable definitions of a particular genre and relaxing into the irresponsibility of family resemblances. As we have seen, communicative purpose has been nominated as the *privileged* property of a genre. Other properties, such as form, structure and audience expectations operate to identify the extent to which an exemplar is *prototypical* of a particular genre.

4. The rationale behind a genre establishes constraints on allowable contributions in terms of their content, positioning and form.
Established members of discourse communities employ genres to realize communicatively the goals of their communities. The shared set of

purposes of a genre are thus recognized – at some level of consciousness – by the established members of the parent discourse community; they may be only partly recognized by apprentice members; and they may be either recognized or unrecognized by non-members. Recognition of purposes provides the rationale, while the rationale gives rise to constraining conventions. The conventions, of course, are constantly evolving and indeed can be directly challenged, but they nonetheless continue to exert influence.

I will illustrate these observations by taking two simple examples: one from administrative correspondence and one from professional interviews. Correspondence, not yet administrative correspondence, itself does not constitute a genre as it does not represent a coherent set of shared purposes. Rather it represents, as a convenient label, a supra-generic assembly of discourse. Within administrative correspondence there are, however, a number of establishable genres. Two closely related ones are the individually-directed 'good news' letter and 'bad news' letter (Murphy and Hildebrandt, 1984). These genres are formal responses to applications, or sometimes complaints. Classic instances are responses to applications for jobs, scholarships or grants. At one level, it might be argued that both kinds of letter constitute a single genre of *responses to applications*, but a little reflection will show that, while the textual environment and the register may be the same, the rationale is sufficiently different to require a separate genre for each.

The rationale for the 'good news' letter is based firstly on the assumption that the information transmitted is welcome. It therefore is conveyed early and enthusiastically, while the rest of the letter is set out in such a way as to remove any remaining obstacles and engender a rapid and positive response. Part of the rationale behind a 'good news' letter is that *communications will continue*. In contrast, the 'bad news' letter is based on the assumption that the information is unwelcome. It therefore is conveyed after a 'buffer' has prepared the recipient for its receipt and couched in language that is regretful and non-judgmental. Part of the rationale of the 'bad news' letter is that it minimizes personal resentment so that no long-term disaffiliation from the institution occurs; another part is to signal that *communications have ended*. For that reason, in 'bad news' letters the negative decision is usually represented as having been taken by some impersonal body, such as a committee, over which the writer gives the impression of having little influence, the purpose being to insinuate that complaint, petition or recrimination will be of no avail. The rationale thus determines what Martin (1985) refers to as the schematic structure of the discourse and also constrains lexical and syntactic choice.

The second illustration is taken from medical consultations and is designed to highlight differences in rationale perception between established and non-established members of discourse communities. Apparently many medical doctors trained in Britain use the system called SOAP to structure their consultations (Jones, 1982):

1. S = Subjective (what the patient says is wrong; what the patient perceives as his or her symptoms)

2. O = Objective (results of tests; symptoms perceived by the doctor)

3. A = Analysis (of the symptoms so as to lead to a diagnosis)

4. P = Prescription (pharmaceutical and/or giving advice or treatment)

However, patients rarely have any conscious recognition that the doctor imposes order on the consultation by the use of a structuring system such as SOAP. Part of the reason may be that other things going on, such as greetings and leave takings and various types of utterance designed to settle and reassure patients and to effect transitions between stages (Candlin, Bruton and Leather, 1976; Frankel, 1984), could appear more salient to patients. Equally, there may be things apparently not going on: the doctor's carrying out of stages O and A may well be a largely silent and private matter.

Understanding of rationale is privileged knowledge, but is neither the whole story nor any guarantee of communicative success. Erickson and Schultz (1982) in their remarkable study of academic counseling sessions make the following observation:

> There is a similar sequential order of discourse topics across interviews – an order which manifests an underlying logic of gatekeeping decision making. But it is not the underlying logic, the interactional *deep structure*, that is essential, for much more is manifested in performance – in communicational *surface structure* – than an underlying abstract logic of gatekeeping. Distinctive packages of social meanings and social identities are also manifested communicatively in each interview.
>
> (Erickson and Schultz, 1982:12)

The point to note here is that even when we grant that surface features and local decisions are highly contributory to the performance outcome, it is still very much the case that for a participant to have a sense of the 'underlying logic' or rationale is facilitative in both reception and production.

5. *A discourse community's nomenclature for genres is an important source of insight.*
As we have seen, knowledge of the conventions of a genre (and their rationale) is likely to be much greater in those who routinely or professionally operate within that genre rather than in those who become involved in it only occasionally. In consequence, active discourse com-

munity members tend to have the greatest genre-specific expertise – as we often see in interactions between members of a profession and their client public. One consequence is that these active members give genre names to classes of communicative events that they recognize as providing recurring rhetorical action. These names may be increasingly adopted first by overlapping or close discourse communities and then by farther and broader communities. Particular attention therefore needs to be given to the genre nomenclatures created by those who are most familiar with and most professionally involved in those genres.

As far as academic genres are concerned, many, if not most, are terms that incorporate a pre-modifying nominal of purpose: introductory lecture, qualifying exam, survey article, review session, writing workshop. Others reverse the order by using a purposive head-noun: grant application, reprint request and course description. Still others indicate the occasion rather than communicative purpose, such as final examination, plenary lecture, festschrift, faculty meeting or graduation address. However, members of the discourse community typically recognize that particular occasional genres have particular roles to play within the academic environment and that, in consequence, the sets of purposes are, on the one hand, evident and, on the other, constrained.

In the previous section that dealt with linguistic contributions to genre analysis (2.3), it was argued that insider metalanguages should certainly be considered seriously, but also viewed with circumspection. Indeed, it was suggested that an appropriate approach for the analyst would be to establish genres based on investigations into actual communicative behavior, two aspects of which, among several, would be participants' naming procedures and elicited categorizations. There are a number of reasons for caution.

One reason is that the naming of communicative events that occur and recur in post-secondary educational settings – to restrict discussion to the main focus of this study – tend to be institutional labels rather than descriptive ones. I mean by this that the timetable or course handbook will identify group activity A in setting X as a *lecture*, and group activity B in setting Y as a *tutorial*. However, as every student in higher education knows one member of staff's 'tutorial' can be identical as a communicative event to another member of staff's 'lecture' and vice versa. Of course, instructors may modify their approach depending on whether they are *supposed* to be giving *lectures* or *tutorials*, but the fact that a communicative event is labeled by the institution as being an event of such-and-such a kind does not necessarily mean that it will be so.

Secondly, names tend to persevere against a background of substantial change in activity. *Lectures* may no longer be the monologic recitations they once were, but actively invite intercalated discussion and small-group tasks. *Tutorials* today may consist of student interaction with a computer program or a tape recorder and no longer involve a 'tutor' in the traditional sense of the term. We inherit genre categories that get passed down from one generation to another.

In direct contrast, genre-naming can equally be generative. While the coining and deliberate usage of new labels for event categories can at times create substance and structure out of an amorphous background, at others the names may reflect empty categories with no claim to genre status. A pertinent instance of these processes can be seen in the advance information for the Nineteenth International IATEFL Conference (*IATEFL Newsletter* no. 84, August 1984:54). The section entitled 'Contributions' quotes at length from *The Working Party Report on Conferences*, April 1984.

> The range of ways in which presentations and workshops could operate might be broadened considerably. If contributors were offered a range of possible formats to choose from, there would be scope for many members who are currently inhibited by the formality of presentation. At the same time many presentations would continue in the well-tried formats of the past.

The *advance-information* then lists and glosses eleven possible suggestions:

1. Basic presentations
2. Haiku sessions
3. Resource rooms
4. Traditional talks/lectures
5. Experimental workshops
6. Creative workshops
7. The buzz-group lecture
8. Curran-style lecture
9. Screening panel lecture
10. The traditional debate
11. Specific interest groups

I think it reasonable to suppose that 11 different formats is decidedly more than the average conference-goer is familiar with, and I would guess that there are very few people in the English-teaching world who could confidently explain what is expected to happen in all 11. Certainly, I had not heard of haiku sessions ('People who have one very good idea to present that can really be properly got across in 10 minutes or one minute') or screening panel lectures ('Before the lecture begins three to five people from the audience come to the front and spend five minutes discussing what they expect to and want to hear from the speaker and what they expect others will want to hear. This allows the speaker to pitch his talk right'). However, I now know what a haiku session or screening panel lecture might be like, even though I have never experienced either of them; and I dare say having read about such possibilities, my interest is raised and so my participation is encouraged. Thus it is that the naming and description of new sub-genres can have pre-emptive force. Oscar Wilde had an inimitable ability to stand the world on its head, and when he observed that 'life imitates art' rather than the commonly-held converse that 'art imitates life', he may have been closer to the truth than his witticism is generally given credit for. Certainly here we seem to have been discussing potential cases where 'conference life imitates format' rather than the converse. On the other hand, relatively few of these genre suggestions seem to have been realized. Documentation from subsequent conferences fails to make mention of the 'haiku' or the 'screening panel' formats, even if others such as 'resource rooms' and 'specific interest groups' have made some headway.

If there are genre names with no genres attached to them, so must there be genres without a name. I believe there is at least one of these that occurs quite commonly in my main professional discourse community and which I am sure many readers will recognize. This is a type of presentation given to colleagues and graduate students which is built around a number of episodes in which participants, often working in pairs or small groups, are asked to reach and then share conclusions on short texts distributed among them. The tasks might involve ranking texts in order of evolution or quality, re-assembling textual fragments into their original order, or using internal evidence to guess a text's provenance. While I have twice experienced the use of such informed guessing episodes in other disciplines (in geology and art history slide-supported presentations), interestingly in both these cases the presenter prefaced his remarks with the same phrase 'Now let's play a party game'. In my own discourse community, I believe that involving others in context-stripped and task-oriented text analysis is viewed as too central and too valuable an activity to be dismissed as 'playing a party game'. And as far as I am aware, presentations of this distinctive and relatively prevalent type have no name.

This section opened with the promise that it would produce an adequate characterization of genre. The working definition that follows may in fact not be fully adequate, but it has I believe benefited from the discussion of the term in allied fields and does represent some advance on my earlier formulations (e.g. Swales, 1981a). Although there remain several loose ends, some to be discussed in the next two sections, my present understanding is summarized below.

Genre defined

A genre comprises a class of communicative events, the members of which share some set of communicative purposes. These purposes are recognized by the expert members of the parent discourse community, and thereby constitute the rationale for the genre. This rationale shapes the schematic structure of the discourse and influences and constrains choice of content and style. Communicative purpose is both a privileged criterion and one that operates to keep the scope of a genre as here conceived narrowly focused on comparable rhetorical action. In addition to purpose, exemplars of a genre exhibit various patterns of similarity in terms of structure, style, content and intended audience. If all high probability expectations are realized, the exemplar will be viewed as prototypical by the parent discourse community. The genre names inherited and produced by discourse communities and imported by others constitute valuable ethnographic communication, but typically need further validation.

3.6   Pre-genres

One of the basic assumptions underlying much of the preceding discussion is that human beings organize their communicative behavior *partly* through repertoires of genres. Thus, it is not the case that all communicative events are considered instances of genres. In fact, there are at least two areas of verbal activity that I believe are best considered to lie outside genres: casual conversation or 'chat' and 'ordinary' narrative.

The nature and role of conversation will be considered first, and Levinson's opening position will serve perfectly well:

> Definition will emerge below, but for the present *conversation* may be taken to be that predominant kind of talk in which two or more participants freely alternate in speaking, which generally occurs *outside specific institutional settings like religious services, law courses, classroom and the like.*

(Levinson, 1983:284, my emphases)

This kind of talk has, of course, been massively studied and discussed, particularly since the advent of the tape recorder (e.g. Grice, 1975; Goffman, 1981; Levinson, 1983; Richards and Schmidt, 1983; Gardner, 1984); and Atkinson (1982) gives the ethnomethodological arguments for the centrality and significance of conversation. As he and many people have observed, 'ordinary' conversation is a fundamental kind of language use: for example Preston (1989:225–6) comments: 'Since conversation in some sense is basic to all face-to-face interaction, it may seem to refer to such a ubiquitous level of speech performance that one would sense a difference between it and anything else one might wish to call a genre'.

Casual conversation presumably occurred early in the evolution of the human race, as it does in a child's acquisition of first language. It takes up, for most of us, a fair part of our days; indeed involvement in conversation can be quite hard to avoid. Further, our sense of the enveloping nature of conversation is brought home when we consider its absence. Therein, after all, lay many of the trials and tribulations of Robinson Crusoe. It is often said that the severity of placing a prisoner in 'solitary confinement' resides as much as anything in the denial of verbal interaction, and a 'vow of silence' is no light undertaking.

Additionally, there would appear to be attestable individual discrepancies between conversational and non-conversational skills. Probably all of us have known people who may be highly effective communicators in certain roles (as teachers, salespeople, joke-tellers, armchair critics and so on) yet who are adjudged to be lacking in the skills of ordinary conversation and thus are thought of as individuals who are 'difficult or uncomfortable to talk with'. Conversely, we probably know people who seem to have a remarkable facility to sustain casual conversation, but who are the first to announce, for instance, that they couldn't stand up and give a vote of thanks to save their lives. These observations all seem to point to the fact that general conversational ability and genre-specific verbal skills may be phenomena of a somewhat different kind.

If these observations have substance, it would seem that ordinary conversation is too persuasive and too fundamental to be usefully considered as a genre. Rather, it is a pre-generic 'form of life', a basis from which more specific types of interaction have presumably either evolved or broken away. The interesting question for the genre analyst is not so much whether conversation is a genre; instead, the interest lies in exploring the kind of relationship that might exist between general conversational patterns, procedures and 'rules' and those that can be discovered in (to give three examples) legal cross-examinations, medical consultations and classroom discourse. In those three cases, are the unfolding interactions best seen as mere extensions and modifications of common conversational practice and thus ultimately parasitic on such practice? Or, alternatively, would we gain a greater understanding of what is happening by considering them as existing independently in separate universes of discourse? Are *Unequal Encounters* (Candlin, 1981) such as normally occur between doctor and patient, lawyer and witness, and teacher and pupil, of a different *kind* to the more equal and less goal-directed encounters that take place in casual conversation?

Another interesting aspect of the putative relationships between the pre-genre and genres occurs in situations where 'ordinary' face-to-face conversation is replaced by telecommunication. Schegloff (1979) has shown that telephone conversations actually open with the ringing of the telephone and that the person lifting the receiver and speaking is *responding* to a summons. He has also analyzed and described the limited range of procedures that Americans use to identify and recognize each other on the telephone (much less of a problem, of course, if you can see to whom you are about to talk). Owen (1981) has written interestingly on the use of 'well' and 'anyway' as signals given by British telephone speakers to indicate a wish to close a topic or a call. However, to establish that a particular kind of communicative event has specific, situation-bound opening and closing procedures is not, in fact, to establish very much, because specificity may well be concentrated at initiation and termination (Richards and Schmidt, 1983:132–3). For example, open-ings like 'Merry Christmas', 'Good morning, Sir', 'Oh, we are smart today', 'Come here often, do you?' reflect particular circumstances that are likely to be of rapidly diminishing importance as the conversation proceeds. Therefore, on present evidence, it would seem sensible to exclude personal telephone conversations from genre status and to consider them, despite their relatively short history, as part of the pre-genre.

In contrast, we can immediately recognize the unusual nature of radio-telephony. Robertson (1985; 1988), for example, outlines the purposes of plane–ground radio-telephony as to:

i)   prevent collisions in the air;
ii) prevent collisions between aircraft and between aircraft and obstructions on the manoeuvering area;
iii) expedite and maintain orderly flow of air-traffic;
iv) provide advice and information useful for the safe and efficient conduct of flights.

(Robertson, 1985:295)

Given these aims it is not surprising that there have evolved especially rigid rules for *turn-taking* (Sacks, Schegloff and Jefferson, 1974) and special conventions for clarifying both rhetorical function and identity. These conventions have to be learnt by native speakers as well as non-native speakers, as the following fragment illustrates:

Control: Sierra Fox 132, correction, Sierra Fox 123,
         what is your flight level?
Pilot: Flight level 150, Sierra Fox 123.
Control: Say again flight level, Sierra Fox.
Pilot: Flight level 150, Sierra Fox 123.

(Robertson, 1985:303)

Radio-telephonic Air Traffic Control meets the criteria for genre status.

If casual conversation is a pre-generic dialogic activity, is there a comparable pre-genre for monologue? The obvious candidate is *narration* (if viewed as a process) or *narrative* (if viewed as product). Narrative, like conversation, is a fast expanding research field (Van Dijk, 1972; Grimes, 1975; Longacre, 1983) and has developed its own disciplinary name, *Narratology* (Prince, 1982). For present purposes I will simply follow Longacre and suggest that narration (spoken or written) operates through a framework of temporal succession in which at least some of the events are reactions to the previous events. Further characteristics of narrative are that such discourses tend to be strongly oriented towards the agents of the events being described, rather than to the events themselves, and that the structure is typically that of 'a plot'. These pre-generic long turns commonly occur in letters and also arise as responses to such prompts as 'How was the vacation?' or 'How did the meeting go?' and so on.

In a way analogous to that described for conversation, specific types of narrative diverge from the pre-generic norm and thus begin to acquire genre status. Thus in news stories the temporal succession is disturbed by putting 'the freshest on the top'. In reports of various kinds, such as those describing scientific work, events rather than agents predominate. Jokes have temporal sequences, agent orientation and plot, but the resolution of the plot is specific: the moment of resolution needs to be overtly signaled (the onset of the punch line) whilst the manner of resolution needs to be unpredictable.

A final point perhaps worth making at this juncture is that the English-speaking world (as one of many) uses *names* to describe classes of communications that quite appropriately operate as higher-order categories than genres. One very common example is the *letter*. This useful term, of course, makes reference to the *means* of communication, but lacks as a class sufficient indication of purpose for genre status. The same observation holds for subsets of the class that refer to fields of activity such as business letters or official letters. It is only when purpose becomes ascribable that the issue of genre arises, as in begging letters or letters of condolence. Category labels like *letters* do not therefore refer to pre-genres in the sense used here, but operate as convenient multigeneric generalizations.

3.7   Differences among genres

If there were only minor differences among genres there would be little need for genre analysis as a theoretical activity separable from discourse analysis, and probably no need at all for an analysis driven by applied concerns. But, of course, it turns out that genres vary significantly along quite a number of different parameters. We have already seen that they vary according to complexity of rhetorical purpose – from the ostensibly simple *recipe* to the ostensibly complex *political speech*. They also vary greatly in the degree to which exemplars of the genre are prepared or constructed in advance of their communicative instantiation (Nystrand, 1986). Typical prepared genres might include research papers, letters of personal reference, poems, recipes, news broadcasts and so on, while at the other extreme arguments and rows typically flare up without malice aforethought. Genres also vary in terms of the mode or medium through which they are expressed; indeed the configurations of speech versus writing can become quite complex (Gregory, 1967). For instance, of the previous examples of prepared genres, most are predominantly written. However, research papers can be presented at conferences in 'manuscript delivery' (Dubois, 1985) or as 'aloud reading' (Goffman, 1981), while references and recipes can in an emergency be communicated by the telephone. Poems in western cultures have in modern times been a predominantly written form, although 'aloud reading' of them is an ongoing tradition and one thought of as requiring uncommon skill in modulated performance (in the case of actors) or in interpretation (in the case of poets reading their own work). In other cultures the converse may apply with poetry as an essentially oral medium, written forms operating as archival repositories. News broadcasts are scripted and then read aloud.

Prepared-text genres like those we have been considering vary also in the extent to which their producers are conventionally expected to consider their anticipated audiences and readerships. However, this variability is somewhat at odds with much current thinking on and research into writing processes. An influential and representative advocate of the interactional orientation to reading and writing processes is Widdowson (Widdowson, 1979; 1983; 1984). He expresses his 1979 position, which has little changed (cf. 1984:220) in this way:

> As I write, I make judgements about the reader's possible reactions, anticipate any difficulties that I think he might have in understanding and following my directions, conduct, in short, covert dialogue with my supposed interlocutor.

(Widdowson, 1979:176)

According to this view, writers, at least competent ones, are trying to second-guess both their readers' general state of background knowledge and their potential immediate processing problems. At the same time (competent) readers are interrogating authors on their present positions as well as trying to predict where the authors' lines of thought or description will lead. There is, as it were, a reciprocity of semantic effort to be engaged in by both sides; a contract binding writer and reader together in reaction and counter-reaction.

Investigations into various genres would, however, suggest that this supposed sociocognitive activity is over-generalized, since a producer's contract with a receiver is not general, but subject to quite sharp genre fluctuations. Of course, the interactional view is obviously both appropriate and useful in certain contexts such as the processing of recipes and news broadcasts. Indeed, Hugh L'Estrange (personal communication) has pointed to the fact that recipe-mongers who fail to be considerate of the reader can contribute to gastronomical shipwreck, as in 'Transfer immediately to a *pre-greased* tin'. And news broadcasts go to quite considerable lengths to ensure that they are comprehensible both by repetition ('Here are the main points again') and by providing background information ('President Kyprianou of Cyprus', 'Faya-Largau, a strategic town in Northern Chad . . .') (Al-Shabbab, 1986). While recipes and news broadcasts may be marginal to the purposes of this book, we can also affirm that a unifying characteristic of instructional-process genres will be consideration for the reader or listener.

However, it remains the case that in certain genres, usually written ones, the writer has the right to withdraw from the contract to consider the reader because of an overriding imperative to be 'true' to the complexity of subject matter or to the subtlety of thought and imagination (Elbow, 1988). Thus we find that in a significant number of genre texts, in laws and other regulatory writings, in original works in philosophy, theology and mathematics (and arguably theoretical linguistics), in many poems, and in certain novels of which Joyce's *Finnegan's Wake* would be an extreme example, there is a diminished consideration for the reader. Joyce, after all, is reported to have commented on *Finnegan's Wake* to the effect that as the book took him 18 years to write he didn't see why the reader shouldn't take as long to read it.

There is in fact a standard defense of the legal draughtsman's practice of using very long sentences containing numerous and elaborate qualifications (all those elements beginning *notwithstanding, in accordance with, without prejudice to* etc.). This defense would claim that it is ultimately more satisfactory for a legal text to reveal clarity after detailed and expert study than to be a text that, however immediately accessible to an educated lay audience, falls into ambiguity upon multiple reading (Bhatia, 1983).

Thus it turns out that certain legal, academic and literary texts all point to another kind of contract that can exist between writer and reader. This is one not based on 'consideration' but on *respect*. If we use Widdowson's device of imagining the thoughts of the writer, it might come out something like this:

> As I write, I am aware that, whatever I do, what I write will be
> difficult for most readers. Because of what I am trying to achieve,
> this is unavoidable. This is why I must convince the readers that
> their efforts will be rewarded; I need to keep their faith that I am
> not making my text unnecessarily difficult.

While Flower (1979) and her co-workers may be generally right in their
theory that the immature writer produces 'writer-based prose' and the
mature writer 'reader-based prose', it would seem equally clear that in
certain genres mature writers also produce 'writer-based prose'.

Genres also vary in the extent to which they are likely to exhibit
universal or language-specific tendencies. On the one hand, it would
appear that the diplomatic press communiqué has developed a global if
devious set of conventions whereby, for instance, 'a full and frank
exchange of views' is interpreted by discourse community members
throughout the capitals of the world as signifying that the parties failed to
agree. On the other hand, one might reasonably assume that marriage
proposals will differ widely from one language community to another
because they are deeply embedded in particular socioeconomic cultural
matrices.

The sociolinguistic literature on the form, structure and rationale of
specific communicative events is vast and falls largely outside the scope of
this book (see Saville-Troike, 1982; Downes, 1984; and Preston, 1989
for overviews). However, there is one investigative area that is directly
relevant to a pedagogically-oriented study of academic English, one
known as *Contrastive Rhetoric*.

The concept of Contrastive Rhetoric was originally elaborated by
Robert Kaplan in a 1966 article entitled 'Cultural thought patterns in
intercultural education' (Kaplan, 1966). Kaplan, who has remained
active in this area, more recently summarized the concept as follows:

> There are, it seems to me, important differences between languages
> in the way in which discourse topic is identified in a text and in the
> way in which discourse topic is developed in terms of
> exemplification, definition, and so on.
>
> (Kaplan, 1987:10)

The notion that the rhetorical structure of languages differs is not only
relevant in itself, but more particularly because much of the work to date
has been based on the study of expository prose (Connor and Kaplan,
1987). Kaplan and Ostler (1982), in a review of the literature, conclude,
despite a minority of studies to the contrary, that different languages
have different preferences for certain kinds of discourse patterns. For
instance, they argue that English expository prose has an essentially
linear rhetorical pattern which consists of:

> ... a clearly defined topic, introduction, body which explicates all but nothing more than the stated topic, paragraphs which chain from one to the next, and a conclusion which tells the reader what has been discussed ... no digression, no matter how interesting, is permitted on the grounds that it would violate unity.
>
> (Kaplan and Ostler, 1982:14)

They then contrast this pattern with the elaborate parallel structures found in Arabic prose, with the more digressive patterns of writing in Romance languages which permit 'tangential' material to be introduced in the discourse, and so on. Clyne (1987), in a particularly careful study, has examined the *Exkurs* or 'digression' in contemporary academic German and is able to show, among other things, that the *Exkurs* is not only institutionalized in certain German genres but has no easy translation equivalent in English.

Comparison of languages is notoriously difficult, especially at the discoursal level (see Houghton and Hoey, 1983, for a specification of *caveats*). Among such caveats it is important to compare texts of the same *genre* in two languages. Ostler (1987), for example, can be criticized for comparing student placement essays with extracts from published texts.

In general terms the existence today of 'invisible colleges' and of transnational discourse communities is likely to lead to universalist tendencies in research genres. A strong form of the universalist hypothesis is offered by Widdowson:

> Scientific exposition is structured according to certain patterns of rhetorical organization which, with some tolerance for individual stylistic variation, imposes a conformity on members of the scientific community no matter what language they happen to use.
>
> (Widdowson, 1979:61)

Najjar's 1988 study of research articles in English and Arabic dealing with agricultural science shows sufficiently few and sufficiently unimportant differences to provide some support for the universalist argument. However, as we have seen, Clyne (1987) provides some counter-evidence from German as does Peng (personal communication) from Mandarin. The jury is still out.

Although universalist tendencies may be apparent in research activities, those who have taught in different higher education institutions around the world have typically been struck by the peculiarities of study modes, teaching styles and of general educational expectations within particular institutions (James, 1980). If we examine, say, the first years of undergraduate study in Faculties of Science, I believe it would be difficult to argue that what goes on in those faculties is part of a universal scientific culture. Rather, we tend to find in this area of scientific activity powerful local influences of many kinds: national, social, cultural, technical and religious. The ways in which such influences form particular 'educational cultures' have been described for various parts of the world: Thailand (Hawkey and Nakornchai, 1980); Iran (Houghton, 1980); the Arab World (Dudley-Evans and Swales, 1980; Holliday, 1984); Asia (Ballard and Clanchy, 1984). There have also been some interesting studies of the 'rhetorical gaps' that apprentice researchers from overseas have to cross when learning English academic style: a Yemeni Arab student (Holes, 1984); a Brazilian (James, 1984a); a Thai and a Japanese (Ballard, 1984). All in all, it looks as though the relativist hypothesis has some substance in teacher–student genres such as textbooks, lectures and tutorials. Nevertheless, we face a difficulty in interpretation. We can either lean towards intrinsic cultural differences, or we can prefer an explanation that would go no further than stress the relevance of recent history. For instance, are the differences between western and Arab educational genres a reflection of differences in rhetorical and ideological codes, or do they signify little more than different stages in an educational cycle? More precisely, would we do better to interpret such differences as deriving principally from, on the one hand, an Islamicized verbalistic tradition and, on the other, a secularized pragmatic European or North American tradition? Or should we conclude that modes of study and modes of expression commonly accepted and practiced in the Arab World today are in surprising numbers of ways similar to those existing in the West 50 years ago (the teacher *qua* teacher as respected authority, a stress on rote-learning, a style of writing in the tradition of *belles-lettres* etc.)? An educational ethos which may, of course, yet revive in the West.

At present, our perspectives on the formative influence of the educational environment rest largely on anecdote, incidental observation and the single-subject case study. Mohan and Lo (1985:515) are certainly correct in their critique of Contrastive Rhetoric when they point to 'a need for greater awareness of students' native literacy and educational experience as factors influencing the development of academic writing in a second language'. It is hoped that the concept of genre developed in this book, especially with regard to features of text-role and text-environment, will contribute to a less narrowly linguistic orientation in Contrastive Rhetoric studies. And indeed, independently, there are signs that this is already happening. Hinds (1987:143–4) has suggested that English-language cultures tend to charge the writer 'with the responsibility to make clear and well-organized statements', whereas in Japanese culture 'it is the responsibility of the listener (or reader) to understand what it is that the speaker or author had intended to say'. Hinds' typology can thus be related, in a cross-cutting way, to the previous discussion on genre-specific differences in the writer's responsibility. Finally, Eggington

(1987) has shown the existence of two rhetorical styles in contemporary academic Korean, one deriving from traditional rhetoric and the other much influenced by English. Although Eggington does not put it in these terms, we can see here the existence of two discourse communities: an elite group of US-educated scholars who are members of the international community of researchers in their specialization, and a larger national community using traditional Korean rhetoric. Indeed, the discourse community concept, as a sociorhetorical construct, offers some general illumination on the difficult and important question of academic language variation across cultures and generations.

4 *The concept of task*

4.1 Task and academic English programs

The third and final concept singled out for special attention is that of language-learning task. However, as this concept brings us closer to pedagogical practice than either *discourse community* or *genre*, we shall consider first how all three might contribute in general terms to the development of academic English programs. Then in 4.2 the merits of various conceptualizations of language-learning *task* will be briefly reviewed against this general framework and a modification suitable for this book's purposes proposed. Finally, in 4.3, I shall attempt to illustrate the approach in the context of some actual academic English teaching materials. The general framework is summarized in Figure 2 opposite.

Like all such diagrams, Figure 2 provides a crude schematization of processes, which in reality are likely to be more overlapping and interconnected than the figure intimates. It suggests, for example, that ethnographic work, of both humble and sophisticated kinds, leads to characterizations of discourse communities, while discourse analysis leads to characterizations of genres. However, as we have already seen, the relationships are much less isomorphic than that, for genres are neither simply texts nor discourse communities simply groups of individuals who share attitudes, beliefs and expectations. The horizontal arrows therefore indicate general propensities rather than bounded investigative territories.

Figure 2 proposes that those concerned with academic English programs in various ways could adopt a four-fold investigative strategy for the realization of their objectives.

I. ETHNOGRAPHY

This strand comprises broadly ethnographic studies (by observation, participation, interview, questionnaire, etc.) of the relevant discourse communities. Although primary targets are the discourse communities that the course participants have joined, are trying to join, or hope to join, secondary targets are the controlling discourse communities of the

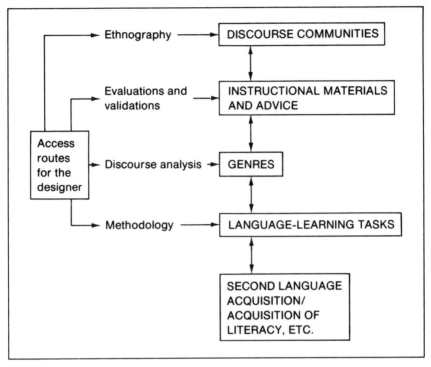

Figure 2   A framework for developing academic English courses

host educational milieu. The pragmatic importance of the latter is now well established (Bridwell-Bowles, 1988; Blair, 1988; Holliday and Cooke, 1982; Swales, 1989).

2.   EVALUATIONS AND VALIDATIONS

One major activity falling within this strand refers to the well-established and sensible practice of reviewing available instructional materials. A subsidiary activity involves the empirical validation of claims made in textbooks, in handbooks and in other sources of advice and direction about the rationales and properties of genres. While such studies are always of value in that they add to our knowledge of how the (English) language is used in the world, they may take on an extra significance in an era when it is apparently becoming increasingly common for textbooks and manuals to rely on secondary data (statements and claims in *previous* textbooks and manuals) rather than on empirical studies of various kinds.

For example, Williams (1988) compared the language used by native speakers of English in business meetings with that taught by business ESL textbooks for use in such meetings. She found considerable discrepancy:

> In general terms the language used in the real meetings differed
> from that used in the tapes and films that accompany courses in
> being often ungrammatical and containing unfinished sentences,
> false starts, interruptions, redundancy, repetition, and lengthy
> explanation. It also lacked the overtly polite forms that were
> taught.
>
> (Williams, 1988:51)

As Williams concedes, the style of the meetings she examined was
distinctively informal because the participants all knew each other. She
also somewhat surprisingly restricted her study to the language produced
by the native speakers in the business meetings. Therefore, there must
remain doubt as to whether her data provides that close an approximation to what we might expect to find in typical NS–NNS or
NNS–NNS business interactions. However, Williams is surely right
when she stresses that materials producers are *accountable* for their
products: 'Working on educated guesswork or hunches when writing
dialogues and transactions for coursebooks or when selecting language
to teach is highly questionable' (1988:53).

Holmes (1988) has compared the expression of doubt and certainty
(via modal verbs, lexical verbs, adverbials, nouns and adjectives) in a few
ESL textbooks and in a range of corpora of spoken and written English.
As we might expect, 'epistemic' nouns (assumption, doubt, possibility,
tendency, etc.) are, according to the corpus data, more frequent in
academic writing, but Holmes concludes that 'nominal constructions are
a rather underrated epistemic category in all the textbooks and learners
are not well served by the range provided' (1988:37).

Other studies have been restricted to particular syntactic or rhetorical
topics. Huckin (1986), was able to show that the well-known Document
Design Center, while advocating principles for the use or otherwise of full
versus reduced relative clauses in technical manuals, failed to follow their
own advice in their own manual. Swales and Najjar (1987) examined
what research paper writing manuals have to say about the advisability
of including a summary statement of principal results at the end of the
introduction sections in those papers. They were able to show that in
published papers from two fields (physics and educational psychology)
the majority of advice was as much honored in the breach as in the
observance. Finally Jablin and Krone (1984) investigated 'bad news' job
rejection letters received by undergraduates against manual and textbook
advice on the one hand and student reaction on the other. The following
is such a letter (slightly adapted to preserve confidentiality):

Dear Michelle:

We appreciate having the opportunity to meet with you during our
recent visit to your campus.

> With respect to any pending offers you may have, we wish to advise you that as of this date we have been unsuccessful in our search to find an open position that would match your qualifications and interests. Your information will be retained in our .... retrieval system.
>
> The interest you have shown in .... is appreciated. Please accept our best wishes for success in your selected field of endeavor.
>
> Sincerely,

Jablin and Krone found that the manual advice was largely corroborated with one glaring exception. The manual advice recommends a personal tone and a personal form of address in rejection letters, but students did not in fact appreciate this in the letters they received. The students felt that the use of first name implied that the corporation had come to know them well, and therefore that the rejection was based on a considered assessment of their personal inadequacy. In contrast, being addressed by title and last name allowed them more easily to believe that the rejection was based on superficial criteria. It wasn't the real 'them' who were being rejected.

The attention given in the last few paragraphs to what I have called validation studies reflects a perception that they represent a promising research area for genre-based approaches to the teaching of communicative competence. They enhance the 'accountability' of the instructional end products. They ground genre studies within the double context of, on the one hand, the prescriptive and advisory elements that may shape the production of exemplars and, on the other, the reactions of recipients to those exemplars. They also lead us towards an awareness that official statements about communicative procedures within discourse communities may not always accord with actual practice. It is well enough known, for example, that the formal requirements for a Ph.D. dissertation are being eroded in the harder sciences by the candidates' prior publication of technical articles (Halstead, 1988). It is well enough known that in the US the 'oral defense' of a thesis or dissertation has become a celebratory rather than inquisitional event; and it is well enough known that in some departments the official requirements for the approval of a dissertation proposal have fallen into abeyance.

3. DISCOURSE ANALYSIS

The third strand of discourse analysis has been sufficiently aired to require little further comment, except to note that the targets of analysis will not be restricted to either finished or professional products. Drafts, plans, revisions and rehearsals of genres central to a discourse community are grist to the mill, as are comparisons of processes and products between apprentice and expert members, and the use of 'specialist informants' (Selinker, 1979) to throw light on those processes and products (see Part III for further discussion of the 'specialist informant' issue).

4. METHODOLOGY

A final strand is methodology, which as Figure 2 shows, is here seen as being configured in terms of language-learning tasks. While the specification of task itself will be considered in the following subsection, the *place* of task can be seen as central to the framework. Tasks are seen as having communicative outcomes, just as genres are seen as having communicative purposes and discourse communities communicative goals. A task-driven methodology thus keeps an appropriate focus on rhetorical action and communicative effectiveness, however much the *means* to those communicative ends may involve, in various ways and to variable extents, the analysis and discussion of text and situation, and the teaching and practice of form. The actual devising of suitable tasks is shown in the figure as being moderated on the one side by considerations of genre and on the other by what we know of first or second language-learning processes.

This role of genre in task-construction would appear to need some justification as it is by no means universally accepted. Hutchinson and Waters (1987) also assign task a central place in their materials construction model. As they say:

> The model acts as a vehicle which leads the learners to the point where they are able to carry out the *task*. The *language* and *content* are drawn from the *input* and are selected according to what the learners will need in order to do the *task*.
>
> (Hutchinson and Waters, 1987:109)

However, in terms of Figure 2, Hutchinson and Waters look only downward for the criteria that will determine the nature and nurture of the task – they look to what we know of the language-learning process in the classroom (Chaudron, 1988). While this may be appropriate enough for the beginning stages, it is less than clear that it is, on the one hand, sufficient and, on the other, necessary for situations in which students are already having to cope with the exigencies of an English-speaking world outside the classroom.

The danger of ignoring genre is precisely the danger of ignoring communicative purpose. Indeed, as I have confessed elsewhere (Swales, 1985c), this is a lesson that I have learnt the hard way. I used to teach an EAP course for students entering the largely English-medium Faculty of Law at the University of Khartoum in Sudan. One of the main genres that

I used were Sudanese case reports, and for this choice I could put forward an elaborate justification. The case reports were relatively short authentic documents; they had certain similarities to the narratives the students had read in their English lessons at school; they introduced in a relatively easy-paced way useful Criminal Law vocabulary; they were situated within Sudanese culture; they had a consistent rhetorical structure consisting of front matter, narrative and judgment; and they were relatively easy to exploit for methodological activities. They thus formed, or so I thought, an excellent basis for a first series of reading comprehension units. However, the comprehension tasks I invited the students to undertake were misconceived because they were designed to help the students to understand the *stories*. It was only when I attended classes given by a Criminal Law professor that I belatedly came to realize that the reading strategy required in legal education was not to understand – and retain the gist of – a narrative, but to spot the crucial fact on which the decision (rightly or wrongly) rested. The problem-solving law professor's questions were quite different to my own. Because I had failed to appreciate the role of the genre in its environment, the reading strategies I was teaching, however well-founded in terms of ESL methodology, were probably doing the students more harm than good.

4.2   Towards a concept of task

At the end of the last section I revealed something of the slowness with which I had come to realize that pedagogical text and pedagogical task need to be inter-related. Prior to that I had concurred with Hutchinson and Waters that task was central to methodology. More generally, the centrality of task is a widely accepted position. Crookes (1986b) in a major cross-disciplinary review opens his summary section with the following conclusions:

> It has been shown that the category 'task', as used by researchers generally, is widely applicable and has psychological reality. Much, if not most, of human activity, whether in employment or in the classroom can be seen as a series of tasks – some having a communicative aspect, others not.

> (Crookes, 1986b:32)

In an earlier section Crookes had discussed a paper by Swaffar, Arens and Morgan (1982), in which the authors accounted for the research failure to show convincingly that one language teaching method is better than another in terms of the fact there are many shared classroom practices that cut across methods. Most of the real differences that exist, differ-

ences perceivable by language teachers as they reflect upon the pragmatics of their classrooms, reside in the nature of the tasks and their
arrangements. 'By their tasks you shall know them.'

Even if there is growing consensus that *task* is an important concept in
language learning – indeed task-based learning has already become
abbreviated to TBL (Samuda and Madden, 1985) – there is little
agreement how task might be appropriately defined. Long (1985) and
Coleman (1987) consider task as broadly equivalent to *activity*, and even
for whose who wish to restrict the context to language teaching, there is
an often expressed wish to generalize the notion of task. Here is Breen:

> Throughout the paper, the notion of 'task' is used in a broad sense
> to refer to any structural language learning endeavor which has a
> particular objective, appropriate content, a specified working
> procedure, and a range of outcomes for those who undertake the
> task. 'Task' is therefore assumed to refer to a range of workplans
> which have the overall purpose of facilitating language learning –
> from the simple and brief exercise type to more complex and
> lengthy activities such as group problem-solving simulations and
> decision-making.
>
> (Breen, 1987:23)

Although the distinction that Breen goes on to make between *task-as-
workplan* and *task-in-process* will be seen to be important, the above
characterization runs counter to one widely held assumption in TBL: that
of *enablement* or *support*. If the 'simple and brief exercise type' is seen as
an end in itself, as it might well be in a structural syllabus, then it does not
reflect a task-based approach. However, if it is so structured as to operate
as directly facilitative of an encompassing 'real' task, as *means* to that
end, then it will be task-based (Edge and Samuda, 1983; Samuda and
Madden, 1985; Hutchinson and Waters, 1987). Breen's characterization
lacks structure because it does not assume that all language activities are
to be related to tasks.

The most elaborate of available definitions of language-learning task is
that of Candlin (1987):

> One of a set of differentiated, sequenceable problem-posing
> activities involving learners and teachers in some joint selection
> from a range of varied cognitive and communicative procedures
> applied to existing and new knowledge in the collective
> exploration and pursuance of foreseen or emergent goals within a
> social milieu.
>
> (Candlin, 1987:10)

Candlin immediately goes on to observe that different readers will give
variable emphasis to such a definition in the light of their different
pedagogical situations and purposes. So be it.

The idea that tasks are 'differentiated' and 'sequenceable' is clearly valuable. The fact that tasks can be seen to have beginnings, middles and ends provides an orientation for learners against the often opaque background of a course or syllabus: in addition they provide clear objectives for learners and establish 'landmarks of achievement' (Hutchinson and Waters, 1987:117). Tasks are clearly 'sequenceable' both in practice and theory, although there currently exist considerable doubts as to the validity of the criteria by which tasks can be ordered (Crookes, 1986b; Kumaravadivelu, 1988). As might be expected, many proponents advocate that tasks should be graded in terms of difficulty or complexity (e.g. Long, 1985; Prabhu, 1985) and in terms of alternating the focus from one that conceives the student as a language user to one that conceives the student as a language learner (Samuda and Madden, 1985; Hutchinson and Waters, 1987). However, at present, the simplicity or the complexity of a task, or the variable need to focus on content or form are not easily predictable in advance and perhaps – and perhaps valuably – never will be. As Breen observes, 'pre-designed tasks are little more than idealized plans for learner work' (1987:38). The *task-in-process* phenomena are not only full of surprises, both good and bad, but equally importantly the study of those phenomena builds up case law in our trial-and-error efforts to discover appropriate sequences of tasks.

Candlin also considers tasks to be 'problem-posing activities'. While task-based communicative language teaching has often emphasized the artful construction of activities that place the learners in a fragmented or disorganized communicative world so that they have to exchange information and otherwise co-operate in order to put that world to rights, I do not believe that 'problem-posing' should as such be criterial for task-status. There seem to me to be several kinds of task that are not problematic in the sense that I believe Candlin to be alluding to. If students have to come up with an answer to a question for which they have been given the relevant information, then I do not see that necessarily this should be considered as a *problem*. Not all questions are problems. More usefully, or so I believe, the activity needs to be *goal-directed* for assignation of task status.

The Candlin working definition then suggests that the activity should in various ways be jointly constructed by teachers and learners. This properly reflects the well-known concern of Candlin and other colleagues at the University of Lancaster to divest the instructor of much of his or her institutionally-given authority. Although the advocacy of joint-planning and class negotiation is surely admirable, and may well be a valuable concomitant of TBL, again I believe that it is unwise to consider it as a necessary condition for a suitable language-learning task. Occasions will surely arise when instructors may feel the need for unilateral action, particularly when a task-sequence is going wrong and a repair-type task seems warranted. In a similar way, I would question the need for the exploration and furtherance of goals to be 'collective', for this would suggest that individual or self-access or out-of-class activities are somehow not to be considered as tasks but merely have some lesser preparatory status. My final comment relates to the final phrase 'within a social milieu'. As far as I can see the phrase is ambiguous. Does 'social' here mean 'socializing', that is, does it refer to a preferred type of classroom dynamic? Or is it to be taken to mean that the *goals* are to be constructed within an actual or simulated operational environment? Or both?

I have given some attention to Candlin's definition partly because he enjoins his readers to do so and partly because it is the best available prototype. My commentary has been negative only in the qualified sense that it has required me to consider an alternative suitable for the genre-based approach advocated in this book. In that context, I suggest that we might think of *task* as:

> One of a set of differentiated, sequenceable goal-directed activities
> drawing upon a range of cognitive and communicative procedures
> relatable to the acquisition of pre-genre and genre skills
> appropriate to a foreseen or emerging sociorhetorical situation.

In the above definition I have, as expected, removed some of the typical characteristics of task-based approaches (negotiated, collective, gap-using) that I do not consider sufficiently criterial to be worth building in. Further, I have – evasively enough – proposed that the activities be *relatable* to genre acquisition. It would, on the one hand, be premature to claim that the activities and their associated procedures are *conducive* to genre skills; on the other, *relatable* allows the task-designer some freedom to experiment with various kinds of analysis and to explore unusual combinations of texts and tasks. I have also placed the task context within a sociorhetorical situation. On some occasions the sociorhetorical situation will in fact be represented by a discourse community, as when the class (including the instructor) meets the criteria established in Chapter 2. These occasions are more likely to occur with disciplinary specific, advanced groups, or in team-teaching situations (Johns and Dudley-Evans, 1980) or in adjunct classes of various kinds (Johns, 1988a; Shih, 1986). On other occasions, heterogeneity requires the construction of sociorhetorical situations for tasks to which individual participants can differentially contribute and in which their engagement may be more or less temporary. The following section, by presenting an actual teaching situation, will I trust, illustrate some of these concluding observations.

4.3   A pedagogical illustration

At the beginning of this chapter on tasks I suggested some major *access routes* whereby an instructor may create appropriate instructional activities. These routes are not *ordered* in any particular way; for example, there is no presumption that exploring discourse communities should precede analyzing genres or that genre analysis should precede the devising of tasks – which is why in Figure 2 the links between the levels have been characterized by double-ended arrows. Sometimes texts present the best immediate opportunity for development, sometimes tasks and sometimes the sociorhetorical situation; at other times it may seem most advantageous to pursue several access routes simultaneously.

I dare say something of this messy non-algorithmic nature of the materials design process will come across in the course fragment presented and discussed below. The fragment comes from a course entitled 'Dissertation, Thesis and Prospectus Writing for Non-Native Speakers'. The course draws an NNS population who have had at least 18 months' graduate experience of studying within an English-medium environment. The participants may come from all the disciplines offered at a major university except rarely from Engineering, for whom an alternative course in Technical Communication is advised.

It was in fact quite early in my first experience with the course that I came to realize that many students were having problems with an area of rhetorical activity that I had not hitherto considered of much significance. This area came to be known as 'Academic Communications' and includes such genres as memos to dissertation committee members, request letters to academics working elsewhere, and application letters for fellowships, assistantships, travel funds and so on. The NNS graduate students, with very few exceptions, said that producing such documents was new to them, and confessed to a limited sense of what their audiences might expect in communications of these kinds. In consequence, their level of confidence was lower in this area than in their more formal or official writing, and they revealed particular anxieties about organization and phraseology.

Although I was initially surprised by these findings, I soon came to see that the general sociorhetorical setting was indeed likely to be problematic. For one thing, there was a conspicuous absence of easily available role models. None of the textbooks, writing manuals or departmental guidelines available discussed how to write memos or request letters. For another, one-to-one communications between students and their perceived superiors were likely to be particularly reflective of the cultural norms that fashion levels of formality and respect across diverse national academic milieux. Thus, even if the students recognized that in the US they could be more to the point and more direct than in their various home academic cultures, this did not mean to say that they were either comfortable about or competent in doing things the American way. Thirdly, it was easy enough to recognize the perils of avoidance strategies. Here was a group of students who were at a crucial stage in their apprenticeships of the disciplinary-specific discourse communities they mostly planned to participate in as their primary career goals. These international communities had become strongly anglophone in their communicative networks, and if the students did not take advantage *now* of the opportunities provided by mentoring and the English-medium environment they might end up being part of what Baldauf (1986) has described as 'the lost generation' of researchers with inadequate English rhetorical skills.

Thus, it seemed to me that a sociorhetorical situation worth incorporating into the materials had become established – alongside more 'expected' elements such as *organizing the prospectus, handling the literature, negotiating knowledge claims,* and so on. The manner in which matters proceeded is perhaps best indicated by the introductory comments in the actual course materials for 'Academic Communications'.

> This section of the course concerns academic correspondence. In particular it deals with the following situations:
>
> I   Requests
> II   Follow-ups
> III Memos
> IV Submissions
>
> I have based the section on fragments of my own personal correspondence. I therefore do not know how typical the correspondence is – or how generalizable are my own reactions to communications from others. But I do genuinely believe the following things:
>
> a) The fact that I have been an active correspondent for many years has greatly helped my own research career.
>
> b) The more a person engages in such correspondence the more easily and the more quickly that person can correspond.
>
> c) Established researchers are *in general* happy to correspond with graduate students *as long as* their interest is aroused and maintained.
>
> I am interested in developing my understanding of this unresearched topic. Please share your experiences with me as fully as you can.
>
> I would like to acknowledge the most useful comments and criticisms made by participants in the ESP Reading Seminar, Fall 1987.

As I imagine readers will have recognized, the tone of the above is somewhat calculated. It is designed to present the instructor, despite surface considerations to the contrary (e.g. teaching ESL!), as comparable to the departmental faculty the students engage with as they go about the business of their research. It advocates communicative activity as being valuable in itself as well as for the membership benefits it may bring. On the other hand, it enters a plea for assistance and enlightenment, ostensibly as a means of developing knowledge, and tacitly as a methodological device for encouraging discussion and comparison among students so dispersed that they are only likely to come in contact through their participation in this particular course. Finally, the introduction ends with an acknowledgement, thus signifying the value of collaboration and the importance of its recognition (see Maimon, 1986 for an excellent discussion of this topic).

The fragment I shall use to illustrate a genre-based approach develops from three short request letters for papers:

a) *Address*

Dear Dr ....,

I have seen a summary of your work on .... in the .... Newsletter, No. 25. I am wondering if there is a longer typescript/reprint that you could let me have. If .... is now back in ...., please give him my regards.

Sincerely,

....

b) *Address*

Dear Professor ....:

I've come across a reference to one of your publications which, unfortunately, is not available in either the .... or .... libraries. From the title, I suspect we're thinking along similar or related lines regarding .... I would be most appreciative if you could send me a copy of the following article:

....

Thank you very much.

Sincerely,

....

c) *Address*

Dear Dr ....,

.... suggested that I write to you and request a copy of some of your recent work, which by all reports would be of much interest to me.

In the meantime I enclose a copy of my .... paper, which may just be of interest to you.

Sincerely,

....

Task One
In pairs answer the following questions.

1. (a) and (b) open in a similar way. How would you describe it?
2. (c) opens in a different way. Do you think that the subject of the first sentence is likely to be a well-known specialist? How much does the status of the 'suggester' matter?
3. There is one other reference to a person in the three texts. Where is it? And what is its function?
4. (b) expresses a belief that (a) does not. What is it?

Task Two
In actual fact, letter (a) was answered slowly, letter (b) was answered very quickly and letter (c) was never responded to at all.

1. What changes might you make to letter (a) to make it more effective?
2. Are there rhetorical reasons why (c) may not have been answered? And if so, how would you change the letter?

Redraft in pairs.

Task Three
One relevant aspect of request letters (as opposed to reprint requests) is that they provide an opportunity to show that you are an active researcher in the field. Letter (c) does this by actually sending a copy of the paper. Maybe you feel it would be less 'pushy' to *offer* to send a piece of your own work along with your request.

1. Under what circumstances would you use or *not* use the following?

   a) I would be happy to send you an unpublished paper on a similar topic that I have recently completed.
   b) I also work in your area – would you like copies of some of my recent stuff?
   c) As it happens, I have recently completed a paper entitled '....................' If you feel it might have a bearing on your own research, I would be pleased to send you a copy.
   d) I have a strong suspicion that you might find a recent paper of mine entitled '....................' of relevance to your work. Shall I send you a copy?

2. Draft a *Request–offer* letter you might be able to use. (It does not have to be about papers: it could be about materials, software, data etc.). In so doing, pay particular attention to the uses of *would* and *could* as illustrated in the previous texts.

Task Four
Look through your correspondence, particularly for short letters you have either sent or received. Do you have any interesting examples you would like to share? Are there any lessons we can learn from your correspondence? If so, call the instructor to discuss how we might arrange the tasks.

The above fragment is only partially representative of the general approach – inevitably some distortion arises from the fact that the section deals with short and relatively straightforward texts. Nevertheless, it does illustrate a number of features of *task* as defined as:

> One of a set of differentiated, sequenceable, goal-directed activities drawing upon a range of cognitive and communicative procedures relatable to the acquisition of pre-genre and genre skills appropriate to a foreseen or emerging sociorhetorical situation.

The emerging sociorhetorical situation is that of moving towards membership of a chosen discourse community via *effective* use of established genres within that community. The 'relatable' procedures include rhetorical analysis, discussion, and anticipation of audience reaction seen as a way of meeting discoursal expectations. The activities are differentiated across two parameters: first, they variously involve critique and composition and, second, they differ in the extent to which the text-task synergies are controlled or controllable by the instructor (obviously less so in the case of Task Four). Finally, in all cases in this fragment, both the illustrative texts *and their rhetorical effects* have been taken from an external world that has nothing directly to do with the actual teaching of academic English.

The methodological and rhetorical value of encouraging participant contributions is hard to overestimate. On one occasion, Task Four produced a series of short request letters written by a Korean doctoral student in metallurgy which were amazingly successful – to the extent of his being able to obtain highly confidential research and development information from certain corporations. Class discussion led to a consensus that perhaps the reasons for the student's success could be attributed to (a) clear statements that the student was a temporary visitor to the US and (b) texts that inadvertently provided clear evidence that the writer was not a native speaker.

Some of the least successful texts that students have volunteered fall into the category of memos to faculty members. Here is part of one:

In connection to our earlier conversations regarding my candidacy exam, I would like to make a clear understanding of certain details.

1. Your role as a candidacy committee member will be to give advice and ask questions related to social aspects of ...

2. Out of the selected papers that you have asked me to read for preparation of the exam, I have not been able to locate/read the following ...

I would appreciate it if you can give me a copy of these articles before the exam or ask questions in a manner that I do not have to depend upon these readings for answers.

The graduate student claimed that he was 'under stress' and observed that in any case he was just following the professor's instructions in a phone call to 'tell me what you want me to do'. Needless to say, the memo gave rise to some need for a repair, which fortunately was successful. These brief characterizations of unexpected high and low points (from a rhetorical point of view) illustrate two general features of the proposed approach. First, student contributions are a continuing source of enlightenment for all the parties concerned. Second, the contributory activity continually adds to the repertoire of genre-centered tasks available for future courses.

Kumaravadivelu (1988) has observed that the general language teaching approach will influence the conceptualization of task. Thus, in *language-centered* approaches learners are likely to be required to perform tasks by utilizing pre-selected grammatical structures and vocabulary items; in *learner-centered* approaches he suggests that students' attention will additionally be drawn to functional or notional properties of language; and in *learning-centered* approaches attention will be focused on negotiation of meaning. In a comparable way, a *genre-centered* approach is likely to focus student attention on rhetorical action and on the organizational and linguistic means of its accomplishment. The extent to which such an approach can find support in the L1 and L2 research literature is the topic of the final chapter in Part II.

5 Genres, schemata and acquisition

As a genre-centered approach gives particular attention to the rhetorical organization of texts, a relevant set of issues concerns the role of *schemata*, their characteristics and their relationships to genre acquisition. The concept of schemata was introduced by Bartlett as long ago as 1932 to explain how the information carried in stories is rearranged in the memories of readers or listeners to fit in with their expectations. In Bartlett's experiments British students re-interpreted Apache folk-tales so that they fitted in with their own schemata, or prior knowledge structures, based on their European folk-tale experiences. Since then there have been many further studies in both L1 and L2 contexts that have shown that human beings consistently overlay schemata on events to align those events with previously established patterns of experience, knowledge and belief (Sanford and Garrod, 1981; Carrell, Devine and Eskey, 1988).

The first set of issues for this chapter then are the origin of these schemata, their nature and their relationships to genres. I suggest that the overall picture might look something like Figure 3 (overleaf).

According to Figure 3, our prior knowledge consists of two main components: our assimilated direct experiences of life and its manifold activities, and our assimilated verbal experiences and encounters. As the arrows show, both types of experience contribute to our accumulated store of facts and concepts. These sources will provide, amongst other things, background knowledge about the content area of a discourse, which in turn allows us to evaluate propositions in terms of their truth, and contributes to the evaluation of appropriacy and relevance. Cognitive activities of this kind are thus invocations of content schemata. They enable us to accept or reject statements such as 'Mexico City is the largest city in the world', 'an increase in price will cause an increase in demand', 'Marilyn Monroe was a great singer' or 'my sister likes ice cream'.

As Widdowson (1983) has shown, it is content schemata that explain the fact that certain apparently empty and tautologous statements can

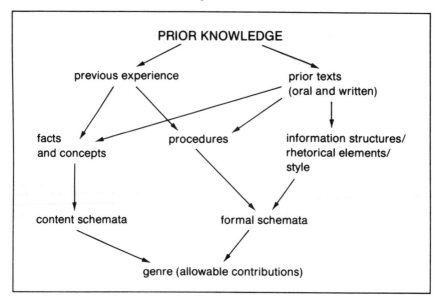

Figure 3

have meaning. Statements like:

a) Boys will be boys.

b) Business is business.

c) The Law is the Law.

work because they invoke both a literal and an interpretive schema so that the second instantiation somehow glosses the first:

a) Young males are typically boisterous, rough and untidy (and don't expect anything else).

b) The world of commercial practice is a world divorced from social and personal loyalties and ties (and don't expect anything else).

c) The system of legal rules is an imposed and elaborate system (but don't expect in consequence that it will be necessarily just or fair).

In most cases, of course, we lack a sufficiently strong interpretive schema to make sense of such tautologies. I dare say few of us are able to negotiate much meaning for the following: 'English teachers will be English teachers' or 'Dentistry is dentistry'.

Prior knowledge not only interprets facts and concepts but also calls up interactive procedures or routines. The latter have, with some relatively small differences in conceptualization, been given a wide range of labels: *scripts* (Schank and Abelson, 1977; Zuck and Zuck, 1984), *scenarios*

(Sanford and Garrod, 1981), *frames* (Van Dijk, 1977) and *routines* (Widdowson, 1983a). Knowledge of such procedures derives from both non-verbal and verbal kinds of experience (as Figure 3 shows) and regulates our behavior in pre-generic settings and in generic ones such as 'Visiting the doctor' or 'Going to a restaurant'. As Thomas (1983) and many others have shown, procedures have to be unlearnt and relearnt in unaccustomed cultural situations where different schemata may be the norm. A common instance of this occurs in meal ordering in unfamiliar countries. British visitors new to the US often find themselves ill-prepared for the number of questions they have to answer in order to obtain a meal. Visitors to Italy are often surprised at the number of questions Italian diners ask about the food. Ordering sequences can vary too. Although there may be a tendency to order food in expected order of arrival, sometimes alternate schemata prevail, such as ordering the main dish first and then the peripherals.

Figure 3 suggests that procedures may derive from both previous experience and prior texts and contribute to the formation of *formal* schemata – 'background knowledge of the rhetorical structures of different types of texts' (Carrell, 1983:81). If, of course, the knowledge of prior texts is entirely secondary (as when it is exclusively derived from fictional sources), it may be sufficiently inaccurate to give rise to inappropriate schemata. It may be the case, for instance, that a citizen arrested for the first time by the police will not behave in the expected manner because of reliance on schemata engendered entirely by detective stories, and police films and television series.

The directive force of procedural routines is often made most manifest by seeing them disturbed. The following short conversation was recorded at the Dry Cleaning establishment where I had become accustomed to a set routine. Brackets refer to significant pauses.

Customer: Two pairs of pants and a sweater.
Clerk: O.K. Name, please?
Customer: Swales . . . S–W–A–L–E–S.
Clerk: First name?
Customer: (   ) John.
           (   ) Will it be Monday?
Clerk: Yes, anytime after 12 on Monday.

The first break in the routine occurred when a new clerk asked for a first name rather than an initial, which led to a surprised pause before the volunteering of information that might be considered unexpectedly personal. The second and longer pause occurred in anticipation of a statement from the establishment's representative regarding pick-up time. Thus it is that variations in procedure may give rise to new procedures, so that I have now become attuned to being asked for my first name and to being expected to know, as a recognized customer, when the clothes will be ready.

So far we have seen that knowledge of prior texts may lead to sufficient recognition of informational and rhetorical structure to invoke a formal schema. The precise mechanism by which this process occurs is debatable. Becker, in the passage below, argues strongly for what can be called a 'particularist' position:

> It is sometimes felt that prior text can be evoked without an image – that we have an abstract set of 'rules' for an opera or a journal entry – or any of the language games we can take part in. The set of 'rules' is felt to be apart from any particular opera or journal entry, just as a grammar is felt to be definable apart from text. That seems backwards: one may formulate an abstract image of an opera or a journal entry, full of necessary and probable features, but the act of formulation is itself a language game, in a particular language, and not a prerequisite to understanding opera or journal entries. One sees opera after opera, and each one frames the next new experience – and these, I would argue, are particular images – not structures but particular in every regard. The real *a prioris* of language are not underlying structures, but prior language, prior texts.
>
> (Becker, 1983:8)

The cited passage usefully emphasizes the well-attested phenomenon that each experience we have of a class of events changes our perceptions of that class. Equally usefully, it points to the strength of textual memory. There are quotations that we use and respond to, just as there are 'catch phrases' that we consider indexical of people well known to us. So it is that memory of *a text* (as opposed to memory of *text*) allows us to make comments like 'The imagery here seems reminiscent of *The Waste Land*' or 'Chomsky's later style has become much more personal'. However, it is less easy to see that we always retain the latest particular image of 'the most immediately prior text' because it is by no means clear that our textual memories are always or even typically of a verbatim nature. While Becker may be right in the way in which a particular discourse may *evoke* other discourses, it is also the case that a particular discourse may *invoke* more abstract properties such as informational arrangement and rhetorical structure and more general features of textuality (Grabe, 1988a).

As we have already seen elsewhere in the first half of this volume, it seems that both content and formal schemata can contribute to a recognition of genres and so guide the production of exemplars. In this particular section, I have tried to indicate how these processes may come about. However, it is. clear that the ways in which the two types of schema – with or without the intervention of interpersonal schemata or procedures – *interact* is at present incompletely understood. In 1983, Carrell, a leading ESL researcher in schema theory, expressed the dilemma in the following way:

> However, the more serious problem is how to measure the separate or interactive contributions of both content and formal schemata when considering the processing of naturally-occurring texts processed in natural (or at least naturalistic) settings. In other words, real people in real language-processing situations encounter texts which have simultaneously a content expressed in a given rhetorical form. What we would need to know in these natural situations with naturally-occurring texts is what the relative contributions are of both prior knowledge of the content area as well as the prior knowledge of the rhetorical form. How facilitative of overall comprehension of the text is each type of background knowledge?
>
> (Carrell, 1983:87)

As put, the question may well not be answerable, or at least not admit of a consistent answer. The available research (e.g. Carrell, 1987) supports the common sense expectancies that when content and form are familiar the texts will be relatively accessible, whereas when neither content nor form is familiar the text will be relatively inaccessible. In the intermediate cases Carrell (1987) concludes:

> When *either* form *or* content is unfamiliar, unfamiliar content poses more difficulties for the reader than unfamiliar form. However, perhaps not surprisingly, rhetorical form is a significant factor, more important than content, in the comprehension of the top-level episodic structure of a text and in the comprehension of event sequences and temporal relationships among events.
>
> (Carrell, 1987:476)

Unfortunately, at least for the arguments in this book, the schema-theoretic research tradition in both L1 and L2 contexts has tended to rely on decontextualized textual samples that fit broad textual categories such as historical narrative or Meyer's five types of expository organization: collection, description, causation, problem-solution and comparison (Meyer, 1975; 1979). There has been in consequence some neglect of communicative purpose and of looking at text in terms of genre-specific organization. Carrell's 1987 texts illustrate these points well enough. She had two groups of ESL students, one of Muslim background and one of Roman Catholic background, work with four texts, all fictionalized versions of historical biographies of religious personages. Two of the texts described the life of a Muslim saint and two of a Catholic one. Each pair of culturally-specific texts (with the same content schemata) was presented in a straight temporal order (assumed to be related to formal schemata) and in an 'interleaved order' (1987:466) in which the early life and late life episodes were mixed up (unrelated to formal schemata).

As with all of Carrell's work, the 1987 paper describes a well-conceptualized and rigorously-conducted experiment. However, a genre-based version would look somewhat different. In the first instance, the texts would have been classified as Hagiographies (or Lives of the Saints) with an identifiable set of communicative purposes including the inspirational, and the role-modeling of the true if exceptional religious life. (The fact that the texts are of this genre is clear enough from some of the causal connections, for example, 'As a young child, because she was born on the Feast of the Annunciation, Catherine loved the Blessed Mother and the Holy Family very much' (1987:479). As far as I am aware, strict chronological order in hagiographic narrative may not be criterial; rather, its identifiable character may rest in its causation (as in the quotation above), in its style and in the exclusion of secular detail (unless used to extol the powers of conversion). Thus, the genre analyst might well approach the construction of a hagiography that breaks the conventions of rhetorical form from a different perspective. Similarly, there would be more attention given to recognition of the text's rationale and of the religious response of the subjects. Admittedly, Carrell does have an item in her questionnaire that asks the subjects to estimate how religious they felt they were, but she does not correlate these self-reports with any aspect of response to the texts.

The foregoing discussion of schema theory has been highly selective not because it has no close intrinsic relationship to a genre-based approach to academic English – indeed the opposite holds – but because the schema theorists have so far been most concerned with the cognitive aspects of text processing. This important and understandable orientation has made the putative distinction between content and form perhaps a more manageable distinction than genre analysts can easily maintain, for the nature of genres is that they coalesce *what* is sayable with *when* and *how* it is sayable. In addition, the schema theorist's emphasis on cognition has tended to isolate the text from its communicative purpose and from its environment. In the former case, the reader's first attempts to match a formal schemata is more likely to be, in the approach proposed here, a search for genre identification and placement. In the latter case, the environment sets up powerful expectations: we are already prepared for certain genres but not for others *before* we open a newspaper, a scholarly journal or the box containing some machine we have just bought. Nystrand (1986) has neatly illustrated these expectations by referring to the well-known process of sorting one's mail before it is even opened: this item is a circular, this is personal correspondence, this is likely to be an inquiry, and so on. As Nystrand says:

> The point of all this is that even before I open my mail I know
> something about it. Once the envelope is open, the trail of clues
> which precedes the text continues. My expectations are pro-
> gressively set and fine-tuned by such details as logos, letterheads,
> typeface, and mode of production (handwritten, typed, or dittos)
> ... These many layers of context which envelop the text provide
> clues to the text's meaning. The skilled reader uses these clues
> systematically to eliminate what the text might be about.
>
> (Nystrand, 1986:59)

And as Nystrand goes on to argue, this process of elimination is a kind of 'wedge' in which the first and broadest stage is to identify genre, the second to identify the topic of the communication and the third is to recognize the sender's stance on that topic. Nystrand in this way usefully identifies procedural routines that operate within the pre- or early textual context and gives genre a watershed role in controlling the reader's expectations.

The studies reviewed so far, such as those collected in Carrell et al. (1988), provide useful evidence for gains in reading comprehension as consequence of the teaching of text structure. However, the experimental studies have tended to view text structure in supra-generic terms such as historical narrative or problem–solution patterns (Hoey, 1983). Where there have been genre-specific investigations, these have tended to be largely qualitative or anecdotal in their pedagogical claims (Stanley, 1984; Zuck and Zuck, 1984; Swales, 1984b; Hewings and Henderson, 1987; Mitchell, 1987). Some shift in the reading research area towards a genre perspective would seem highly desirable.

A comparable situation currently exists in the area of writing. Swales (1990) shows that teaching non-native speakers the rationale and conventions of a common type of research article introduction can lead to the production of texts that sufficiently match the reader's formal schemata to override particular processing difficulties brought about by non-standard language. However, the data here is of an elaborate case study type. There is no control group comparison which would allow us to compare the textual products of those who had not received a genre-based treatment, nor indeed is there any before-and-after data from the students who actually participated in the class. For reasons that are not hard to seek, the genre analysts have largely concentrated on the textual analysis *per se*, while the schema-theorists and composition researchers have been more concerned with the experimental design. The case for merging the strengths of each group is urgent and strong.

In Part II, I have so far discussed such concepts as discourse commu-nity, genre and schema predominantly in relation to groups who had already experienced at least 15 years of schooling. In so doing, I may have given an impression that genre analysis and its applications are somehow *only* relevant to such groups. Before the general discussion closes, it may therefore be useful to comment briefly on the role of genres at earlier educational and developmental stages.

My understanding of trends in developmental psychology is that the traditional view (Piaget, 1962; Vygotsky, 1962) that small children's speech is egocentric or pre-social is becoming eroded, perhaps partly because of the much greater interest in recent years in discourse processing. In contrast, the typical small child is now seen as an interactive organism seeking out social stimulation. In some cases, this may be strengthened by direct tuition, especially at ritualistic turns in social events ('Don't forget to say "thank you very much for having me"'). In others, the child's grasp of properties of linguistic structure offers entrée into a world of coherent discourse. While they early respond to yes/no questions ('Are you warm enough?') with agreement or disagreement, they do not respond to negative *why* questions ('Why don't you go and play outside?') with *because* because they recognize them as suggestions (Shatz, 1983). Nelson and Gruendel (1979) argue that nursery children can carry out dialogue rather than engage in egocentric utterance when they have possession of both knowledge of conversation structure and sufficient content knowledge of the social world. Further Poulsen et al. (1979) have obtained strong evidence to indicate that four-year-olds already had some knowledge of conventional narrative schemata and were actively employing this knowledge in story understanding. Shatz's (1984) study of the stories of a child of that age indicates that they resembled mature stories in many ways except that the main discourse markers were not of narrative's *and then* type but were borrowed from the highly conversational *Guess what?* Overall, there would seem to be some evidence that children acquire some genre skills quite early because 'children are able to internalize models of language and of genres which have been provided through repeated conversational interactions' (Painter, 1986:81). Some of these early genres in my culture are bedtime stories, nursery rhymes and role-plays of the 'doctors and nurses' type.

Painter (1986) goes on to relate the acquisition of spoken genres to that of written ones:

> It is necessary for teachers to have a clearly formulated idea as to what kind of writing is being worked towards at a particular point in their programmes. It is not good enough simply to have 'expectations' that children will experiment with a variety of different functional genres, and to provide lists – often ridiculously ambitious – of suggestions of different types. Children do not learn to master a new *spoken* genre, such as making purchases in a shop or ordering a meal in a restaurant, just by suddenly being expected to do it. If they have not had any occasion to internalize a model of such a text type, whether spoken or written, how can they be

expected to construct it? In any event, just 'expecting' children to produce a variety of written genres, or leaving them 'free' to do so, will simply be restricting the possibility of success to those children whose out-of-school experience has given them some opportunity to gain familiarity with a discourse type.

(Painter, 1986:92–3)

The concerns expressed by Painter have been shared by many others who have seen the teaching of writing to be over-dominated by teacher emphasis on 'creativity' or 'originality' and under-concerned with genres other than narrative (e.g. Martin and Rothery, 1986). While few would advocate the elimination of story-writing, its preponderance in school writing classes has surely caused neglect of other genres that we can anticipate will be of greater service to students in their later activities, both educational and otherwise.

Although advocacy of varied genre-based instruction does raise the potential danger of formulaic and ideological indoctrination (Lemke, 1985), the danger is diminishable, as we saw earlier, by allowing sufficient space for the critiquing of genres. Kress (1982) articulates such a strategy well:

> The fact that few people's lives are so constructed as to permit them to exercise creativity, imagination, criticism is a fault not of the teaching of writing but of society. Given the lives that most school-learners will lead, I believe that there are, in addition to these, other skills with which the teaching of writing should provide them. They should have practice in the genres which will impinge most on their lives. The ideological contents of the various forms, genres, of writing should become the subject of overt discussion and direct teaching. In this way it could be that all school-learners would gain some insight into the meanings of their own and others' writing, to understand the content of the messages to which they are subjected, and to provide them with the essential skills necessary to manipulate, control, and organize language for their *own* purposes.

(Kress, 1982:13)

In this final chapter of Part II I have attempted to show how prior knowledge can, by diverse routes, give rise to the identification and control of genres. I have alluded to the important role of schemata in discoursal processing and production, but I have also observed that schemata alone reflect a microcosmic cognitive world dangerously adrift from communicative purpose and discoursal context. I have also noted that *hard* evidence for the value of genre-based approaches to the development of communicative competence is not yet readily available, although indirect support for such approaches comes from a number of areas: from schema-theory itself, from explorations into the power of prior texts, from acquisitional psychology and from the limitations of a narrowly expressivist view of reading and writing developments. At the end of the day, we may come to see that genres as instruments of rhetorical action can have generative power (Himley, 1986); they not only provide maps of new territories but also provide the means for their exploration. Yet the empowerment they provide needs to be accompanied by critical reflection in order to ensure that our students, as they journey forward, are not blind to the social consequences of their own actions and of those who have been there before them.

PART III   RESEARCH-PROCESS GENRES

In 1.2 I outlined the structure of Part III and gave a number of reasons for prioritizing research-process genres. Of these genres principal attention is given here to the *research article* or *research paper*; I shall not attempt to distinguish between the two. The research article or paper (henceforth often RA) is taken to be a written text (although often containing non-verbal elements), usually limited to a few thousand words, that reports on some investigation carried out by its author or authors. In addition, the RA will usually relate the findings within it to those of others, and may also examine issues of theory and/or methodology. It is to appear or has appeared in a research journal or, less typically, in an edited book-length collection of papers.

The fact that the research article usually appears within the covers of a particular journal means, of course, that it is not an independent *sui generis* text – some fixed and inexorable inscription of reality – but rather an end product that has been specifically shaped and negotiated in the author's efforts to obtain acceptance. Journals declare policies and requirements, some of which have become highly elaborated with the passing of time and the development of disciplinary paradigms. Bazerman (1987) for example has chronicled the remarkable growth in the American Psychological Association's *Publication Manual* from six and a half pages in 1929 to about 200 pages in 1983. This shaping process has several aspects. The most ostensible of them is a concern to maintain 'quality' via some form of refereeing process. Another is the obvious need to maintain an acceptable level of consistency among articles in a journal with regard to sectioning, style or referencing and so on. Somewhat less obviously, the shaping process also reflects the perceptions of journal editors and their advisory boards as to areas and types of research activity which they wish to promote or demote, since journals, especially important ones, are not simply passive reflectors of trends but also quiet instigators of policy.

One of the main reasons for giving attention to the research article is its quantitative and qualitative pre-eminence. Approximately half of the researchers who have ever lived are alive and active today. Most typically, the product of their research is the published research article, although of course a hard-to-estimate minority of research reports remain unpublished: they may be classified documents, they may be internal to a corporation's research division, or they may be ephemeral technical reports aimed at tackling a temporary problem. Alternatively, the reported research may be so flawed or so trivial that it will never appear in print. However, on the whole this is somewhat unlikely since most established researchers seem in the end to find a journal somewhere that will accept their papers. For instance, Relman (1978), the editor of the highly-regarded and prestigious *New England Journal of Medicine* (NEJM), analyzed what happened to the manuscripts rejected by his journal in 1975. On the average NEJM accepts at most 15% of the articles submitted. By using follow-up questionnaires (a 50% response rate), Relman was able to show that 85% of 151 articles rejected in 1975 either had been or were about to be published elsewhere, in the great majority of cases with only minor changes to the text. A further 5% had been submitted for publication. There remained only 15 papers (10%) which their authors had abandoned as a result of the painstaking NEJM refereeing process. As Relman observes:

> What seems clear is that the highly selective reviewing practices of the JCI (Journal of Clinical Investigation) and the NEJM mainly influence *where* papers will be published, not *whether* they will be published. Far from acting as *filters* or gatekeepers, these two journals seem to be functioning ... primarily as traffic officers directing the flow of papers either toward or away from themselves.
>
> (Relman, 1978:59)

The other side of the coin, the determination to keep on redrafting until success is achieved, is nicely illustrated in a case study by Myers (1985a) of two well-established biologists at the University of Texas. Both researchers wanted to move into a slightly different area but both had great difficulty in doing so. One sent his article to *Nature* (twice) and *Science* before it was accepted in a revised version at the *Journal of Molecular Evolution*. The other offered his paper to *Science* (twice), *Nature*, and *The Proceedings of the National Academy of Sciences* before it was finally accepted at *Hormones and Behaviour*. Each article had been through no less than four reviews and as Myers observes, 'the authors rewrote the articles each time, so that the published versions are hardly recognizable as related to the first submissions' (1985a:594).

Either way then, either by redrafting or by serial submission down a pecking-order list of journals, researchers are able to force themselves into print. The motivations to do so are extremely powerful. As Ziman (1968) and many others haved noted, research is not considered complete *until* it is made available to the wider research community. Further, publication is the major route to tenure, promotion, research grants and so on. Given all this, it comes as no surprise to find that 'where there is a will, there is a way'.

Such pressures have undoubtedly contributed to the exponential growth of research journals and articles in the last few decades. Blickenstaff and Moravcsik (1982) estimate that there are now 70,000 journals devoted to the sciences and technology around the world. If we add another third to cover all the other research areas, we approach Garfield's upper limit of 100,000 (Garfield, 1978). Some of these journals will be slim and intermittent, others will be frequent and enormous. Bazerman (1984a) has calculated that the *Physical Review* for 1980 contained a total of about 30 million words. Hence if somebody were to attempt to read *all* of the *Physical Review* their task in terms of wordage would be the equivalent of reading a substantial novel every day. The annual total of research articles themselves is even more uncertain, but if we take a (conservative) average of 50 articles per journal per year the total would be somewhere around five million. Thus, the research article is a gargantuan genre – in the printed medium unrivaled in number of exemplars, except perhaps for news stories in newspapers. One consequence of this growth is that the research article has become the standard product of the knowledge-manufacturing industries (Knorr-Cetina, 1981).

6 *The role of English in research*

6.1 General perspectives

This enormous RA production raises two inter-related questions that need to be addressed in a book of this purpose and scope: first, how much of this production is in English as opposed to other languages and, second, how is it globally distributed? Then in the following section (6.2) we will consider what the answers to such questions might mean for researchers who do not command native or near-native skill in English and/or who are located in 'off network' parts of the earth.

Until recently such language issues have been surprisingly neglected in the relevant literatures. As Baldauf and Jernudd (1983a) comment:

> Although language of publication is an inescapable feature of scientific communication, it is most often treated as background noise, a variable in which neither information specialists nor scientists have shown much interest, nor is it, as far as we can tell, a problem which linguists have examined.

> (Baldauf and Jernudd, 1983a:97)

In an effort to provide some redress, they re-examined Wood's 1967 study of the language used in original articles abstracted by the major science abstracting and indexing services in 1965 and, as far as possible, attempted to replicate the study using 1981 data. (The 1965 and 1981 figures are not exactly comparable because the abstracting services have both modified their names and their procedures as a consequence of increasing computerization.) The advance made by English is both striking and consistent. A simplified version of their findings is given in Table 1 overleaf.

Baldauf and Jernudd were able to show that in their data the gain in English has been largely achieved at the expense of the major European languages. Japanese and Chinese both increased in percentage terms, although the latter from a minute 1965 base line. Maher (1986b), in a detailed study of the medical literature, largely reaches the same conclusion except that he notes a small decline in the Japanese percentages beginning sometime between 1970 and 1975. Even higher percentages

TABLE I. PERCENTAGES (TO I%) OF ABSTRACTED
ENGLISH LANGUAGE RAS

	1965	1981	Gain
Chemistry	50	67	17%
Biology	75	86	11%
Physics	73	85	12%
Medicine	51	73	22%
Maths	55	69	14%

for English have been found in more specialized sectors. Baldauf (1986), in a study of the four leading journals devoted to cross-cultural psychology published between 1978 and 1982, found an English-medium publication percentage of 97%.

The upshot of all these figures would seem to suggest that the anglophone grip on published research communications is both strong and tightening. However, this English domination may in fact not be as real as it appears; indeed, typical claims that 80% of the world's scientific production is written in English (e.g. Garfield, 1983) may be decidedly on the high side. The major difficulty is one of bias in the data bases. The Institute of Scientific Information's (ISI) largest bibliometric tool is the *Science Citation Index* (SCI), which scans about 4,000 journals. While, with an estimated world total of 70,000 science journals, considerable selectivity is clearly necessary, there is evidence (as there is in other US data bases) of a tendency to select journals emanating from the most developed countries in the northern hemisphere and publishing in English. These dual tendencies in effect constitute a kind of 'double-whammy' for non-anglophone Third World research. Indeed, the ISI itself sponsored an investigation into The Coverage of Third World Science and concluded that it may be under-representing worthwhile research from lesser developed countries (LDCs) by a factor of two (Moravcsik, 1985). A particularly striking case is that of Brazil which, according to Arvanitis and Chatelin (1988) publishes 149 scientific periodicals, only four of which are currently included in the ISI data base. Najjar (1988) claims that not even one Arab world science journal was consistently entered in the data base in the 1980s.

Nor are 'peripheral' English-speaking countries necessarily immune from deselection. Byrne (1983) in an article trenchantly entitled 'How to lose a nation's literature: database coverage of Australian research' showed that (apart from education) at most only a third of Australian journals in various social sciences and humanities were represented in international data bases.

There have been a number of attempts to get round the problem of bias. Throgmartin (1980) used UNESCO's *International Bibliography of the Social Sciences*, fearing that an American (and hence largely anglophone) abstracting service would under-represent non-English items. His relatively small (1000–1100) samples from sociology, economics, political science and anthropology show English percentages of between 39% and 51% with consistent double-figure percentages (14–26%) for French. Analogously, Baldauf and Jernudd (1983b:247) analyzed in detail a sample from *Aquatic Sciences and Fisheries Abstracts* 'because of its international sponsorship (i.e. UNESCO and based in Zurich) and because it appeared to abstract articles on fisheries in a wide variety of languages and from a wide variety of sources'. Here, however, English continued to be by far the most important language of publication (75%) with French (5.5%) and Spanish (4%) coming a long way behind.

Arvanitis and Chatelin (1988), in an impressive recent study of tropical agriculture, used PASCAL, a large French multidisciplinary data base, in another attempt to get round the problem of English-language bias. However, like Baldauf and Jernudd (1983b) they found even here that three-quarters of the publications were in English, with French (10%), Portuguese (7%) and Spanish (5%) falling far behind.

A rather different kind of evidence comes from the meticulous bibliography of the literature on schistosomiasis, (Warren and Newill, 1967). The bibliography covers the period from 1852 to 1962, contains nearly 10,000 articles on the subject and represents a truly global search, the most significant figure being that these articles have been garnered from no less than 1738 different periodicals including those publishing in languages as peripheral as Albanian. The Warren–Newill bibliography thus provides a fully comprehensive listing without any bias either in terms of RA language or in terms of provenance. Not surprisingly, the language distribution of RAs is a little different to that which we have

TABLE 2. LANGUAGE DISTRIBUTION OF
SCHISTOSOMIASIS RAS 1957–62

Language	Total	%
English	750	45.5
Portuguese	230	15
Chinese	200	12.5
Japanese	160	10
French	140	9
Spanish	40	2.5
German	30	2
Italian	20	1
Other	40	2.5
Total	1610	

come to expect. Table 2 is an approximate adaptation of part of the graphs in Warren and Goffman (1978: 34–5).

Undoubtedly, certain percentages have been skewed by the specialized topic – as they are likely to be in any specialized bibliography. For instance, the high percentages for Portuguese and Chinese are almost certainly due to the fact that schistosomiasis is endemic in parts of both Brazil and China. It may be further objected that the reason for the lower percentage of English-language articles is simply caused by a relative lack of interest in the disease in the United States, but even here American concern with tropical diseases is known to be strong in both the missionary and military fields. While the Warren–Newill bibliography is now 25 years old, it still represents the most complete bibliography that I know on any research topic. It thus represents a useful partial indicator of the role of English in an area of very broad and long-standing international concern.

We are now in a position to attempt an answer to the first question regarding the importance of English. While there is no doubt that English has become the world's predominant language of research and scholarship, the extent of that predominance may have been exaggerated. High overall percentages can indeed be extracted from the major US-located international data bases, but these data bases are themselves predisposed to English-language sources. Arvanitis and Chatelin, writing from Venezuela, draw the consequence with considerable irony: if one relies on the SCI data base, they argue 'one cannot be surprised to learn that the US produces 40% of the international production and receives 60% of the citations, or that 80% of the world scientific production is written in English' (Arvanitis and Chatelin, 1988:114). An overall figure of 80% is almost certainly too high.

More important than any overall figure is the small but growing body of evidence that the role of English is variable. We have already seen this in very high percentages for cross-cultural psychology and in much lower ones for schistosomiasis research. There may be special language-preservation efforts as in French-language sciences, or in German-language psychology (Becker, 1984). Najjar (1989), in a study of journals published in the Arab world, found Arabic predominantly in social science RAs, occurring about 25% of the time in agriculture but hardly at all in medicine. Finally, Jernudd and Baldauf (1987) contrast the strong effect of English on Scandinavian psychology with its very weak effect on articles concerning the teaching of Swedish. In the latter case, the medium of scholarly communication has predominantly been a Scandinavian language for the last 40 years (overall about 93%). In more general terms, it may be hypothesized that research fields relying on localized input (archaeology, agriculture, literature, religious studies) are more likely to resist or escape the domination of English than those that do not (chemistry, genetics, physics etc.). A useful study might be made, for example, comparing language use patterns of research into a spottily-distributed rural disease of great antiquity like schistosomiasis and a very recent and increasingly-global urban disease like AIDS.

The final aspect of the first answer pertains to the future. At present all the available studies indicate that the predominance of English is currently growing (e.g. Table 1). However, as Maher (1986b:208) observes, 'language is maintained or declines in response to the amount of (new) information that it carries'. A time will surely come in the future, as it always has in the past, when one premier language for the exchange of knowledge and information will give way to another. Indeed a presage of this may be detected in the role of Japanese as the language of the fifth-generation computer (Grabe, 1988b).

The new field of *linguistic scientometrics* (Baldauf and Jernudd, 1986) might also be expected to provide answers to the second group of questions: where are (English-language) RAs coming from, and how many are being produced by non-native speakers of English? These are harder questions to answer than the first set; in consequence, the answers must be more partial and more tentative.

Baldauf and Jernudd (1983b) in their fisheries study, estimated, on the basis of the institutional affiliation of the first author, that four-fifths of the English-language articles originated in countries where English is either the national language or the official language. Two-thirds of the remaining 20% appeared as outcomes of international conventions or as the work of multinational organizations such as the International Whaling Commission. The remaining 6% were submitted from locations where English was a foreign language, but very few of these were outside Western Europe or Japan.

Swales (1985b) attempted to estimate the percentage of NNS or 'probably' NNS authors in a selection of RAs taken randomly from journals in health sciences and economics available in a British university library. Again, the overall percentage was around 20%. However, of the 117 locations traced for NNS or probable NNS writers, only 21 were in the Third World, and 'ten of these were from institutions in the Indian subcontinent with its strong tradition of using English as the language of scholarship, and five from Israel where the data is particularly suspect because of the large amount of US–Israeli academic traffic' (Swales, 1985b:98).

The two studies reviewed above suggest that published research from peripheral countries (non-anglophone, LDC etc.) is minimal. Work on tropical agriculture by Arvanitis and Chatelin (1988), however, throws doubt on the general validity of such a conclusion. Their investigations into the 1983 PASCAL tropical agriculture data base suggest that perhaps up to half of the research in this field – one of course with a high

Third World priority – is being published from southern hemisphere locations, even when important anglophone contributions from Australia, New Zealand and South Africa are excluded. They further show that LDCs have evolved somewhat different national traditions for agricultural research publication. Of the Third World's agricultural research 'big three', Brazil tends towards national publication in the national language, Egypt towards national publication in English rather than Arabic, and India towards international publication in English.

Support for at least the Brazilian and Egyptian findings can be seen in more localized studies. Velho and Krige (1984) investigated the publishing activities of a group of Brazilian agricultural scientists. The group published 55 RAs in national Brazilian journals in 1982 (none on the ISI SCI list) and only seven abroad. This result is in marked contrast to other findings such as those of Rabkin and Inhaber (1979), who concluded that the Latin Americans published 74% of their work in 'advanced country' journals. However, Velho and Krige were working *within* the Brazilian context rather than relying on US data bases and almost certainly have more complete and more reliable information. Although Velho and Krige are not explicit about the matter, they certainly imply that the preference for domestic journals is related to the opportunity thus afforded to write in the native language, Portuguese, as well as to the opportunity of making a more direct appeal to the leaders of their agricultural community.

Najjar (1989) was able to corroborate the fact that Egyptian agricultural researchers have a strong tendency to publish locally but in English. In Jordan, on the other hand, the picture is more complex. At one of the two major agricultural research institutions, the University of Jordan, the trend remains to publish mainly locally, and largely – but by no means exclusively – in English. At the other institution, the University of Yarmouk, researchers tend to publish internationally. The explanation for the difference is in fact quite simple; the University of Jordan produces a suitable scholarly journal of its own, but Yarmouk does not.

The answer to the second set of questions is considerably less clear than it is to the first set of questions, partly because of the technical difficulties in getting at reliable data. However, both answers share a common danger. If we rely exclusively on the major US data bases we will fulfill the prophecy, in the first case, that English is overwhelmingly predominant and, in the second, that published research activity outside the northern hemisphere is minimal. However, when we go beyond such data we see that published research activity in peripheral contexts is not so much minimal, as largely invisible to the leading specialized discourse communities. Certainly, this seems to be the case with agricultural science in Brazil and in much of the Arab World.

Naturally enough, such conclusions raise in turn legitimate concerns about bias and lack of equity. There already exist intractable imbalances between the north and the south in such areas as GNP, quality of health care, life expectancy, educational opportunity, level of literacy and so on. Is it inevitable that we have to add to this list disregard for valid Third World research and scholarship? And if not, what role could our own discourse communities play in making research activity around the world a more equitable field of endeavor? These issues are taken up in the next section.

6.2   Individual perspectives

One of the aims of *linguistic scientometrics* 'is to develop an understanding of how language acts as a barrier in various disciplines, and what language correction procedures are able to solve them' (Baldauf and Jernudd, 1986:388). Although there exist a few localized studies of how non-native speakers of English manage to survive in an increasingly English-dominated research world, such as St John's investigation into the behaviors of Spanish scientists at the University of Cordoba (1987), much work remains to be done. Some of the most dramatic findings are the self-reports elicited by Jernudd and Baldauf (1987) from Scandinavian psychologists. The findings are dramatic because Scandinavians are in English-language terms one of the more privileged NNS groups. The advanced Scandinavian countries have highly-developed and largely successful foreign-language educational components and their leaders have a keen sense of the need to foster polyglot citizenries in order to maintain connections with Western Europe and beyond. And yet for the psychologists, all of whom have published in English-language international journals, communication in English represents a heavy burden:

- It is constantly depressing to be confronted by one's shortcomings in foreign language.
- It is meaningless to publish original research in psychology in Swedish.
- I regard the language barrier as a central problem for Norwegian researchers in my professional field.
- One year in England/USA – even as a street sweeper – would likely mean more to a scientific career than half a million crowns in the form of a research grant.
- It is important for those of us who are non-native speakers to create some understanding among many researchers that English is not their natural (or obvious) language of communication.

(Jernudd and Baldauf, 1987:150)

There may be other burdens as well. All non-native English speakers must take additional time out of their academic and research careers if they wish to acquire and maintain high-level English-language skills (Lewin and Jordan, 1981). Further, the general increase in research production is leading to high journal rejection rates, currently reaching 80–95% in the arts and humanities, which in turn means increasing pressure on manuscripts that betray evidence of non-standard English.

In fact, the Scandinavian psychologists are probably relatively well-placed in comparison to all those researchers in more isolated, more 'off-network' and generally less supportive research environments. In those situations, library resources may be limited, with the result that only the leading journals will be carried. One important consequence of this is that disadvantaged researchers may not even *know* of the existence of journals (particularly newish ones) which might in fact be eager to publish their contributions. Access to good English-language assistance may be limited, and advice on rhetorical differences in research writing in the mother tongue and English non-existent or even misleading. And finally, there is the question of bias against submission from 'obscure' places. In a somewhat notorious study, Peters and Ceci (1982) claimed to have established such bias even within the confines of the United States. They took 12 leading American psychological journals (all with a 'nonblind' refereeing policy) and resubmitted to each an article that each published 18–32 months previously. The only changes they made were to use fictitious author names and to substitute institutional affiliations of somewhat dubious credibility such as 'The Tri-Valley Institute for Human Growth'. Of the 12 papers, just three were recognized by the journals as having been previously published by them under other names. Of the other nine, one was accepted, but eight were rejected.

There may be other more unexpected perils facing the under-resourced researcher. Here are the comments of an editor of an international journal as reported to me:

> We get single copies of these papers from India. They are manually typed with an old ribbon on that grey recycled paper. As they won't photocopy there is I'm afraid little that we can do with them.

For want of a nail then.

The most serious attempt so far to situate the NNS researcher within a general framework is that of Jernudd and Baldauf (1987:164). As they say, 'we would argue that if one could understand the process by which the individual scientist makes choices, language correction procedures could be developed to improve communication and presumably specific language "products", which would lead in turn to an increase in information exchange which is related to the level of human resource development possible in any community'. A simplified version of their model of this process, and one also somewhat translated into the key concepts of this book, is presented overleaf as Figure 4.

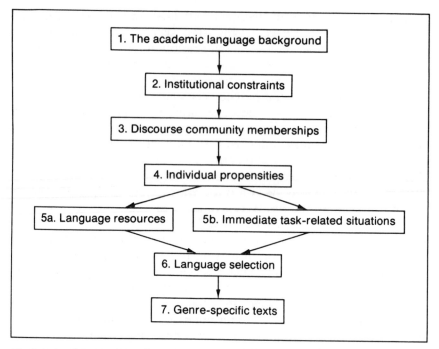

Figure 4   Language selection in research (adapted from Jernudd and Baldauf, 1987:172)

I shall discuss the operation of this process model by referring to the situation in the Arab World. The academic language background (Stage 1) in the Arab World reveals a not untypical sociolinguistic setting in which the main regional language, Arabic, co-exists with one or two imported and ex-colonial international languages. Arabic itself has several varieties, from pure colloquial sub-regional forms to the traditional literary and religious language of classical Arabic (El-Hassan, 1977). The variety relevant to research is MSA or Modern Standard Arabic, a modernized version of classical. Not all educated speakers of Arabic command MSA with equal facility and conviction, and the genre development of MSA as a language of research communication may not yet be complete (Najjar, 1988). By and large, English is the alternative language for research communication in areas that fell under British influence during the first half of this century (Iraq, Sudan, Saudi Arabia etc.), while French is the alternative language in areas of historic French influence (Syria, the Maghreb etc.). However, the neat distinction between French and English has broken down somewhat in the last decade or two, partly as a result of crossover patterns of individual advanced training and collaboration, but these can be handled under Stage 4.

Stage 1 shows that Arab researchers are likely to have two choices as the vehicle for their research publication: MSA, on the one hand, or English or French, on the other, (or possibly both if the researcher is Lebanese or Egyptian). These choices may be affected by institutional constraints (Stage 2). The National Research Council may have a language policy for its publications. The universities may impose constraints: at the University of Jordan promotion is not possible without at least one publication in Arabic, while at the University of Khartoum in Sudan, promotion may be blocked without publication in international refereed journals.

Stage 3 attempts to characterize the discourse communities that the individual researcher belongs to. If these are purely local, opportunities will be limited to the contacts available to that local community. However, membership in regional or more distant communities may bring valuable advantages of collaboration (including co-authorship), access to funds, and useful advice about where and how to submit a manuscript. Stage 4 then characterizes the individuality of the researcher. In the Arab World, for instance, quite a number of Arab researchers have received doctoral training in Russia or Eastern Europe and may therefore be as prepared to write in Slavic languages or in German as in English or French. Additionally, Stage 4 accounts for the important nationalistic variable, since, as Najjar (1989) shows, researchers vary considerably in the extent to which they feel a commitment to advance the cause of Modern Standard Arabic.

Stages 1 through 4 allow us to characterize the general language orientation of a researcher. Stages 5 through 7 relate to the immediate specifics of the communicative tasks in hand. One researcher might, for instance, have decided to write his or her research in Arabic but has recently recognized that additionally an abstract in English needs to be provided. Are there English-language resources (human, textual or both) in his or her environment to facilitate this task? And if there are, could they later be employed to produce an English-language paper based on another aspect of the research? Finally, the selection of a particular language as vehicle at Stage 6 then invites consideration (Stage 7) of both language-specific genre requirements (as was discussed in 3.7) and of the specific expectations of targeted journals. Thus, in these ways, linguistic choices are made and publications and presentations in particular languages constructed.

This model of language selection in research is a generalized one, and in reality a number of 'cut-outs' may operate. For example, the researcher may receive an *invitation* to participate in a communicative event with a previously established linguistic choice. More importantly perhaps, the model as it now stands fails to account directly for the variable of perceived quality. This variable is probably significant as there is strong anecdotal evidence from around the world that many NNS researchers try to publish what they consider to be their 'best' research in a major international language, leaving their 'lesser' findings to appear in local or regional language format.

Although the process typified by the model is otiose for the native speaker of English, it definitely may not be for the non-native speaker. In particular, Stages 3 and 5a may be crucial. If these boxes are largely unfilled or infertile, then the chances of a researcher's output being reduced in both quantity and visibility are increased. As Baldauf (1986) observes, there may be a 'lost generation' of cross-cultural psychologists out there who have only a reading knowledge of the English language, the overwhelmingly dominant vehicle for information exchange in this subfield.

The geopolitical implications of being 'off-networked' are themselves not trivial. They raise serious questions about the effectiveness of the investments being made by LDCs in doctoral scholarships held by their nationals in the USA and Europe. They raise questions about the scientific, scholarly and developmental value of research scholarships and visitorships offered to LDC nationals by American, European and Russian governments and other sponsoring agencies. They raise questions about whether advanced country training is as relevant as it might be and about whether *institutional* mechanisms for initiating NNSs into appropriate discourse communities need to be strengthened. And finally they raise questions about the policies of academic English programs abroad – in particular with regard to their largely exclusive concern with undergraduate education. In consequence, we may perhaps legitimately ask whether these programs should not also be concerned with mitigating post-doctoral 're-entry shock' and with providing alternative frameworks for those not selected for advanced training outside of their local environments.

In Chapter 6 I have tried to assess our current knowledge about the role of English in contemporary research. The fact that reaching even a provisional assessment has occupied several pages should not, I believe, be seen as mere scholarly fussiness. Facts about the medium of communication, as about the medium of instruction, are *always* important because decisions to use a particular language inevitably confer advantage on some and disadvantage on others. For this reason I have been at pains to look at the available evidence from the perspectives of both the privileged and the less privileged, from the viewpoints of users of major bibliometric resources and from those of their critics, and from the stance of general survey and that of local investigation.

The role of English in research that has been depicted in this chapter offers a number of opportunities for action. One is to consider whether there is anything we can do to modify, where necessary, the attitudes of

NS scholars, researchers and students so that they are more tolerant of non-native speakers, more willing to accept them into their discourse communities and more aware of the extra burdens which they carry. A second is to resist a mindset which associates quality with location – a mindset, to take a real example, that would likely deny the possibility that a group of lecturers at the University of Tabriz in north-west Iran could have produced the most elegant ESP course design so far constructed (Bates, 1976). A third would be to ask whether we have the skills and interests to foster 'lesser' languages as vehicles for research communication, particularly by engaging in collaborative ventures aimed at developing and consolidating genres such as the research article in those languages. Fourthly, and as the most direct form of affirmative action, we may consider what roles we may play as teachers *of* and *about* research English.

As it happens, the texts cited throughout this chapter are very well suited for such an instructional purpose (Swales, 1987b). Themes such as the anglophone grip on contemporary research will be of direct relevance and concern to non-native speakers and are, at the least, educative for native speakers. The fact that the themes concern language makes them amenable to English-language instructors. The straightforward quantitative nature of many of the studies, such as tabulating locations of authors in a sample of RAs, may appeal to scientists and offers a methodology that can easily be replicated on a small-scale for class projects. Further, the methodology itself engages participants in searching and scanning processes (Bazerman, 1985) that can be valuably generalized for other purposes and tasks. Finally, the texts themselves, particularly those with a quantitative orientation, are prototypical exemplars of the RA genre. Figure 5 overleaf is part of one such text.

The text might be utilized in the following way:

a) The first objective is to get the class 'into' the text. An obvious place to start is with the interpretation of *North, Periphery* and *South*. So, blank maps of the world are distributed and individuals or pairs are asked to divide the main areas of the world up into these three categories. Discussion towards consensus follows, the instructor using a copy of the full article for reference.

b) A second priming activity is to raise consciousness about the data base. On the limited textual evidence, what is it? Where is it located? Is PASCAL a clue?

c) A preliminary writing task would be to supply the missing data-comment paragraph for Table 2. Pointers to possible items for written discussion might be: is the Portuguese/Spanish order surprising? Does PASCAL adequately cover the Far East? Mandarin, Thai, Bahasa? Paragraphs are compared – and compared to the original.

Findings

Agricultural sciences in 1983 were represented by 9398 references in the PASCAL data base, in those sections that we selected. Of these, 2040 references (21.7%) concerned a tropical environment or a tropical country. Table 1 shows the distribution of this production by areas.

TABLE 1. ORIGIN OF PUBLICATIONS ON TROPICAL AGRICULTURAL SCIENCES

North	420	21%
Periphery	536	26%
South	1042	51%
Others	42	2%
Total	2040	100%

The South produces half of the research on tropical areas – that is, 11% of the total of world research in agricultural sciences. This figure surpasses the traditional 'near to 6%' usually admitted for Third World countries. The Periphery produces about a quarter of tropical agricultural research, and the North a little less. The 'Others' represent difficult-to-identify references, anonymous items, affiliation to international institutions, and so on.

The linguistic distribution is shown in Table 2.

TABLE 2. LINGUISTIC DISTRIBUTION OF TROPICAL AGRICULTURE RESEARCH

English	1530	75%
French	204	10%
Portuguese	143	7%
Spanish	102	5%
German	20	1%
Others	41	2%
Total	2040	100%

Figure 5   Language and location in research (Arvanitis and Chatelin, 1988: 118–19)

d) Matters are now ready for a real task orchestrated as a class project (Hutchinson and Waters, 1987). The class divides into self-selecting fields of interest. The groups go to the library to obtain data from journals in their fields on origin of articles and language of publication. Group results are tabulated and presented orally; cross-group figures are assembled and discussed; comparisons are made with previous research; methodological procedures (and problems) are written up, as are suggestions for further research. A multi-author small research paper is constructed. NS colleagues are invited to attend a formal conference-type presentation and then to participate in a NS–NNS panel discussion on the issues of language barriers in research communication.

7 Research articles in English

I have divided this chapter into several sections. It opens with a necessarily brief and episodic account of the history of the research article over the last 300 years or so. The purpose of this section is to place the main synchronic analysis against a diachronic framework, for, like all living genres, the RA is continually evolving, and future developments may find part of their explanations in present or previous rhetorical practice. The second section examines and tries to inter-relate several case studies of the processes whereby research articles were actually constructed. Both the first and the second sections are therefore evolutionary, although in very different ways. Sections 7.3 to 7.6 constitute a textual analysis of the genre itself, taking each of the main sections of the RA (Introduction, Method, etc.) in turn, while 7.7 attempts to summarize our current state of knowledge. Despite considerable research activity, conclusions must at present be considered tentative, partly because the enormous size of the genre means that the number of texts examined represents extremely minute proportions of the whole, and partly because we still experience considerable difficulty in making well-validated decisions about how that whole should be divided up.

7.1 Episodes in the history of the research article

The scientific RA emerged, albeit in embryonic form, contemporaneously with the establishment of the first scientific periodical, *The Philosophical Transactions of the Royal Society*, in 1665. According to Ard (1983), the genre of the scientific article developed from the informative letters that scientists had always written to each other – and still do. Thus, many of the early contributions to the *Transactions* took the first person descriptive narrative form associated with letters, some even having the salutation 'Sir' at their outset. However, as the *Transactions* and subsequent journals began to assume a role of providing a regular arena for discussion, the new and recurring rhetorical situation that emerged led to the creation of a new genre increasingly distinct from its letter-writing origin. In Bazerman's words:

> By talking to each other in a specific format scientists were figuring
> out how to talk to each other and changed the format according to
> what they were figuring out.
>
> (Bazerman, 1983:1)

Another powerful force that shaped the early scientific article came from
the existing tradition of published scientific treatises; most immediately,
from the efforts of Robert Boyle and his fellow experimentalists in the
decade preceding the appearance of the first issue of the *Transactions* to
establish a proper foundation for scientific knowledge (Shapin, 1984).
According to Shapin, Boyle and his colleagues sought to transform claims
and speculations into generally-accepted knowledge by way of the
experimental *matter of fact*. In order to achieve this transformation,
Boyle would appear to have developed a largely self-conscious and highly
complex set of strategies. Some of these strategic elements are as follows:

a) The key apparatus for his pneumatic experiments was the air pump.
   At that time air pumps were very expensive, elaborate and tempera-
   mental; they were thus rare and well beyond the means of the great
   majority of potential users. Boyle presented his machine to the Royal
   Society to ease the problem of access and to pre-empt objections that
   might be based on traditional opposition to alchemical secrecy or to
   aristocratic aloofness. (Boyle was a son of the Earl of Cork.)
b) In Boyle's program of work the capacity of experiments to yield
   matters of fact depended less on getting the apparatus to do certain
   things than on securing the agreement of the relevant community that
   these things had, in fact, been done. He needed witnesses, the more
   the better and the better qualified the better. Experiments were
   performed before an audience at the Royal Society and members were
   encouraged to sign a register as witness that they had seen what they
   had seen.
c) Boyle also recognized that witnesses could be multiplied by encouraging others to replicate experiments. Although he strongly advocated this practice, he came soon enough to realize that many
   attempts at replication would fail.
d) According to Shapin, Boyle's most important way of trying to
   establish facts was by what Shapin calls *virtual witnessing*: 'the
   technology of virtual witnessing involves the production in a reader's
   mind of such an image of an experimental scene as obviates the
   necessity for either its direct witness or its replication' (1984:491).
   Boyle set out to achieve this objective by a variety of methods:
   i) If there were to be illustrations of apparatus in his published
      work, Boyle was insistent that these should be realistic, exact and
      detailed.

ii) He wrote deliberately elaborate and prolix accounts of his experiments so that the reader would be encouraged to believe that he was getting a full and honest account.

iii) He offered his readers circumstantial accounts of *failed* experiments.

iv) He deliberately avoided philosophical speculation.

v) Boyle wrote very cautiously and made much use of what today have become known as 'hedges' (e.g. Lakoff, 1972). As Boyle himself put it, 'in almost every one of the following essays I ... speak so doubtingly, and use so often *perhaps, it seems, it is not improbable* and other such expressions, as argue a diffidence to the truth of the opinions I incline to ...' (quoted by Shapin, 1984:495).

e) A further important aspect of Boyle's contribution to the rhetoric of science was his attempts to regulate scientific disputes; in particular he insisted that disputes should be about findings and not about persons. In this way he stood out against the common *ad hominem* style of arguing at that time. As he elegantly puts it, 'I love to speak of persons with civility, though of things with freedom' (Shapin, 1984:502).

Of course it is sometimes thought that the facts 'speak for themselves'; that is, a scientist's description of natural reality, if it is carefully and competently done, is simply a reflection of that reality. However, if this were to be the case, then Boyle's complex strategy would have been unnecessary. Rather, even the foregoing short summary of Shapin's analysis seems to show clearly enough how hard Boyle and his collaborators had to work to *make* a rhetoric – to *develop* a convincing style for the research report. It would appear that phenomena only acquire fact-like status by consensus and that consensus may not be achievable without rhetorical persuasion. The art of the matter, as far as the creation of facts is concerned, lies in deceiving the reader into thinking that there is no rhetoric, that research reporting is indeed 'writing degree zero' (Barthes, 1975) and that the facts are indeed speaking for themselves.

Boyle was a great researcher, and at least a small part of his greatness lay in the subtle and imaginative perceptions he developed about the relationships between doing research and writing about that research. We can see what happened to the research article on a more mundane level by taking up Bazerman's study of developments in the *Transactions* during the period 1665–1800, which focuses particularly on changes in the presentation of the experiment. This study is neither simply a piece of literary nor a piece of scientific history. As the author says:

> I hope to show that the story of the experimental report is not one of simple accretion, but an evolving response to an evolving

> discourse situation. As literature and knowledge represented by the
> literature accumulated and locuses of discussion emerged, the
> discussion itself changed in character.
>
> (Bazerman, 1983:4)

Bazerman's first finding was that relatively few early items in the
Transactions were actually experimental reports, and even by 1800 such
reports still amounted to less than 40% of all the articles published. In the
early days, the majority of the items were reports of noteworthy natural
events such as earthquakes, or of observations made by means of
telescopes or microscopes or by anatomical dissection. Further, Bazerman is able to show that 'the definition of experiment moves from any
made or done thing, to an intentional investigation, to a test of theory, to
finally a proof of or evidence for a claim' (1983:5). In this process of
evolution, the scientist's relationship with nature gradually changed from
a view that the nature of things would be easily revealed by direct or
manipulated observation to a view that nature was complex, obscure and
difficult to get at. Inevitably enough, this changing view also meant that
more care began to be taken in describing how experiments were done, in
explaining why particular methods were chosen, and in detailing precisely what results were found. All this was necessary because it was
becoming more and more clear that minor differences in procedure could
produce major differences in findings. The supposedly modern concept of
controlling the variable is not far away.

By the end of the eighteenth century, these developments (and others
such as the demise of communal witnessing) had led to a reconfiguration
of the RA:

> As phenomena began to be treated as more problematic, articles
> began to take on a different organization, opening with an
> introduction to the problematic phenomenon, often substantiated
> with the story of an experiment that did not go as expected. With
> the problem established, the article would chronologically describe
> a series of experiments aimed at getting to the bottom of the
> mystery. Transitions between each two experiments would draw
> conclusions from the previous experiment and point to the
> rationale or need for the subsequent one. In the highly developed
> continuity we see the experimenter gradually come to an adequate
> understanding of the phenomenon, which would then be pulled
> together in a concluding synthesis or explanation of the
> phenomenon, as in Hewson's investigations into the nature of
> blood (60:368–83).
>
> (Bazerman, 1983:16–17)

This description of a typical RA offers, I would suggest, a striking
vindication of Boyle's attempts 100 years earlier to establish a rhetoric

for experimental description. There are, of course, certain quite marked differences between the eighteenth and the twentieth century RA; among them a decidedly more casual approach to the previous literature and some continuation of the epistolary convention of first person narrative. This kind of writing has almost totally disappeared from the contemporary RA, although it exists in other scientific genres such as Nobel Prize acceptance speeches (Ard, 1983). According to Ard, the use of 'I' in early scientific discourse is related to the fact that the observer played a more central role at that time, at least partly because observations, especially with untried apparatus, relied much on individual skill. (And we could well remember that early instruments were handmade and were far from being the standardized products in use today.) However, as we have seen, a further – if connected – reason for the continuing reliance on first person pronouns derives from the insistence of Boyle and other pioneer experimentalists for a style of writing that would project both personal honesty and modesty. This style should avoid the presumptions which the passive voice would bring that others either could or (worse) could not replicate the methods and results with ease. However, the issue of impersonality in scientific writing, despite its apparent innocent simplicity, turns out to be complex and vexatious, and is yet to be fully understood.

The only substantial study known to me that traces the *textual* development of the RA in the present century is Bazerman (1984a). Bazerman investigated a selection of Spectroscopic articles in the *Physical Review* from its founding in 1893 to 1980. As he says, 'this period marks the rise of American physics from backwardness to world dominance, reflected by the journal's rise from a local university organ to the primary international journal of physics' (1984a:166). Some of his main conclusions are summarized below:

a) ARTICLE LENGTH

From 1893 to 1900 the average length of articles fell from around 7,000 words to around 5,000. With some fluctuations they continued to average about 5,000 words until 1940. Thereafter average article length has steadily increased and reached about 10,000 words by 1980. So much then for the common belief that scientific articles have become more compact during this century.

b) REFERENCES

Referencing trends over the 1893–1980 period reveal an intriguing story. In the early years references were quite common (about 10 per article) but rather general, rarely relating to specific findings or to the specific topics investigated by the authors. As Bazerman says, these characteristics 'weaken the sense of a coherent, moving research front' (1984a:173). By

1910, the number of references had become severely curtailed, but the very few that remained were all recent, had dates and were of direct relevance to the research being reported. From then on, the number of references has trended upwards, whilst maintaining specific relevance to the work at hand. Thus, new work becomes increasingly embedded in the spectroscopic literature. A further sign of this is that references are no longer concentrated in the Introduction but are distributed throughout the RA, so that every stage of the document both relies on and relates to the work of others. And it is this development that provides at least part of the explanation for the doubling of average article length over the last 40 years.

c) SYNTACTIC AND LEXICAL FEATURES

Bazerman found no important variations in sentence length. The averages of sentence length of around 25 words accord closely with those of other investigators (Barber, 1962; Huddleston, 1971). He did find, however, that relative clauses declined in frequency, whilst both noun clauses and temporal and causal subordinate clauses have become more frequent. The rise of the latter (also corroborated by Huddleston, 1971) indicates a shift from description to explanation, thus suggesting increasing intellectual complexity. On the lexical level, subjects of main clauses have over the period become more abstract. Concrete subjects like *substance, apparatus*, and so on, have tended to give way to nouns of process or quality such as *ionization* and *correlation*. Significant changes in the function of the main verb were also found:

> The decrease in reporting verbs (for example, 'Smith reports ...') and increase in active verbs (for example, 'temperature increases ...') suggest that the finding or theory has increasingly been brought into the central grammatical position, whilst the publishing scientists have been given a back seat, thus adding density to the discussion and integrating source material into the continuity of the argument.
>
> (Bazerman, 1984:177)

d) NON-VERBAL MATERIAL

The same trends towards abstraction and integration can be seen in the changing nature of the graphic material. During the period, there was a decrease in the number of apparatus drawings and in the number and size of tables. In compensation, there were increases in the number and complexity of both graphs and equations.

e) ORGANIZATION

Before 1950 only about 50% of the articles were formally divided into section titles; after 1950 section headings became a regular feature. Up till 1930, if sections were used they usually ended with Results thus implying that the findings could stand alone without further comment. Since then, Discussion and Conclusion sections have not only become much more common but they also have greatly increased in length and complexity. On the other hand, the proportion of space given to Method and Apparatus sections has generally declined (c.f. Huckin, 1987).

In this pioneering study, Bazerman assembles considerable discoursal evidence for a number of general trends: growing abstraction, the deepening integration of present work within the relevant literature, the increasing foregrounding of research as opposed to researcher, the increasingly uphill struggle to incorporate more and more information, and a steadily more focused argumentation. The finer rhetorical and linguistic detail of these outcomes will be discussed in later subsections.

The fact that Bazerman's investigation *is* pioneering means that we are faced with very real problems of extrapolation and generalization. Is the *Physical Review* typical of other important American physics journals? Would the findings apply to comparable journals from elsewhere? What about chemistry, psychology or sociology? Physics is a large, central and long-established field – would similarities be found in a field that had none of these characteristics?

In an attempt to throw a little light on at least the last of these questions, I analyzed main articles in the first 20 years of the *TESOL Quarterly*, the flagship publication of the US-based association of Teachers of English to Speakers of Other Languages (Swales, 1988b). From the early 1970s, average article length – of the main text – has remained relatively stable, centering around a mean of very approximately 5,000 words. However, the articles look longer because of steady upward trends in the amount of non-textual material (principally tables) and in the number of references. The average number of references had grown from four in 1968 to 34 in 1986. In addition, the period was also characterized by a proportional decline in citations of books (particularly ESL textbooks) and a rise in citations of shorter works (particularly articles, and chapters in scholarly edited collections). Further signs of the adoption of a social science (as opposed to humanities) paradigm have been the consistent subsectioning of articles, increasing co-authorship and a wider employment of statistics. In addition, the fact that authors in *TESOL Quarterly* have increasingly tended to cite previous work published in it may be taken to imply the existence of a number of coherent and established research fronts. On the other hand, there was no sign of the drift towards graphs that Bazerman noted from the *Physical Review*, and I eventually abandoned my efforts to trace increasing lexical abstraction due to a lack of firm evidence. (Syntactic features were not investigated.)

Overall, this vignette of RA history in the embryonic ESL field evinces a determination to *professionalize* – a particularly pressing and understandable concern given the folkloristic belief that anybody who knows a language well can teach it. The clearest rhetorical evidence of this lies in an increasingly standardized main article product which meets a number of requirements, such as the formulation of research questions sited within a rhetorically-established framework of previous work, and the presentation and discussion of data. One consequence of all this can, especially in the light of the comments made in Chapter 6, be seen as unfortunate. Although the teaching of English to speakers of other languages has become a major global activity, the leading journal in the field has remained one which publishes contributions from authors based in North America – even by 1986, articles from outside the US and Canada constituted less than 20% of the total.

7.2   The constructing of research articles

The continuum from a gleam in the researcher's eye to the distribution of the published paper may not be easily breakable into segments, but one possible staging is into the processes of writing prior to submission to a journal (internally-moderated changes) and into those that may occur subsequently (externally-moderated changes). Myers' (1985a) study – already mentioned at the opening of Part III – of the struggles of two biologists to get their papers published would fall into the latter category. For Myers all researchers are faced with decisions about the level of claim they might wish to make. The higher the level of claim, the more likely that it will involve contradicting large bodies of the relevant literature and will challenge assumptions embodied in important ongoing research programs. On the other hand, the lowest level claims may contradict nothing, but may also add very little to what is accepted and established within the given research field. Thus, high-level claims are likely to be important but risky, whilst low-level claims are likely to be trivial but safe. Both of Myers' biologists consistently sought to make the highest-level claim that they could persuade a particular journal to accept, but in both cases they eventually had to settle for the publication of much more limited and lower-level claims than they had originally hoped for (and perhaps still hope for). Concomitantly, they had to settle also for a more limited and more specialized readership; in aggregate they made no fewer than six attempts at publication in *Science* and *Nature* before abandoning these two highly visible and widely-read journals.

   If we turn to the earlier stages of the composing process, the preparation of a manuscript prior to review, we can also find impressive evidence that any vision we may have of the scientist-researcher working away in the lab or in the field and then retiring to a quiet place to type up quickly the experimental report according to some stereotyped format is decidedly at odds with reality. Evidence for what really happens can be gathered from three recent book-length studies that are largely concerned with the construction of research papers. Two are case studies of important US laboratories (Latour and Woolgar, 1979; Knorr-Cetina, 1981), the third is an analysis of a controversy in biochemistry (Gilbert and Mulkay, 1984). All three books are significant products of a relatively new school within the sociology of science in which discourse is topic rather than resource. As Gilbert and Mulkay put it, the approach concentrates 'on describing how scientists' accounts are organized to portray their actions and beliefs in contextually appropriate ways' (1984:14).

The most directly relevant of the three is Knorr-Cetina, for in one of her chapters she presents an extensive textual study, including facsimiles and additionally supported by direct observation and interview, of what transpired between the first rough notes for and the final draft of one paper produced at a large government-financed research center in Berkeley, California during 1977. The subject of the paper is the recovery of protein from potatoes, a process of some significance for the food industry.

The first significant point to emerge is that the public story as told in the drafts is a reversed, rather than revised, version of what actually took place within the confines of the laboratory. In the lab, the scientists responded opportunistically to an incidental finding, rather than consciously planned to try and solve a particular problem. (The problem would, in fact, turn out to be finding a method of extracting valuable potato protein which would require less energy than the current acid/heat treatments and which would also increase nitrogen solubility.) As one of the main researchers commented:

> No. I think I was not clever enough originally to see that it would be better to recover protein without applying heat treatment. I probably first read about the ferric chloride . . .
>
> (Knorr-Cetina, 1981:101)

In the laboratory realizing that ferric chloride coagulation could occur without heat eventually led to the establishment of an alternative method, whilst *in the paper* the story opens with the need to produce a better method and then offers ferric chloride coagulation as a resolution of this need. Of course, this reversal of the research dynamic is *in its context* neither deceitful nor misrepresentative — although it might be thought so if the *laboratory notes* themselves had been revised in this way. This is because the *research paper* is a quite different genre to the laboratory record and has its own quite separate conventions, its own processes of literary reasoning and its own standards of argument, within all of which one powerful shaping paradigm is that of the problem–solution text type (Hoey, 1979).

But the story of the Introduction does not end here, because there is a further world of difference between the first full version and the final version. In the first there is a clear succession of increasingly specific paragraphs starting with observations about the large quantities of valuable potato proteins available in the world and how these are under-utilized. A description of current recovery methods follows with considerable emphasis on their drawbacks. The Introduction ends with a discussion of a major alternative coagulant (ferric chloride), which would turn the disadvantages of the current methods into advantages. The final sentence then generalizes the method search:

> The aim of this work was to find an alternative precipitation
> method resulting in a yield comparable to that of protein recovered
> by means of the most commonly used acid/heat treatment method,
> while achieving a more acceptable quality of the PPC needed for
> the application in human foods.

(Knorr-Cetina, 1981:157)

As Knorr-Cetina observes, the switch at the close to the Past tense suggests that the method was actually found, although it is not identified at this point in the paper.

Several months and drafts later, a final version emerged after considerable discussion with and comments from colleagues, including the Director of the Institute. The straightforward and somewhat dramatic unfolding of the first version has almost entirely disappeared. The general–specific structure (zeroing in on the solution) has been abandoned for a series of paragraphs that discuss various topics at approximately equivalent levels of detail, thus producing a more discursive and less goal-directed text. Further, many 'dangerous' claims have been eliminated; for instance, only one of the several first-version statements about the 'disadvantages' of the prevailing protein recovery method has survived. There has also been a considerable increase in 'hedging'; *should* becomes *could, is* becomes *has been suggested as possible, good* solubility becomes merely *enhanced* and so on. The cautiousness and rhetorical diffuseness of the final version is neatly illustrated by the very different closing sentence of the Introduction:

> The purpose of this study was to compare the effectiveness of HCl,
> $FeCl_3$, and HCl combined with heat, as precipitants of potato
> protein in the laboratory, as well as under pilot plant conditions,
> and to evaluate some compositional, nutritional and functional
> characteristics of the protein concentrates recovered by these three
> methods.

(Knorr-Cetina, 1981:165)

Thus, the pre-announcement of a new method has been toned down to a comparative analysis, and the early exuberance of the primary research-ers has become the careful understatement of a wider group. In Myers' terms, the level of knowledge-claim has been reduced, perhaps partly in order to limit damage to the Institute's reputation should subsequent work go awry. Throughout, rhetorical considerations have had a per-vasive role – first in reconstructing events in the laboratory, and secondly in the long process of generating the final draft. However, it is not quite as though the lab notes could not have been built on in a linear manner, nor that the first version is clearly unpublishable (its main author had already published 40 papers). Rather we seem to see a process of technical critique and social control operating both in the particular research setting and in a wider half-imagined world of 'what other scientists will think'. Knorr-Cetina herself offers a stronger version of this observation: 'the published paper is a multilayered hybrid *co-produced* by the authors *and* by members of the audience to which it is directed' (1981:106, original emphasis).

Unlike the Introduction, the Method and Materials section remained virtually unchanged in succeeding full drafts except for the eventual deletion of one or two statements of purpose. A sample of Method discourse is given below:

> **Methods for analysis and functional properties**
> The standard AOAC methods (AOAC, 1975) were used for the determination of total solids, nitrogen, crude fat, ash and vitamin C. Total sugars were determined by the method of Potter et al. (1968) and the total carbohydrates (in terms of glucose) were assayed according to the procedure of Dubois et al. (1956). The method of Kohler and Patten (1967) was followed for determining amino acid composition.
>
> (Knorr-Cetina, 1981:167)

The above text is a bald Past tense narrative with agentives realized by the method rather than by the protagonists (the contrast with Boyle's reporting style as described in the previous subsection is patent). There are no problems, no matters of discussion, no questions of choice (even though some of the procedures involved several months of testing and modification), no evidence of failure, and no statements of rationale. The contrast with the Method sections in the 'soft' social sciences is also patent. As Knorr-Cetina observes, 'compared with the relevant work in the laboratory, where the *making* of selections dominates the scene, the paper offers a curiously *residual* description, constituted by what is *not* at stake in the research (such as the brand names of devices, or the origins of a technique) than by what is' (1981:115). In fact, the Method sections of RAs often seem increasingly not to be 'reports' in any normal sense;

rather, they are highly abstracted reformulations of final outcomes in which an enormous amount is taken for granted.

This conclusion inevitably belies the common belief that the purpose of Method sections is to permit replication. As it happens, Knorr-Cetina's informants – as well as numerous others – deny that replication is really possible. On one occasion, Knorr-Cetina asked whether a reader could work out the reason for an unglossed change in method. The reply she received was as follows:

> He could in principle ... but it would require a lot of thinking.
> And he would have to presuppose that I did a lot of thinking too
> ... In practice, he simply would not know.

(Knorr-Cetina, 1981:129)

Apparently, there are many virtually indescribable matters of technique (which require 'know-how', 'laboratory skills', 'a good pair of hands') that ostensibly make up much of the difference in the way laboratory events turn out.

The Results and Discussion section of the paper also creates a different reality to that observed by Knorr-Cetina in the laboratory. In the laboratory the rhetorical division into the various article sections was, to all intents and purposes, non-existent. For instance, Knorr-Cetina noted that 'methodological constructions' were continuously interpreted and discussed; she also found that the researchers recognized that method and result were mutually inter-dependent. And yet in the published account, the Method section is a 'listing of procedural formulae' whereas the Results is largely taken up with statements of similarity and difference. Interestingly, in the rewriting of the Discussion a comparable process took place to the one we have already described for the Introduction. Evaluation was gradually squeezed out, and no speculations were attempted beyond those previously adumbrated in the opening section. Although the final version of the Discussion, extrapolating from the described results, implicitly argues for a change in the existing practice of recovering potato protein, no longer are there any explicit proposals.

In all then, at the close of this commentary on a splendid but individual case study, we can carry forward two main empirical findings: first, we have seen a long process of rhetorical construction leading to the drafting of the first full version; secondly, an equally long process of rhetorical reconstruction leading to the published paper. In this way we have seen once again how the ultimate published product attempts to create a reader-environment in which the tentative facts can be allowed to 'speak for themselves'. However, we can also see, on some occasions at least, that the creation of such a linguistic artifact is neither simple, nor short, nor particularly natural.

The 1979 Latour and Woolgar study of the Salk Institute in California is somewhat less concerned with rhetorical processes and more with the role of language itself in the scientific enterprise. They note, *inter alia*, that the denizens of the Institute spend the greater part of their days making or reviewing inscriptions: they code, mark, correct, read and write. The aim of all this documentary activity is not to preserve administrative records, but to make contributions to the research front in the form of published papers:

> Firstly, at the end of the day, technicians bring piles of documents from the bench space through to the office space. In a factory we might expect these to be reports of what has been processed and manufactured. For members of this laboratory, however, these documents constitute what is yet to be processed and manufactured. Secondly, secretaries post off papers from the laboratory at an average rate of one every ten days. However, far from being *reports* of what has been produced in a factory, members take these papers to be the *product* of their unusual factory.
>
> (Latour and Woolgar, 1979:47)

Of course, this laboratory also produces other things; most obviously, small quantities of rare and valuable natural and synthetic substances. However, these are not sold (Latour and Woolgar estimate that their market value would about cover the Institute's expenses); rather, they are exchanged as part of various kinds of deal or in return for various kinds of favor. Thus their real value lies, as we might now have come to expect, in their *potential* for generating further papers.

Latour and Woolgar then point out that the oral discussion in the laboratory also is largely taken up with discussion of documents: 'almost without exception, every discussion and brief exchange observed in the laboratory centered around one or more items in the published literature ... In other words, informal exchanges invariably focused on the substance of formal communication' (1979:52). For Latour and Woolgar, then, the laboratory is constantly performing operations on statements; citing, borrowing, criticizing, making stronger or weaker knowledge-claims in respect to prior statements. In addition, 'members of our laboratory regularly noticed how their own assertions were rejected, borrowed, quoted, ignored, confirmed or dissolved by others' (1979:87). Therefore, for Latour and Woolgar the laboratory is no longer so much in confrontation with recalcitrant *nature*, but in open competition with other research groups. However, these kinds of argument lead them to adopt the extreme subjectivist position that reality is the outcome of the settlement of a dispute, that facts are always constructed, and that − at least by implication − substances, physical mechanisms and so on do not exist until they have been identified.

Naturally enough this view has been challenged. Bazerman (1980) in particular has observed that *laboratory life* conflates fact with statement of fact. The documentary world of Latour and Woolgar rather conveniently ignores the real substances (and animals) left behind as description moves progressively forward from raw data to the Results sections of papers. In the end, experimental reporting in science is not a collective flight of the imagination, nor a mere matter of shooting down the opposition, but is tethered, however tenuously and obliquely, to an experiential world of substance.

In contrast to the two other books, Gilbert and Mulkay (1984) offer an analysis of the various ways in which a major controversy in biochemistry is described and discussed by the leading protagonists. The accounting for 'the facts' seems to vary along two major dimensions. The first relates to where a particular researcher stands *vis-à-vis* the currently fashionable position. More specifically, Gilbert and Mulkay are able to show the tension between a need to recognize good work by others – however unpalatable – and a need on the researcher's behalf to protect his or her 'investment' in time, equipment, money, effort and kudos. The second major variation in accounting relates to public and private statement – more specifically to the difference between what is said in formal published papers and what is said in informal interviews with the two sociologists. Thus, Gilbert and Mulkay argue that the ordered variability of scientific discourse can be explained by recognizing the existence of two repertoires: the *empiricist* and the *contingent*. The former is typically used in the research literature:

> As we have seen, in research papers experimental data tend to be given chronological as well as logical priority. Neither the author's own involvement with or commitment to a particular analytic position nor his social ties with those whose work he favors are mentioned. Laboratory work is characterized in a highly conventionalized manner, as instances of impersonal, procedural routines which are generally applicable and universally effective. Although the content of experimental papers clearly depends on the experimenters' actions and judgments, such papers are overwhelmingly written in an impersonal style, with overt references to the author's actions and judgments kept to the minimum. By adopting these kinds of linguistic features, authors construct texts in which the physical world seems regularly to speak, and sometimes to act, for itself. Empiricist discourse is organized in a manner which denies its character as an interpretative product and which denies that its author's actions are relevant to its content.

(Gilbert and Mulkay, 1984:56)

This depiction of the empiricist repertoire has, on the one hand, much in common with Knorr-Cetina's description of the RA product, while, on the other, it contrasts sharply with the accounts that scientists produce when they discuss their work informally. In interviews, a *contingent* repertoire was manifest in which the impact of a range of factors not directly concerned with the world of biochemical phenomena was admitted. In interviews 'scientists presented their actions and beliefs as heavily dependent on speculative insights, prior intellectual commitments, personal characteristics, indescribable skills, social ties and group membership' (1984:56).

Further, Gilbert and Mulkay engagingly demonstrate that one kind of humor in the research world depends on playing off one repertoire against the other, a *locus classicus* being those lists pinned on research students' walls which contrast what is written with what 'really' happened. A version perhaps appropriate for readers of this book is given in Figure 6.

Empiricist	**Contingent**
A sample of 139 reprint requests was assembled.	My own and Bob's down the corridor.
The return rate was only 34%.	Actually a bit higher but two forms were returned about a year later, long after I had done the analysis.
An intermediate group of students was chosen as especially suitable.	We were already teaching them.
There is evidence that NNS graduate students are concerned about academic correspondence.	At least some of mine either panicked or indulged in avoidance strategies.
Short introductions were used for the preliminary analysis.	I wanted to be able to spread out single-page texts.
It has long been known that ...	I haven't been able to remember where I read it.

Figure 6   The two repertoires

The Gilbert and Mulkay study is itself artificially restricted (Halfpenny, 1988) since the division into just two repertoires is a direct consequence of the dual nature of their investigation: formal papers and semi-structured informal interviews. However, as linguists and rhetoricians know, language is always relatable to context, and we would therefore expect that other settings would give rise to additional repertoires. Indeed, Mulkay has gone on to do this by considering other genres such as scientific correspondence and Nobel Prize speeches (Mulkay, 1985). Another problem is that, as Gilbert and Mulkay observe but Latour and Woolgar do not, eventually 'the truth will out'; for instance, the relevant discourse communities will eventually agree that 'cold fusion' does or does not occur. A third is that sociologists of science not unnaturally need for the growth of their discipline to find – and perhaps stress – *sociological* aspects of both the processes and products of hard science experimentation. Thus, the accounts we have may not themselves be immune to the encroachment of contingent elements; we have yet to have in this area an ethnography of an ethnography (cf. Lury, 1982).

Despite these minor caveats, the three major studies reviewed in this section indicate in their slightly different ways the strength of the genre-specific conventions that constrain and shape the research article. Consequently, and despite appearances to the contrary, we find ourselves far away from a world in which it is expected that researchers will 'tell it as it happened'. Despite the conventional sectioning of the research article, we are far away from a world in which the research itself is comparably compartmentalized. Despite an objective 'empiricist' repertoire, we are far away from a world in which power, allegiance and self-esteem play no part, however much they may seem absent from the frigid surface of RA discourse. And yet we find the research article, this key product of the knowledge-manufacturing industry, to be a remarkable phenomenon, so cunningly engineered by rhetorical machining that it somehow still gives an *impression* of being but a simple description of relatively untransmuted raw material.

There is one other kind of rhetorical transformation that needs to be considered at this juncture: the translation of the RA into various kinds of more popular account. Dubois (1986) has traced the process whereby articles in journals like the *New England Journal of Medicine* (which we have already met at the outset of Part III) appear as news items in local papers through the mediation of science journalists working for the Associated Press wire service. As might be expected, the very clear differences in anticipated audience have profound rhetorical effects. Not only do we find expected changes such as the removal of jargon and the diminution of qualification, but the structure of the medical news item takes on the organizational form of journalistic genres. The main conclusions now occur in the opening sentences, while summaries of method are placed at the end (where they may be cut by local editors without causing the story as a whole to lose coherence). Further, 'publication of the scientific article is treated itself as a news event, with the result that the status of the scientific information may appear to be elevated to that of unalterable fact' (Dubois, 1986:243).

Fahnestock (1986) has also studied 'the fate of scientific observations as they pass from original research reports intended for scientific peers into popular accounts aimed at a general audience' (1986:275). She again traces translation into ordinary language, loss of careful qualification and a greater concern to capture human interest. She also observes:

> With a significant change in rhetorical situation comes a change in genre, and instead of simply reporting facts for a different audience, scientific accommodations are overwhelmingly epideictic: their main purpose is to celebrate rather than validate. And furthermore they must usually be explicit in their claims about the value of the scientific discoveries they pass along. They cannot rely on the audience to recognize the significance of information.
>
> (Fahnestock, 1986:278–9)

Fahnestock's genre shift is dramatically underlined by Myers (forthcoming), for he is able to establish major differences between original versions and their appearance in such prestigious science magazines as *Scientific American* and *New Scientist* – periodicals of course often believed by English teachers to *represent* contemporary scientific writing. Myers argues that the popularizations tell a different story and have a different view of science to the originals:

> These two views of science are apparent in textual differences in narrative structure, in syntax, and in vocabulary. The professional articles I study create what I call a *narrative of science*: they follow the argument of the scientist, arrange time into a parallel series of simultaneous events all supporting their claim, and emphasize in their syntax and vocabulary the conceptual structure of the discipline. The popularizing articles, on the other hand, present a sequential *narrative of nature* in which the plant or animal, not the scientific activity, is the subject, the narrative is chronological, and the syntax and vocabulary emphasize the externality of nature to scientific practices.
>
> (Myers, forthcoming:1–2)

Myers then goes on to show how this dichotomy works its way through differences in titles, abstracts, overall organization, introductions and illustrative material.

There are a number of pedagogical messages to be drawn from this review of what we know about the processes of constructing (and reconstructing) research articles. For example, the findings of Dubois, Fahnestock and Myers strongly suggest that we need to be aware of what we are doing if we are to introduce texts of the *Scientific American* type into our classes. We need to recognize that they constitute a different genre to the original RAs from which they derive. While, as Fahnestock (1986) argues, there may be a place for engaging students in exercises of technical journalism of this kind, they must be recognized as such and not seen as helping students to enter primary discourse communities of researchers. Indeed, there may be gain in getting students to test out Myers' two narratives proposals with material from their field or to follow controversies that arise from the over-simplifications of original conclusions.

Other easily communicable messages include the sheer importance of the writing aspect of research activity, its rhetorical complexity even within well-established genres, and the often elaborate nature of the revision process. Many of the longer quotes cited in this subsection are directly suitable for discussion, comparison, analysis and matching tasks, as I attempted to show in Swales 1987b.

7.3 Textual overview of the research article

The immediately preceding section offered several case histories of the processes whereby research articles get constructed. These case histories may in fact be somewhat one-sided in that they consistently point to the long-drawn-out and complex nature of these processes. Unfortunately I do not know of studies which document instances where RAs were 'dashed off', even though the very high productivity of certain researchers would indicate that such instances very probably occur and recur. Perhaps all we can conclude at the present time is that it would be erroneous to assume that the writing of a RA is *necessarily* a straight-forward task even for full and established members of discourse communities.

The reason for disassociating process and product is encapsulated in Murray's celebrated dictum that 'process cannot be inferred from product any more than a pig can be inferred from a sausage' (Murray, 1982:18). However, while the admonitory strength of this is obvious enough for those who would study the ways and means of the compositional process, the analogy does not affect the fact that the world itself evaluates the end product. The sausage succeeds or fails on its own merits. Although there may well be some correlation between the quality of the materials (plus the time and care given to their processing) and the acceptability of the outcome, the consumer makes a judgment on the thing itself. Similarly, editors and reviewers evaluate the product they receive, and do not encourage accompanying accounts of how long or how agonizing the construction processes were. In the RA genre the amount of effort is ultimately deemed not material, as it is similarly deemed in a book like this. This is not to say, of course, that matters are always of an open or shut character. We may, with varying degrees of formality, distribute or even submit *drafts* for comment – as the prefaces to this and many other books signify – but these are subsequently viewed by their recipients as being drafts and treated accordingly. Accompanying commentary will tend to refer to the draft as being 'rough' or 'incomplete' rather than refer to the amount of time or effort expended. At the end of the day, it is the product that counts.

I believe that sections 7.1 and 7.2 should have convinced many that the RA is anything but a simple genre. It is thus quite surprising to find that there have been very few attempts to define an appropriate procedural methodology for approaching texts of this kind (unlike in spoken discourse, e.g. Ellis and Donohue, 1986; Potter and Wetherell, 1987). The most important set of proposals is probably that of Bley-Vroman and Selinker (1984) in which they advocate the following five-step approach to 'an optimum research strategy':

1. Practical problem areas and current tools
2. 'Quick and dirty' analysis
3. Explicit initial assumptions
4. Highly-valued texts
5. Subject-specialist informants

(Bley-Vroman and Selinker, March 1984:4)

As far as I am aware, the first three steps have received general assent. In Step 1 Bley-Vroman and Selinker advocate that research in the grammatical/rhetorical tradition – as pertaining to academic genres – should be grounded in a perceived inadequacy in extant teaching materials, in a perceived dissatisfaction with current methods of applied discourse analysis, or in a perceived dissatisfaction with our state of knowledge of a student-relevant text type. Under Step 2 they recommend a rough-and-ready survey of relevant texts in order to ascertain the incipient problems of procedure, sampling, text-division and so on. For Step 3 they state that it is necessary 'to establish and *explicitly state* the initial series of assumptions which will guide the researcher studying the unit in the text(s) under observation' (January 1984:2) – and this concern for validating assumptions is both emphasized and extended in Crookes (1986a). So far so good.

However, Bley-Vroman and Selinker then suggest in Step 4 that the analytic work be limited to an apparently restricted number of 'highly-valued' texts that can be established – by inquiry, interview and so on – as central to a given field, either by virtue of content or by virtue of form. There are, I believe, a number of difficulties with this notion. First, important papers may often be written by powerful luminaries who are consequently able to ride rough-shod over many of the accepted linguistic and rhetorical conventions in their given field; Ard (1983), for instance, has pointed out that Chomsky's later writings (written when he had already achieved a considerable degree of fame) display very much greater use of first person pronouns than his early publications. Therefore, there is a very real danger that the 'content' version of a highly-valued text may be stylistically atypical, thus offering a misleading role-model to those trying to embark upon a career as research writers. Apparently, Bley-Vroman and Selinker take 'form' in the somewhat abstract sense of referring to standard 'argument' or representative rhetorical organization. However, as the two authors nowhere make any reference to corpus-building or establishing a representative sample, this method of ascribing 'high value' seems prone to circularity. After all, we do not know what a model in terms of 'form' may be *unless* and *until* some survey has established that a particular text is generally representative of exemplars of the genre. It seems to me that the concept of *highly-valued* texts may have considerable significance in studies that trace the intellectual and/or rhetorical history of an area; however, in our attempts to develop genre-specific skills among apprentices we may do better to operate on and with texts that are not extraordinary by virtue of import, authorship or whatever, for then they are more likely to be *prototypical* exemplars.

Step 5, eliciting the help of a specialist informant in text-selection, category-establishment and interpretation, offers at first sight a convincing way out of the subjectivist dilemma. However, if we are to give credence to the findings of Gilbert and Mulkay and others we have to recognize that discussions with specialist informants may fall squarely within the *contingent repertoire*. Those discussions will hence be subject to all the subjective features of personality, allegiance, status and so on that this repertoire exhibits. Although Selinker (personal communication) is clearly right to point out that without specialist informants genre analysts may be in danger of 'not knowing what they don't know', over-reliance on specialist informants may invite the opposite danger of analysts 'believing all that they hear'. Further problems are that specialist informant work can be very time-consuming (Huckin and Olsen, 1984), and that it raises uncertainty when comparing RAs from different disciplines (where instability is inevitably created by relying on *different* informants for each discipline). We might conclude, then, that the role of the subject specialist informant in RA genre analysis remains, given the current levels of evaluated experience, somewhat controversial. Certainly the evidence is mixed. There is at least one purely textual study that has been subsequently confirmed by re-analyzing the data with the aid of a specialist informant (Selinker, Tarone and Hanzeli, 1981:52); and yet there must be myriad instances of language specialists 'misreading' specialized texts when working on their own. Even more confusingly, there is one case (Huckin and Olsen, 1984) in which the original author offered a rather different interpretation of his text to that provided by the subject specialist informant in Selinker (1979).

If there are discernible figures in this carpet they would suggest the following. Firstly, there is always a partial and supportive role for the specialist informant: useful for certain types of analysis, for certain parts of texts, for testing formulated hypotheses and findings. Secondly, the general need for a specialist informant may be in inverse proportion to the degree of relevant experience possessed by the genre analyst. Thirdly, there is a strong suggestion in the literature that the value of specialist informants increases when they are not only conceived of as sources of information and insight, but also as objects of ethnographic study themselves as they negotiate textual material within their own environments (Pettinari, 1982; Bhatia, 1983; Zumrawi, 1984; Huckin, 1987). It remains the case, however, that the field still lacks effective studies that evaluate the use of informants in terms of the trade-off between the rewards of 'behind the scenes' insight and professional confirmation, and the penalties of extra time and narrowed scope.

The literature that explores the textual properties of RAs is quite extensive. Moreover, there is considerable variation amongst the papers in the scale of research, in the level of analysis (from the straight counting of surface linguistic features to the search for underlying structure), and in the methodological and linguistic approaches devised or drawn upon. Useful part characterizations of this variety are provided by Widdowson (1979) and Jarvis (1983). In fact, some of this research attempts to describe scientific writing in general: research articles, textbooks, specialized reports, and sometimes various kinds of scientific journalism. Those investigations that have conflated genres in such a way that information specific to the RA is irreconstructible will not be considered further in this section. This may seem arbitrarily dismissive, but I believe it is a not unreasonable position to adopt in a book whose major premise is that genre differentiation provides the opening strategy in elucidating the characteristics of recurring and regularized communicative events. Some of the more important pieces of work that have been 'lost' in this way are Barber (1962), Huddleston (1971), Selinker et al. (1976) and a series of articles on lexis such as Salager (1983).

Because of the complexity of the remaining literature, I will first offer a summary overall listing of studies before discussing detailed findings. Thus, in Table 3 the studies are principally arranged by *coverage* – all of the RA or one or more of its parts – and secondarily by main *feature* selected for study (tense, voice, etc.). Under the latter heading I have used the cover-term 'structure' to encompass investigations that deal with a wide variety of *patterns* of rhetorical, informational and conceptual organization. I have also tried to show wherever possible both the size of corpus and the discipline or disciplines covered, the asterisks indicating

TABLE 3. OVERVIEW OF THE TEXTUAL STUDIES OF THE ENGLISH RA

a) *The RA as a whole*

Author(s)	Date	Feature(s)	Corpus (no. of RAs)	Field(s)
Lackstrom et al.	1972	tense, etc.	*	engineering
Lackstrom et al.	1973	paragraph development and tense	*	science and engineering
Inman	1978	types of lexis	40	range/ undifferentiated
Lackstrom	1978	modals	*	general science
Ewer	1979	modals	18	range/ undifferentiated
West	1980	*that*-nominals	15	biological science
Tarone et al.	1981	voice	2	astrophysics
Tomlin	1981	voice and clause	*	*
Wingard	1981	verb forms	5	medicine
Ard	1982	tense and aspect	*	*
Darian	1982	definitions	*	*
Dubois	1982	NP-development	5	zoology
Heslot	1982	tense	16	plant pathology
Hill et al.	1982	structure	1	psychology
Ard	1983	personal pronouns	*	*
Een	1982	tense	9	geotechnical engineering
Adams Smith	1984	authorial comment	6	medicine
Stanley	1984	structure	1	engineering
Weissberg	1984	paragraph development	60 (paras)	agriculture/ botany/ engineering
Adams Smith	1987	variation	6	medicine
Jacoby	1987	citation patterns	6	literary research
Malcolm	1987	tense	20	medicine
Popken	1987	topic sentences	35	range/ differentiated
Tinberg	1988	variation	2	economics

TABLE 3. OVERVIEW OF THE TEXTUAL STUDIES OF THE ENGLISH RA

b) *Introductions*

Author(s)	Date	Feature(s)	Corpus (no. of RAs)	Field(s)
Hepworth	1979	structure	*	*
Oster	1981	tense	2	engineering
Swales	1981	structure, etc.	48	range/ differentiated
Trimble and Trimble	1982	tense	*	science/ engineering
Zappen	1983	structure	*	engineering
Kinay et al.	1983	concluding sentences	50	range/ differentiated
Cooper	1985	structure	15	electronics
Hopkins	1985	structure	5	agriculture engineering
Crookes	1986	structure	24(96)	range/ differentiated
Swales and Najjar	1987	results statements	110	physics/ educational psychology

c) *Methods and Results*

Wood	1982	structure	10	chemistry
Bruce	1983	structure	*	medicine

d) *Discussions*

Belanger	1982	structure	10	neuroscience
McKinlay	1984	structure	30	medicine
Peng	1987	structure	10	chemical engineering
Hopkins and Dudley-Evans	1988	structure	12	range/ differentiated

that information is not available. The use of 'range' in the final column refers to a spread of fields or disciplines; the *range* may be undifferentiated (i.e. the findings are consolidated) or differentiated (i.e. similarities and differences between fields can be traced).

Before we examine some of the more interesting findings, a few general observations on Table 3 may be useful. In some of the studies, there are comparisons between genres, such as Heslot's study of experimental and review articles or Adams Smith's 1987 search for differences and similarities between original RAs and their popularization. Typically, I have excluded the data that is less prototypical of the RA. Secondly, it is easy to see that some fields are much less well represented than others; for example, there is very little on disciplines such as economics and sociology. Third, I have not thought it worthwhile to incorporate in Table 3 papers that have already been quite extensively discussed for other purposes (Bazerman, 1984a; Huckin, 1987), although relevant aspects of these fine studies will not be neglected. Finally, the listed papers vary considerably in their analytic perspective. Bruce, Dubois, Weissberg and Wood have been influenced by the *Functional Sentence Perspective* of the Prague school; Stanley and Jacoby by the *Clause Relations* of Winter (e.g. Winter, 1986); and Oster, Tarone and others by the *Rhetorical–Grammatical Approach* associated with Lackstrom, Selinker and Trimble. A number of other studies have attempted to develop an analysis which reflects the characteristics of the genre itself – a posture already recommended more than once in this volume.

A number of papers have attempted an account of the conceptual macrostructure of the research article: Stanley (1984) proposes a problem–solution structure, Bruce (1983) suggests that the Introduction–Method–Results–Discussion format follows the logical cycle of inductive inquiry, and Hutchins (1977) offers for the RA a modification of Kinneavy's cycle of *Dogma–Dissonance–Crisis–Search–New Model* (Kinneavy, 1971). However, little textual evidence is put forward to justify such configurations and, as the previous section has made clear, there can often be considerable distance between research actuality and its formal presentation. Perhaps then a more manageable starting-point for a discussion of shape of macrostructure is the hour-glass diagram (Figure 7) proposed by Hill et al.

Although this schematic diagram is apparently derived from but a single paper in psychology – and one with an off-beat content at that – it intuitively accords with much of the discussion in the previous two sections. As the authors say, 'research papers make the transition from the general field or context of the experiment to the specific experiment by describing an inadequacy in previous research that motivates the present experiment' (1982:335). The Method and Results sections (subsumed under Procedure in Figure 7 overleaf) then continue along a narrow, particularized path, whilst the Discussion section mirror-images the Introduction by moving from specific findings to wider implications.

The findings of West (1980) and Heslot (1982) can now be fitted into this scheme. West studied the occurrence across sections of *that*-nominals (elements of the type in italics in the following example sentence): 'We

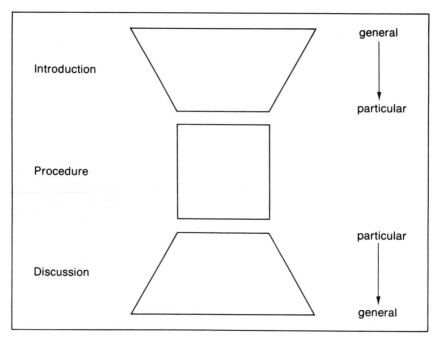

Figure 7   Overall organization of the research paper (Hill et al., 1982).

have shown *that genres have considerable generative power'*. He found 306 such structures in the 15 biology RAs he examined. As might be expected, they were distributed differently across the Introduction– Method–Results–Discussion (IMRD) structure; very rare in Methods, fairly uncommon in Results, frequent in Discussions and most frequent in Introductions. He provides the following explanatory comment:

> Because that-nominalization relegates statements to secondary positions in other statements, that-nominals are used when making claims about other statements rather than simply making state- ments. The Introduction section, as the rhetorical section that motivates the study, normally includes a review of previous research. The fact that a primary function of the Introduction section is to make claims about statements from other research accounts for the high density of that-nominal constructions. Similarly, the Discussion section, as the rhetorical section whose primary function is to explain the statistical findings in non- statistical English, makes many claims about the research findings and therefore contains many that-nominals. The Results section, which describes the process of manipulating the data obtained from the Methods section and makes only limited claims about the statistical tests, has fewer that-nominals. The Methods section, which simply describes the process of obtaining the data, rarely

makes claims about other statements and consequently has almost no that-nominal constructions.

(West, 1980:486–7)

Of course, commenting on the work of others can be expressed by a variety of syntactic devices other than that-nominals (West himself mentions the infinitive), and at this stage we might not want to accept too readily West's descriptions of the purposes of the various RA sections; nevertheless, the statistical differences in regard to this linguistic feature are both striking and indicative.

Heslot (1982), in a useful paper, examines tense, voice and 'person markers' across the four sections in 16 RAs from the journal *Phytopathology*. Again the distributions are highly significant (percentages have been rounded where not 0.5).

TABLE 4. TENSE AND VOICE PER SECTION IN 16 RAS (after Heslot)

	I %	M %	R %	D %
Simple Present	48.5	4.0	6.0	48.5
Simple Past	35.0	94.0	94.0	39.0
Active	67.0	17.0	72.0	83.5

Both the procedural M and R sections in this sample are almost exclusively 'past', but the former strongly favors the passive whereas the latter equally strongly favors the active. The I and D sections are similar in showing a smallish preponderance for the present and in having combined percentages for the two main tenses in the 80–90% range (as opposed to 98–100% for M and R), thus suggesting that other verb forms, such as the Present Perfect and modal complications, tend to occur principally in these two sections.

Heslot also comments that first person forms did not occur in M and R, but did so in I and D, although she does not give any figures. This finding conflicts with that of Tarone et al. (1981) who showed that *we* was widely distributed across the (more complicated) sectioning of two astrophysics RAs – indeed, if anything, it occurred *less* frequently in the opening and closing sections. If there is a simple explanation for this anomaly, it may lie in the fact that astrophysics papers have no obviously procedural sections but largely consist in descriptions of and arguments for an increasingly refined set of equations to account for astrophysical phenomena.

Leaving aside the Tarone results, further support for the emerging conclusion that the different sections perform different rhetorical functions and thus require different linguistic resources to realize those functions is provided by Adams Smith, who investigated 'author's comment' in (amongst other genres) six medical research papers. The relevant part of her figures is given in Table 5 below.

TABLE 5. INSTANCES OF AUTHOR'S COMMENT PER RA SECTION
(simplified from Adams Smith, 1984)

	Instances of author's comment	No. of lines	Comment/ line ratio
I	58	173	1:3
M and R	18	385	1:21
D	202	436	1:2,2

Again we see a marked contrast between I and D on the one hand, and M and R on the other; in this particular case a difference close to an order of magnitude. According to Adams Smith, the main way in which I- and D-clustered authorial comment is introduced is by modal auxiliaries, of which *may* and then *should* are the most frequent. (In Adams Smith's sample *can* is rare, although Huddleston (1971) remarks that it is common in physical science papers.) In fact, modality accounted for about half of the instances of *comment*, the other half being expressed by adverbs and adjectives of 'probability' such as *possible, certainly*, and so on (about 15%) and by a wide range of 'attitudinal markers' (the remaining 35%) such as adverbs like *surprisingly*, marked choice of noun (*view* v. *hypothesis*), switch to first person, and unusual use of metaphor or analogy. Functionally, by far the most common type of authorial comment in the six RAs in the sample is epistemic, that is, relating to the probability (from 0 to 100%) of a proposition or a hypothesis being true. The three other uses that occurred with any frequency were recommending, emphasizing and evaluating. If we put these preliminary findings together we get an overview as in Figure 8.

The evidence thus suggests a differential distribution of linguistic and rhetorical features across the four standard sections of the research article. By and large, we have seen evidence for a two-way division into 'simple' M and R and 'complex' I and D – and at this juncture we could bear in mind Knorr-Cetina's observation that in her case study it was the Introduction and Discussion that were serially redrafted whilst the M and R drafts survived to publication virtually unchanged. The following sections will examine each of the four parts in more detail by con-sidering, *inter alia*, the rationale behind such findings, exceptions to them, and cross-disciplinary variation. This, however, is a suitable point

Feature	I	M	R	D
Movement (Hill et al.)	outside-in	narrow	narrow	inside-out
Reporting statements (West)	high	very low	low	high
Present Tense (Heslot)	high	low	low	high
Past Tense (Heslot)	fairly low	very high	very high	fairly low
Passive Voice (Heslot)	low	high	variable	variable
Authorial comment (Adams Smith)	high	very low	very low	high

Figure 8   Features across the IMRD sections

to indicate one or two linguistic and functional features that occur very rarely, if at all, in *any* section of a RA. Progressive or continuous forms are extremely rare (Barber, 1962; Wingard, 1981). Second person pronoun forms are absent (in contrast to textbooks), except for the occasional imperative verb in comments on non-verbal data or in footnotes. Explicit definitions (again unlike textbooks) are very rare (Darian, 1982; Swales, 1981a).

7.4   Introductions

Introductions are known to be troublesome, and nearly all academic writers admit to having more difficulty with getting started on a piece of academic writing than they have with its continuation. The opening paragraphs somehow present the writer with an unnerving wealth of options: decisions have to be made about the amount and type of background knowledge to be included; decisions have to be made about an authoritative versus a sincere stance (Arrington and Rose, 1987); decisions have to be made about the winsomeness of the appeal to the readership; and decisions have to be made about the directness of the approach. If we add to the above brief catalogue the assumption that first impressions matter (especially in an era of exponentially-expanding literature), then we are not surprised to note that over the last 10 years or so there has been growing interest in the introductory portions of texts. As far as the RA is concerned, part of this literature has been listed in Table 3.

One possible approach is to view RA introductions as encapsulated problem–solution texts. This, for instance, is the position adopted by Zappen (1983) who, following Toulmin (1972), argues that researchers in their writing need continuously to address the context of the intellectual discipline wherein they are located. More specifically 'the researcher addresses the goals, current capacities, problems, and criteria of evaluation that derive from and operate within that discipline' (Zappen, 1983:130). As Figure 9 shows, Zappen's analysis follows this series of sub-contexts: *goal* in the first paragraph, *current capacity* (the best we can do at the moment), *problem* (However, ...), *solution* (In the present work, ...) and *criteria of evaluation*.

While the emphasis on the disciplinary audience in this characterization is both salutary and necessary, and while the five-part rhetorical division is itself plausible, the labeling of those divisions suggests a rather flat and certainly sunny world in which the empiricist repertoire of logic, objectivity and reason strongly predominates. However, if we examine a little more closely the Figure 9 text that Zappen himself chose to illustrate his approach, we can see that this short introduction is firmly embedded within the localized field of the researchers' previous work. Eight of the nine references cite previous papers by the first author. All but one of the self-citations are positive, the exception being (9), while the solitary outside reference (8) is considered to make a less 'practical' proposal than the authors' own. The exception to the positive evaluation of their own work lies in Zappen's Problem section where the authors need both to motivate their present work and to justify its publication by showing that their contribution to the discipline, whilst previously established as significant and reference-worthy, is as yet incomplete. In addition, the story that Neelakantaswamy and Hong tell is not without its rhetorical interest. They open their account with the bold claim that they have developed not a 'number' nor a 'series' but a 'class' of instruments – and one that has been given a class name. These are 'compact' and 'simple', have 'practical utility' and are 'non-invasive'. Unfortunately, this class of instrument does produce a 'significant amount of spherical aberrations', but in the latest version as presented in the current paper 'the spherical aberration effects are relatively minimized'. (But not eliminated completely.)

Thus, this 'simple' and short engineering introduction is rich in evaluative commentary that not only reveals the authors addressing the

GOAL

In the recent past, Neelakantaswamy et al. (1–4) developed a class of microwave radiators termed as 'Gaussian-beam launchers' to produce a focused exposure field in biological experiments for partial-body irradiations. These compact and simple structures with their ability to focus the microwave energy in a very small region indicate their practical utility, in the areas of biological researches and medical applications of microwaves, such as for selective heating of diseased/cancerous tissues. These launchers can also be used in noninvasive beam-wave reflectometric and spectrometric instrumentations for measuring complex permittivity of biological material at microwave frequencies, as indicated by Neelakantaswamy elsewhere (5–7).

CURRENT CAPACITY

When compared to the microwave beam-launching system described in (8), which consists of a plane-wave irradiated dielectric sphere (lens), the launcher formed by combining a scalar horn and dielectric sphere (1) is a more practical source of microwave Gaussian beam. However, the use of a

PROBLEM

dielectric sphere as the focusing lens results in a significant amount of spherical aberrations in the focal field, as indicated by Neelakantaswamy et al. in (9) ...

SOLUTION

In the present work, a Gaussian-beam launcher is formed by placing a dielectric hemisphere (instead of a full sphere) at the aperture end of corrugated circular waveguide (scalar horn). This enables a reduction in the path length of the ray in the lens-medium, and hence the spherical aberration

CRITERIA OF EVALUATION

effects are relatively minimized. Further, by using a hemisphere in the place of a full sphere, the launcher structure becomes less massive and smaller.

(from P. Neelakantaswamy and F. Hong. 1979. Dielectric Hemisphere-Loaded Scalar Horn as a Gaussian-Beam Launcher for Microwave Exposure Studies. *IEEE Transactions on Microwave Theory and Techniques. MTT*, 27:797)

Figure 9   A problem–solution model of article introductions (Zappen, 1983)

expectations of the discourse community (as the Toulmin–Zappen model suggests) but also addressing the development of their research area particularly as it relates to their *own* contributions, past, present and future. Although the level of self-citation in the text may be abnormally high, scientist colleagues consistently respond to my queries with comments like 'you cannot avoid citing your previous work in science'. This suggests, amongst other things, that part of the difficulty with fitting a problem–solution schema onto introductions is the fact that 'problems' or research questions or unexplained phenomena are the life-blood of many research undertakings. Adams Smith (1987) cites her informant as follows:

> Biomedical research, he said, is not a matter of problem-solving. Rather it is the observation of something interesting that does not seem to fit the pattern, followed by the observation of this phenomenon over a period of time, and the recording and explanation of the findings. It is common for a piece of research to answer the question it has set out to clarify while at the same time it raises other questions to be accounted for in the course of further investigation.

> (Adams Smith, 1987:19–20)

Perhaps it is not therefore surprising that Adams Smith (1987) found that the medical RAs she examined either failed to contain a recognizable *problem* or tended not to foreground it. In contrast, the derived popularizations emphasized problem or controversy, partly by placing the issue early (presumably for reasons of 'newsworthiness' discussed in the previous section).

My earliest attempt to offer an alternative *sui generis* model to account for the rhetorical movement in article introductions was Swales, 1981b. Although the '4-move' model presented in that monograph has had some little influence (sometimes more than I would wish), certain defects have become increasingly apparent. Several analysts (Lopez, 1982; Bley-Vroman and Selinker, 1984; Crookes, 1986a) have commented on the difficulties of separating Move 1 and Move 2. The fact that the original corpus was deliberately restricted to *short* introductions led to the creation of a separate citational category (Move 2 – Summarizing Previous Research) clearly at odds with the increasing practice of spreading references throughout the introduction (Jacoby, 1986). A further consequence of the corpus choice was neglect of the recycling possibilities in longer introductions. In addition, the range of options in the final two moves was overly restrictive (Jacoby, 1987; Cooper, 1985).

In the revised *Create a Research Space* (CARS) model (Figure 10) I have taken the ecological analogy rather further than hitherto, because it seems to me that it adequately captures a number of characteristics of RA

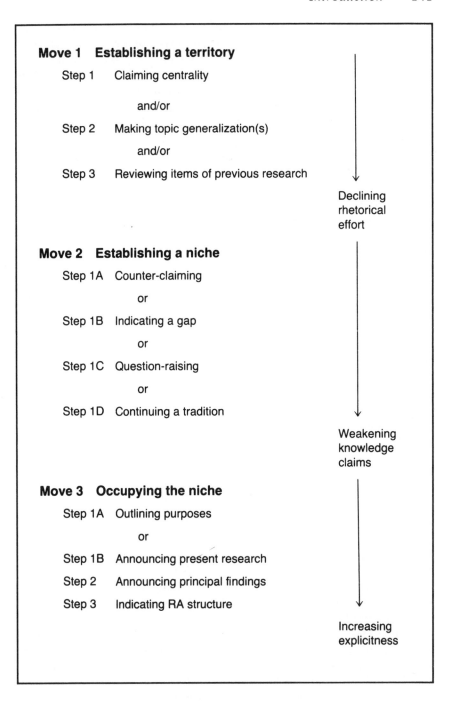

Figure 10   A CARS model for article introductions

introductions: the need to re-establish in the eyes of the discourse community the significance of the research field itself; the need to 'situate' the actual research in terms of that significance; and the need to show how this niche in the wider ecosystem will be occupied and defended. It follows that the amount of rhetorical work needed to create such a space depends on the existing ecological competition, on the size and importance of the niche to be established, and on various other factors such as the writer's reputation.

If we apply this model to the Zappen text (Figure 9) we can see that Move 1 is coterminous with *goal* and *current capacity*, Move 2 with *problem* and Move 3 with *solution of criteria of evaluation*. We would ascribe Move 1 as containing only a Step 3 because there are no opening generalizations of a type to be discussed shortly. However, the Step 3 (literature items 1–8) is, as we have already seen, quite marked by upbeat expressions of significance and relevance, presumably because of the self-citational nature of the review. The single sentence Move 2 can be identified as a Step 1B (indicating a gap). A possible alternative would be to take Move 2 as a Step 1D (continuing a tradition) but the use of the adversative *however* suggests otherwise.

The four options for Move 2 can be illustrated as with the following versions of the Figure 9 text:

Step 1A (Counter-claim)	However, the use of . . . results in such a degree of spherical aberration that radical design changes have become necessary.
Step 1B (Gap)	However, the use of . . . results in a significant amount of spherical aberrations . . .
Step 1C (Question)	However, it is not clear whether the use of . . . can be modified to reduce spherical aberration to acceptable levels.
Step 1D (Continuation)	The remaining issue is to find a way of better controlling spherical aberration.

Finally, we can assign the third paragraph to Move 3, the first sentence being Step 1B, and the final two being Step 2.

Figure 11 offers a sample Move–Step analysis of a slightly longer, 14-sentence introduction, but again from the hard sciences area. Both the text itself and the issues it raises for the genre analyst are quite intriguing. In the first place, the establishment of territory in Move 1 utilizes all three step options, again suggesting that we would be unwise to come to any swift conclusion that science and engineering RA introductions tend to avoid (or do not need) the more rhetorical options. In fact, the opening two sentences represent a prototypical instance of both the 'narrowing' effect and of what I have called *claiming centrality*:

I Introduction

(1) The increasing interest in high-angle-of-attack aerodynamics has heightened the need for computational tools suitable to predict the flowfield and the aerodynamic coefficients in this regime. (2) Of particular interest and complexity are the symmetric and the asymmetric separated vortex flows which develop about slender bodies as the angle of attack is increased. / (3) The viscous influence on the separation lines and the unknown three-dimensional (3D) shape of the vortex wake are some of the main flow features that must be modeled in the construction of a computational method to properly treat this problem.

MOVE 1 — STEP 1 / STEP 2

(4) Among the many potential flow methods developed in attempting to solve body vortex flows are early two dimensional (2D) multivortex methods,[2–4] 2D time-stepping vortex models that include boundary-layer considerations,[5–8] and a quasi-3D potential flow method[9] that uses source and vortex elements. (5) Linear, unseparated potential flow models as well as purely viscous models, are not mentioned here. (6) A survey of the various methods may also be found in Ref. 10. (7) The potential flow methods are of special interest because of their ability to treat 3D body shapes and their separated vortex flows using a simple and relatively inexpensive model. / (8) However, the previously mentioned methods suffer from some limitations mainly concerning the treatment of the vortex wake formation and its interaction with the body. (9) The first group of methods [2–4] cannot treat 3D flows and is limited to very slender bodies. (10) The second group of computational methods[5–8] is time consuming and therefore expensive, and its separation prediction is not sufficiently accurate. (11) Both the methods in this group and the method in Ref. 9 suffer from the dependency on too many semiempirical inputs and assumptions concerning the vortex wake and its separation. (12) The steady, 3D nonlinear vortex-lattice method,[11–12] upon which the present method is based, eliminates many of these limitations by introducing a more consistent model, but it can treat only symmetrical flow cases. / (13) The present work extends the use of the last model to asymmetric, body-vortex flow cases, thus increasing the range of flow problems that can be investigated. (14) In addition, an effort is made to improve the numerical procedure to accelerate the convergence of the iterative solution and to get a better rollup of the vortex lines representing the wake.

STEP 3 (MOVE 2) — STEP 1B — MOVE 3 — STEP 1B

(D. Almosino. 1985. High Angle-of-Attack Calculations of the Subsonic Vortex Flow in Slender Bodies *AIAA Journal* 23 (8):1150–6)

Figure 11   A sample Move–Step analysis

I am grateful to Changyu Yang for bringing this text to my attention.

S1   The increasing interest in ... has heightened the need for ...

S2   Of particular interest and complexity are ...

Centrality claims are appeals to the discourse community whereby members are asked to accept that the research about to be reported is part of a lively, significant or well-established research area. Some typical examples of the linguistic exponents – and signals – of centrality claims are given below in abbreviated form. In all these cases, and in subsequent ones, the examples have been taken from actual RA texts, unless indicated otherwise.

Recently, there has been a spate of interest in how to ...

In recent years, applied researchers have become increasingly interested in ...

The possibility ... has generated interest in ...

Recently, there has been wide interest in ...

The time development ... is a classic problem in fluid mechanics.

The explication of the relationship between ... is a classic problem of ...

The well-known ... phenomena ... have been favorite topics for analysis both in ...

Knowledge of ... has a great importance for ...

The study of ... has become an important aspect of ...

The theory that ... has led to the hope that ...

The effect of ... has been studied extensively in recent years.

Many investigators have recently turned to ...

The relationship between ... has been studied by many authors.

A central issue in ... is the validity of ...

As the above list indicates, authors of a RA can make a centrality claim at the introduction's outset in a number of ways. They can claim interest, or importance; they can refer to the classic, favorite or central character of the issue; or they can claim that there are many other investigators active in the area. In the two corpora that I have examined in detail (Swales, 1981b; Swales and Najjar, 1987) the exercise of the Step 1 option was comparatively common, averaging a little under 50% for the combined sample of 158 introductions. It also seems quite widely distributed across various disciplinary areas, although exercised somewhat less in the physical sciences. Possible rationales for utilizing or avoiding a centrality claim remain an unexplored but interesting research area. Among the variables that might turn out to be relevant are the disciplinary area itself; some felt sense of the expectations of particular journals; the nature of the research itself (as when authors might want to

enhance with centrality claims a particular piece of research or scholarship that others might conceive of as marginal); or individual rhetorical
predispositions for or against marked rhetorical activity of this type.

Centrality claims are typically communicated in a single sentence, but
can, as Figure 11 shows, extend over two or more sentences. They are
also typically, but not inevitably, introduction initial. In the following
case, for instance, Steps 1 and 2 have been reversed:

> S1   An elaborate system of marking social distance and respect is
>   found in the morphology of Nahautl as spoken in
>   communities of the Malinche volcano area in the Mexican
>   States of Tlaxcala and Puebla. (Step 2)
>
> S2   The complexity of the morphology involved, the semantic
>   range of the elements, and variation in the system of use *raise*
>   *questions of considerable interest* for our understanding of the
>   form and function of *such systems*, both in Nahautl itself *and*
>   *in other languages*. (Step 1, my emphases)
>
> (J. H. Hill and K. C. Hill. 1978. Honorific Usage in Modern Nahautl.
> *Language* 54:123)

This introduction opens with a topic generalization of a Step 2 type, and
as such does little to appeal to any but those with a specialized interest in
Mexican languages. The 'repair', if one is needed, immediately follows,
for the elements that I have italicized make a strong claim that the
about-to-be-described findings are of central interest to sociolinguists of
whatever areal specialty. It would doubtless have been possible to
reverse the order in some way, or to have incorporated the substance of
S1 into S2, although at the probable cost of increased syntactic complexity. My reading of the introduction as a whole suggests that the unusual
order may be relatable to the authors' concern to establish early that their
study was based on very extensive field work. This would explain the
early circumscription to 'as spoken in communities of the Malinche
volcano area', which in turn would explain the difficulty of initiating the
introduction with Step 1.

The more general point raised by this particular text is that there are
good general and applied reasons for assigning numerical sequence to
textual elements that occur in suitably robust preferred orders. In the case
of RA introductions the three moves occur at a high frequency in their
assigned order. Swales and Najjar (1987) found, for instance, only 10 out
of 110 introductions beginning with a Move 3. An anomaly percentage
of under 10% is well within acceptable bounds in discoursal and textual
studies for, even more than syntax, discourse is a phenomenon of
propensities. Discourse generalizations are permeable to exceptions, and
are not consequently falsified by limited numbers of counter-instances.
Further, the occasional recurrence of minor dispreferred structures is

itself a phenomenon of interest both intrinsically and in terms of what it may reveal about the rationale behind the major preferred ones.

Step 2 has been labeled as *making a topic generalization* and represents a more neutral kind of general statement than Step 1. Step 2s can take a variety of forms, but generally fall into two categories: statements about *knowledge or practice*, or statements about *phenomena*. Representative authentic but abbreviated examples of the first group are:

The aetiology and pathology of . . . is well known.

There is now much evidence to support the hypothesis that . . .

The . . . properties of . . . are still not completely understood.

A standard procedure for assessing has been . . .

Education core courses are often criticized for . . .

Typically, these Step 2s express in general terms the current state of the art – of knowledge, of technique, or as in the case of the Figure 11 text, of current requirements for further progress. The second group of topic generalizations refers to phenomena, such as:

. . . is a common finding in patients with . . .

An elaborate system of . . . is found in the . . .

English is rich in related words exhibiting 'stress shifts'.

There are many situations where . . .

As these examples indicate, there is a strong tendency for *phenomena* topic generalizations in particular to establish territory by emphasizing the frequency and complexity of the data – indeed I suspect that if territory cannot be easily established in this way a Step 2 of this type would be dispreferred. Consider these alternates:

a1) English is *rich* in related words exhibiting 'stress shifts'.

a2) English is *poor* in related words exhibiting 'stress shifts'.

b1) There are *many* situations where examination scripts are marked and then re-marked by another examiner.

b2) There are *few* situations where . . .

In the case of (a2) the bald announcement of the relative absence of the phenomenon would seem, *prima facie*, to surrender territory; we would therefore be more inclined to expect that the author would attempt to regain ground with something like:

a3) English is *surprisingly poor* in related words . . .

for we can now expect some interesting account of the *reasons* for the impoverished phenomenon. The (b) example, which is discussed in detail in Swales (1987b), is the opening sentence from an experiment in exam re-marking. In that context, it would make little rhetorical sense to imply (by using 'few') that the phenomenon under investigation is of marginal status. On the other hand, territory might be established via the insertion of a couple of small words that carry implications of being 'state of the art':

b3) There are *as yet* few situations where …

The author may then be in a position to advance a knowledge claim that the innovation is provisionally promising.

Indeed, we see the precise mirror-image of the frequency requirement in studies that purport to be case reports. Here is a skeletalized version of an introduction in a medical journal:

S1   Primary malignant … lymphomas of … are very rare.

S2   In the Department of …, this diagnosis has been made in only ten patients during the last fifty years.

S3   Retrospective analysis showed that one of these cases showed a very uncommon …

S4   A review of the recent literature yielded only two reports of …: both of these reports paid little attention to clinical details.

S5   L… reported fourteen cases, … but in this report, too, clinical data are not given.

S6   In the present report we shall describe the chemical … findings in a case of … lymphoma … with an uncommon clinical course.

It is often believed that straightforward research reports begin with a straightforward thesis statement or statement of purpose. While it might have been possible for the authors of this article to have so begun by opening with S6, study of the above text shows clearly enough why they chose to establish both a territory and a niche before S6. Most obviously, given the fact that they had one case to report – and presumably one dug out of the archives at that – they were under some rhetorical pressure to establish its rarity and possibly near uniqueness. After all, the chances of being able to publish in a RA (as opposed to a textbook) a description of a single standard case of a standard disease are likely to be very slim. Hence, we are not surprised to find the authors' endeavoring to establish in the first three sentences the rarity of the phenomenon in their own medical institution, and then to go on to note that the mere 16 cases found in the literature lack clinical details. The complex establishment of the first five sentences thus prepares the discourse community to accept that there is indeed a niche being occupied in the introduction's final sentence.

The third step in establishing a territory is the review of one or more items deemed by the authors to be relevant to that establishment. Apart from at least one exceptional disciplinary area, minimal reference to previous work is the obligatory step in Move 1, while the other steps, from a corpus perspective, are discretionary. One exception to a strong literature-citation requirement was discovered by Cooper (1985) in her study of IEEE publications dealing with advances in computer technology. Four of her 15 introductions did not contain a Step 3, and she suggests that there may be a number of special circumstances that account for the light referencing: the fact that the field is relatively new and has little accumulated research tradition; and the fact that there is heavy commercial involvement in the field; and the fact that work tends to be product-related rather than concerned with hypotheses *per se*. Cooper's findings are interesting because they suggest that evolving discourse communities on the periphery of the academic world may be developing alternative conventions for their central genres.

The Step 3 is one of the main occasions where the RA author needs to relate *what has been found* (or claimed) with *who has found it* (or claimed it). More precisely, the author needs to provide a *specification* (in varying degrees of detail) of previous findings, an *attribution* to the research workers who published those results, and a *stance* towards the findings themselves. My earlier attempts (e.g. Swales, 1981b) to provide a useful account of the attribution variables – and their typical tense correlates – have not fully withstood the test of critical commentary (particularly by Jacoby, 1987) and I now offer a modified position. The basic distinction I would wish to make is between *integral* and *non-integral* forms of citation. The distinction has the merit of being easily applicable because it depends merely on recognizing surface features of text. An integral citation is one in which the name of the researcher occurs in the actual citing sentence as some sentence-element; in a non-integral citation, the researcher occurs either in parenthesis or is referred to elsewhere by a superscript number or via some other device. The main patterns are illustrated with constructed examples in Figure 12.

The integral citations show the name of the researcher as subject (Ia), passive agent (Ib), as part of a possessive noun phrase (Ic and d) and as what Tadros (1985) calls 'an adjunct of reporting' (Ie). The non-integral citations show three parenthetical citations and two superscripted ones. In Figure 12 the citations all in fact occur at sentence-final position, but scrutiny of technical RA introductions will reveal instances of other placements, especially when groups of researchers and related topics are introduced (as in sentence 4 of the Figure 11 text). The final type of non-integral citation listed in Figure 12 (Nf) was, to my knowledge, first discussed in the discourse analysis literature on RAs by Jacoby (1986).

Integral		Non-integral	
Ia	Brie (1988) showed that the moon is made of cheese.	Na	Previous research has shown that the moon is made of cheese (Brie, 1988).
Ib	The moon's cheesy composition was established by Brie (1988).	Nb	It has been shown that the moon is made of cheese (Brie, 1988).
Ic	Brie's theory (1988) claims that the moon is made of cheese.	Nc	It has been established that the moon is made of cheese.[1-3]
Id	Brie's (1988) theory of lunar composition has general support.	Nd	The moon is probably made of cheese (Brie, 1988).
Ie	According to Brie (1988), the moon is made of cheese.	Ne	The moon may be made of cheese.[1-3]
		Nf	The moon may be made of cheese (but cf. Rock, 1989).

Figure 12   Integral and non-integral citation

She labeled such references as 'contrastive' because they go against the drift of the conclusions being reached in the sentence itself. Contrastive references seem very unevenly distributed in academic writing. They are, for example, very uncommon in the scientific areas, but quite common in scholarly legal commentary. In the humanities, they seem to form part of some academics' writing style, but rarely, if ever, occur in the writings of others. Of Jacoby's six texts dealing variously with literary research, only two made much use of contrastive references but these two texts employed them quite consistently. They are worth further study.

Jacoby (1987:55) also proposes a category of reference which she calls *summary*: 'In these references no particular research predecessor is named, as a rule, but clear reference to the state of previous research as a whole or to the state of consensus knowledge can be identified'. I have not adopted this particular proposal. In cases where no previous researchers are specifically cited, I see no reason not to assign the text to Step 2 (topic generalization). In cases where specific previous researchers are cited, text elements can usually be assigned to one of the categories illustrated in Figure 12. As Jacoby implies, the problematic cases occur when the writer refers to groups or 'schools' of researchers and scholars. Compare the following:

a) Generative grammarians have recently modified their position.

b) Generative grammarians influenced by Chomsky have recently ...

c) Chomskyan grammarians have recently ...

d) Chomsky and his co-workers have recently ...

Even in the case of (d) the most workable assignment procedure would seem to be one that asks whether there is an actual citation or not. If there is, as in:

e) Chomsky and his co-workers (e.g. Napoli, 1988) have recently ...

then it falls under one of the Figure 12 categories (i.e. Nd). If there is none, as in (d), then it is not a citation.

The final column in Figure 12 is labeled +R or −R. The +R citations are *reporting*; that is to say the RA author employs a 'reporting' verb (show, establish, claim, etc.) to introduce previous researchers and their findings. In the lower sections of the figure, the citations are *non-reporting* (−R). The dichotomous classification works fairly well except for uncertainties that can arise with a small set of verbs, particularly *find* and *be associated with*. For example, we can give two possible readings to the sentence: 'X was found to be impaired' (Sang et al. 1972). We could read this as reporting:

a1) X was found by Sang et al. (1972) to be impaired.

a2) Sang et al. (1972) found that X was impaired.

Alternatively we could read it as *non-reporting*:

b1) X was impaired (Sang et al., 1972).

b2) Impairment of X occurred (Sang et al., 1972).

This existential reading has affinities with such common uses of *find* in the passive as: 'Coal is found in the ground' (i.e. coal occurs in the ground).

As we have already seen, Bazerman (1984a) noted a firm trend from reporting to non-reporting citations in the *Physical Review* during this century. However, this trend may be partly due to the fact that the *Physical Review* uses a numerical/superscript system. Such systems do not easily permit integral reporting choices:

? Reference 3 established that the moon was made of cheese.

In 16 biological and medical RAs from the 1970s, I found that the non-reporting/reporting ratio was only 40–60 (Swales, 1981b) whereas Jacoby (1987) found a 25–75 ratio among her literary critics. The survival of both integral and non-integral *reporting* structures can fairly clearly be attributed to their considerable discriminatory power. In the first place, the repertoire of reporting verbs that an author can draw on is quite large (around 50 possible candidates) ranging from highly frequent choices such as *suggest*, *report* and *show* to rarities like *asseverate*. Secondly, this class can be broadly divided into two main groups; those whose use asserts the author's commitment to the attendant proposition (*show, demonstrate, establish*, etc.) and those whose use carries no such commitment (*suggest, propose, examine*, etc.). The distinction is a powerful rhetorical tool in authors' attempts to create research spaces for themselves, because it allows them to signal early whether claims are to be taken as substantiated or not. Thirdly, the incorporation of a reporting verb concomitantly involves a choice of tense, the selection of which may be highly indicative.

In fact, EAP studies of references to previous research have tended to focus on providing an account of tense and aspect usage (Lackstrom et al., 1972; Swales, 1981b; Oster, 1981; Ard, 1982, 1985; Een, 1982; Trimble and Trimble, 1982; Malcolm, 1987). These studies have examined in particular the use of the three forms, the Past, the Present Perfect and the Present Simple, that together realize over 90% of all finite verb usages in citational statements. There are, I believe, three broad kinds of response to the issue of tense usage in this literature. One is to say that the 'general rules' are largely adequate (Ard, 1982 and 1985; Malcolm, 1987). A second approach, best illustrated by Oster (1981), proposes a special set of explanations of tense/aspect that are closely associated with the nature of the claims being made about the previous literature. The third approach (Swales, 1981b; Een, 1982) has argued that the use of tense/aspect in referenced statements is best explained in terms of where and how the reference to the previous researcher is introduced into those statements.

We might begin with the commonly-made observation that the 'general rules' for the Past, Present and Present Perfect seem to be less powerful in expository texts than in narrative ones, this being presumably due to the fact that time-lines and time-sequences, which are important elements in the traditional explanations, are more prominent in narratives. Thus in a *story* the following three statements might easily be explained in terms of 'general rules':

A disagreed with B.

A has disagreed with B.

A disagrees with B.

However, in the context of a report on an academic debate with, say, A being Halliday and B Chomsky, we can see, as Lackstrom et al. (1972) have observed, that the three statements are typically interpreted not in terms of increasing present-ness or increasing relevance to the present, but in terms of increasing *generality*. It is the perceived role of such concepts as *generality* and *relevance* that has led to the second approach, which so far has reached its fullest published form in Oster (1981). She proposes the following principal hypotheses:

> i) The Present Perfect tense is used to claim *generality* about past literature. The Past tense is used to claim *non-generality* about past literature.
>
> ii) The Past tense is used when it refers to quantitative results of past literature that are *non-supportive* of some aspects of the work described in the technical article. The Present tense is used when it refers to quantitative results of past literature that are *supportive* or *non-relevant*.
>
> iii) The Present Perfect tense is used to indicate the *continued discussion* of some of the information in the sentence in which the Present Perfect tense occurs.
>
> (Oster, 1981:77)

Although Oster's sample is small (two articles from chemical engineering), she is able to show that the above hypotheses apply quite well to her texts. The first hypothesis, of course, fits well with general accounts – and we have already seen many instances of the Present Perfect in broad centrality claims and topic generalizations. Of the other two hypotheses, the third is the more interesting because it provides a discoursal rather than a semantic/sentential explanation via its suggestion that the Present Perfect can operate as a *signal* to the reader to expect further discussion of the topic. In Swales (1981b) I attempted to validate this claim in 16 biological and medical papers, but without much direct success. However, I did find several instances of a corollary to Oster's hypothesis: the Past tense following a Present Perfect (or series of Present Perfects) in a discussion of a particular piece of research is apparently used to indicate that discussion is *terminating*.

The more general difficulty of an account such as Oster's, particularly from a pedagogical point of view, is that of deciding what is going to 'count as' *continued discussion* and so forth. In order to provide a simple 'safe rule' alternative (Selinker et al., 1985) I provided a correlational match that, in terms of the updated classification of references provided here, would look like Figure 13.

	Integral	**Non-integral**
reporting	*Past* Brie (1988) showed that ...	*Present Perfect* It *has been shown that* ... (Brie, 1988)
non-reporting		*Present (or modal)* The moon may be made of cheese (Brie, 1988)

Figure 13   Reference and tense

This account matches tense with an easily identifiable structural feature and thus offers a serviceable 'rule of thumb' to non-native writers. However, it only exhibits statistical tendencies: Een (1982) in a follow-up study of geotechnical texts found confirmation as far as non-reporting and non-integral reporting citations were concerned, but in integral reporting citations in introductions the occurrence of the Past fell to 50%.

Malcolm (1987) adopts the usefully eclectic position that there is need for both 'general' rules (as outlined by Celce-Murcia and Larsen-Freeman, 1983; Comrie, 1985; etc.) and 'special' ones. She proposes, for instance, that 'an adequate theory of tense usage in EST discourse needs to account not only for obligatory constraints on tense usage, but also for strategic choices that provide authors with the capability of manipulating temporal references for their own rhetorical purposes' (1987:32). Although Malcolm, unlike Swales, starts from a generalist perspective, her findings on the use of tense in citational text – based on the *Journal of Pediatrics* – turn out to be comparable. She puts forward three hypotheses:

1. Generalizations (as indicated by verbs without researcher agents) will tend to be in the Present tense. (Found to be 74% true in her sample.)
2. References to specific experiments (as indicated by a researcher agent and a footnote to a *single* study) will tend to be in the Past tense. (Found to be 61% true in her sample.)
3. References to areas of inquiry (as indicated by agents and/or foot-

notes to more than one study) will tend to be in the Present Perfect tense. (Found to be 74% true in her sample.)

As Een (1982) also found, the greatest variability occurred in the data for hypothesis 2. This is not surprising because commentary on a single paper is a key location for strategic tense choice:

a) Malcolm pointed out that there is both constraint and choice in tense usage[4].

b) Malcolm has pointed out that ...

c) Malcolm points out that ...

Ard (1985) correctly warns us – note use of tense! – against attempting to determine a rationale for such choices in specific instances, but I believe most readers would see the progression from (a) to (c) as being one of some kind of increasing proximity. The reasons for an author choosing the more remote (a) form may (or may not be) complex: choice could relate to placing the cited author's work in a chiefly historical context; it could emphasize concern with text rather than content; it could de-emphasize relevance to present concerns; or it could prepare the way for critical discussion. Whatever the reasons, the tense choice may indicate something of the author's *stance* towards the cited work, and it is probably this facility, allied to a rich choice of lexical verbs, that continues to make reporting structures attractive to RA authors.

We can now consider in a little further detail Move 2 of the CARS model (Figure 10). We can begin with the introduction illustrated in Figure 11, for this provides an elaborate example of the rhetorical work undertaken to establish a niche for about-to-be-presented research. The key signals are repeated in skeletal form below:

S8   *However,* the previously mentioned methods *suffer from some limitations* ...
S9   The first group ... *cannot* treat ... and is *limited to* ...
S10 The second group ... is *time consuming* and *therefore expensive,* and its ... is *not sufficiently accurate.*
S11 Both ... *suffer from the dependency on* ...
S12 The ... method (upon which the present study is based) eliminates many of these limitations by ..., *but* it can treat *only* ...

As we can see, the move opens with an adversative sentence-connector. Across various samples of RA introductions, about a quarter of Move 2s are initiated with such signals, most commonly *however* but also *nevertheless, yet, unfortunately* and *but.* The type of Move 2 is clearly 1B – that of *indicating a gap.* The author does not counter-claim that the previous work is hopelessly misguided, but rather 'suffers from some limitations'. Most of the gaps are signaled lexically in the verb (*suffer; is limited to*) or in adjective phrases (*time consuming; expensive; not sufficiently accurate*). There is also a case of verb negation in S9 (*cannot treat*).

In fact, the linguistic exponents of establishing a niche are extremely interesting and have not yet received the attention they deserve either from a general or an applied perspective. In a 'quick and dirty' survey of 100 Move 2 instances drawn from a range of fields (physics, geology, psychology and composition) the means of niche-establishment broke down into the following categories, which are listed in order of decreasing frequency.

a) *Negative or quasi-negative quantifiers* (28 instances)

no	12
little	7
none (of)	4
few / very few	4
neither ... nor	1

Interestingly, these quantifiers either occurred sentence-initially (or following an adversative), or were merely preceded by existential *there*, as in: 'However, there is little research that ... '. It is quite possible, therefore, that the somewhat preferred choice of the negative quantifier format may be connected, at some level of consciousness, with a wish to signal *early* that a niche is now being established.

The other common exponent employs lexical negation or quasi-negation.

b) *Lexical negation* (26 instances)

Verbs	15	(fail 5, lack 2, overlook 2, plus 6 single instances)
Adjectives	7	(inconclusive, complex, misleading, elusive, scarce, limited, questionable)
Nouns	3	(failure 2, limitation)
Other	1	(without regard for)

The subtlety of the verbal repertoire available at this juncture is probably connected with the frequency of its adoption. The RA author may opt for a trenchant *fail*, imply oversight with *neglect, overlook* or *underestimate*, suggest complacency with *be content to*, impute a certain narrowness of vision with *concentrate on, be restricted to* or *be limited to*, or offer rather more sympathetic understanding with *constrain*.

c) *Negation in the verb phrase* (16 instances)

not	14
rarely	1
ill	1

The relative infrequency of this type of exponent, at least compared to so-called 'general English', might suggest that it is somewhat contra-indicated when referring to the work of others. It is possible that the use of *not* in conjunction with many verbs is seen as providing a potentially hostile depiction of previous work. Indeed, this possibility is strengthened when we note that as many as five of the 16 instances employed *we* as the subject as in 'We do not yet know ...'. The inclusive *we* obviously includes the present authors as co-members of the unsuccessful group.

The remaining minor ways of establishing a niche can be listed together.

d) *Questions* (8 instances)

Direct   6
Indirect   2 (e.g. 'A question remains whether ...')

e) *Expressed needs/desires/interests* (8 instances)

e.g. 'The differences need to be analyzed ...'
     'It is desirable to perform test calculations ...'
     'It is of interest to compare ... '

f) *Logical conclusions* (6 instances)

Must   3 (e.g. 'This must represent ...')
Seem/appear   2
'One would intuitively expect ...'

g) *Contrastive comment* (6 instances)

'The research has tended to focus on ..., rather than ...'
'They center mainly on ..., rather than on ...'
'Studies most often contrast ..., rather than ...'
'Researchers have focused primarily on ..., as opposed to ...'
'Emphasis has been on ..., with scant attention given to ...'
'Although considerable research has been done on ..., much less is known as to ...'

h) *Problem-raising* (2 instances)

'The application presents a problem ...'
'A key problem in many ... is ...'

An (e) or (f) format seems to be chosen when there is a weaker challenge to the previous research, as we most typically find in a *continuing a tradition* Step 1D. Clear evidence of this is the quite frequent co-occurrence of the sentence connector *therefore* (rather than *however*) in these contexts. Formats (e) and (f) were much commoner in physics and, to a lesser extent, in geology than in psychology or composition. On the other hand, most of the instances of what I have called *contrastive comment* (g) occurred in composition research. The milder tone of the (g) examples may be connected to the fact that composition researchers comprise a relatively small and mutually supportive discourse community and one not without its external antagonists and detractors.

The underlying theme that has linked this discussion of the RA introduction has been a felt sense that the typical introduction is a crafted rhetorical artifact. At the published textual level, the introduction is a manifestation of rhetorical maneuver. The extent of this rhetorical work can often be seen when we compare expert and non-expert products. The text presented in Figure 14 was written by a Japanese masters student as an exercise in writing research introductions for one of my courses (Swales, 1990).

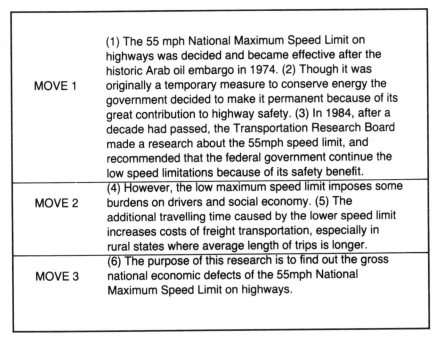

Figure 14   An NNS introduction

The above text is, I would suggest, a quite effective piece of writing, especially if we bear in mind that the student had had no prior English-medium academic experience and was only two months into a US degree program. Certainly it suffers from few of the orientation problems found in Scarcella (1984) in NNS introductions; there is little unnecessary background information and there is adequate use of attention-getting devices. Although there are occasional 'off-register' elements such as *made a research about* in S3, the text moves smoothly, swiftly and quite authoritatively towards the announcement of the research topic in the final sentence.

However, it remains the case that the introduction remains somewhat flat in the second half. The author seems to have somehow missed an opportunity to highlight the gap between surmise and substantiated opinion, and between present qualitative judgments and potential quantitative ones. We can see this if we compare the original final three sentences with more 'modulated' variants (Latour and Woolgar, 1979).

S4-original
However, the low maximum speed limit imposes some burdens on drivers and social economy.

S4-modulated
However, *it would seem* that the low maximum speed limit imposes *a certain amount* of burden on drivers and the social economy.

S5-original
The additional travelling time caused by the lower speed limit increases costs of ...

S5-modulated
In particular, the additional travelling time caused by the lower speed limit *can be expected* to increase costs of ...

S6-original
The purpose of this research is to find out the gross national ...

S6-modulated
The purpose of this research is to *arrive at a preliminary quantitative estimate* of the gross national ...

The relatively minor alternatives that I have been proposing take fuller advantage, I believe, of the opportunity to create a research space via more precise specification of the gap and of the attempt to fill it.

The final issue with regard to Move 2 is its cyclicity. A number of investigators (Cooper, 1985; Crookes, 1986a; Hopkins and Dudley-Evans, 1988) have pointed out that niche-establishment does not necessarily occur only at the end of a literature review, but may follow reviews of individual items, so that cycles of Move 1/Step 3 and Move 2 recur. Consider the Figure 11 text for a final time. As we have seen, the author of this text opted for a composite 'chunked' Move 1/Step 3 followed by a composite Move 2. He could have opted instead for a cycling solution to his effort to create a research space (Figure 15).

In our present state of knowledge, it is not possible to do more than speculate about the factors that might predispose authors to choose composite or cycling configurations. It is likely that the length of the introduction plays some part, so that the longer the introduction the greater the probability of some recycling (Crookes, 1986a). It is also likely that choice is influenced by how the research field is perceived. If the relevant research tradition is viewed as linear and cumulative, then a composite arrangement may work well. However, if the field is viewed as

1–3	Among the many potential flow methods developed in attempting to solve body vortex flows are early two-dimensional 2D multi-vortex methods. [2–4] / However, these methods cannot
2–B	treat 3D flows and are limited to very slender bodies. / An alternative is time-stepping vortex models that include
1–3	boundary-layer considerations, [5–8] / but these are time consuming and therefore expensive. In addition, their
2–B	separation predictions are not sufficiently accurate. / A third possibility is a quasi-3D potential flow method[9] that uses source
1–3	and vortex elements. / Unfortunately, this method, like the previous ones, suffers from the dependency on too many
2–B	semiempirical inputs and assumptions ...

Figure 15   An example of cyclicity

branching – consisting of several loosely-connected topics – then a cyclic approach may be preferred. The combination of length and divergence may contribute to the cyclicity more evident in the social sciences, and brevity and linearity to the compositeness more characteristic of the natural and life sciences and of engineering.

We can now turn briefly to Move 3, which I have labeled *occupying the niche* (Figure 10). The role of Move 3 is to turn the niche established in Move 2 into the research space that justifies the present article. The link between the moves is a strong one. Whenever a Move 2 occurs – and there is a minority of instances in which it does not (Swales, 1981b; Cooper, 1985; Crookes, 1986a) – the ensuing Move 3 variously offers to substantiate the particular counter-claim that has been made, fill the created gap, answer the specific question or continue the rhetorically-established tradition.

The obligatory element in Move 3 is Step 1. This can take one of two predominating forms:

Step 1A   The author or authors indicate their main purpose or purposes.

Step 1B   The author or authors describe what they consider to be the main features of their research.

In both cases the opening step is a kind of promissory statement, and in both cases its onset is typically marked by (a) the absence of references to previous research and (b) the use of deictic references to the present text. The more common deictic elements, in approximate decreasing order of frequency, are: *this, the present, we, reported, here, now, I* and *herein.* Typical examples culled from RA introductions are:

a) This paper reports on the results obtained ...

b) The aim of *the present* paper is to give ...

c) In *this* paper *we* give preliminary results of ...

d) The main purpose of the experiment reported *here* was to ...

e) *This* study was designed to evaluate ...

f) The *present* work extends the use of the last model ...

g) *We now* report the interaction of ...

There are a number of comments that can be made about the language of Move 3s. First, there is a strong tendency for the deictic signal to occur *early* – as the above examples show – and, in general, the only items that precede them are occasional linking phrases such as 'In view of these observations'. Of the 48 introductions in the 1981 corpus, there was only one in which the deictic *in this paper* phrase occurred at sentence-final position. However, apprentice writers, both NS and NNS, are more prone to delay the Move 3 signal – and by doing so likely to create uncertainty in the reader. Secondly, there may be an opportunity, depending somewhat on style-sheet instructions, for using either a standard descriptive form or a *collapsed* structure:

a) In this paper, we argue that ... (standard)

b) This paper argues that ... (collapsed)

Although collapsed structures are quite common, there are little-understood constraints on the co-occurring verb:

This paper utilizes the notion of ...

? This paper hopes to show that ...

?? This paper measures the extent of ...

There is also some evidence that the co-occurrence of inanimate subject and animate verb varies in its acceptability from one language to another. Kojima and Kojima (1978), for example, argue that it is dispreferred in Japanese and concomitantly produce evidence that Japanese scientists tend to avoid collapsed structures when they write in English.

A third observation concerns tense in purposive Step 1s. In cases where the deictic refers to the *genre* (paper, report, note, review, etc.) tense is restricted to the present. However, in cases where the deictic refers to the type of *inquiry* (investigation, study, experiment, etc.), authors may choose between *present* and *past*:

The purpose of this investigation is to ...

The purpose of this investigation was to ...

For reasons comparable to those discussed in connection with reporting previous research, there seems to be a strong preference for a Present tense copula, presumably because it encourages an impression of contemporary relevance.

Many, perhaps most, RA introductions end with a Move 3–Step 1. There are, however, two further options. One is to follow the Step 1 with a summary announcement of the principal findings. Swales and Najjar (1987) investigated this option in terms of quite a large sample (110 introductions) drawn from two very different fields: physics and educational psychology. They found that the Step 2 option was utilized 45% of the time in physics but only 7% of the time in educational psychology. We seem to see here, then, a quite marked disciplinary divergence that has not so far been attested for either type or form in Step 1.

A final option in the introduction is to indicate in varying degrees of detail the structure – and occasionally the content – of the remainder of the RA. If Step 3 occurs, it is always at the end of the introduction. Examples are:

a) We have organized the rest of this paper in the following way ...

b) This paper is structured as follows ...

c) The remainder of this paper is divided into five sections. Section II describes ...

Cooper (1985) found a Step 3 in as many as 10 out of her 15 IEEE introductions and was further able to report that specialist informants in the computer technology field both expected and welcomed such indications of organization. In most other fields, the percentage of introductions closing with Step 3 seems to be much lower. The high incidence in Cooper's study may well be connected to the absence of an established schema for research reporting in a new and rapidly evolving field.

In this section I have made some fairly bold claims about the rhetorical organization of RA introductions across a range of fields. The most obvious way of validating these claims is to test them out on new data. To this end, I have examined how well the model fits with the RAs in the latest journal I received at the time of writing. That journal was *Research in the Teaching of English* for February 1988, RTE also incidentally covering a disciplinary area (composition research) little studied in the literature on introductions. The February 1988 issue contains four research articles, the first exceptionally long, the other three of normal length. The basic 'facts' about the four introductions are given in Table 6.

The introduction to the long 35-page opening article (Berkenkotter et al.) follows closely both the Move–Step sequences and the linguistic signals that previous research tells us to expect.

TABLE 6. FOUR INTRODUCTIONS FROM RTE

Author(s)	No. of paras	No. of lines	No. of refs (including repeats)
1. Berkenkotter et al.	5	71	22
2. Slater et al.	13	129	43
3. Cordeiro	4	44	7
4. Roen and Willey	9	125	39

RA I OUTLINE STRUCTURE

	Move–Step		Signals (my emphases)
Para. 1	1–1	(S1)	*Recently* there has been *considerable* interest in ...
	2–1B	(S3)	*Yet* there is a *dearth* of information
	2–1C	(S4/5)	(2 direct questions)
Para. 2	1–3	(S1)	The existence ... may be inferred from recent studies ...
	1–3	(S2)	The work of these researchers sheds light ...
Para. 3	1–3	(S1)	Composition scholars Bizzell (1982c, 1983b) and ...
	2–1B	(S3)	*Yet* understanding ... is only part ...
	1–3		...
Para. 4	1–2	(S1)	Understanding ... appears, therefore ...
	2–1C	(S2/S3)	(2 direct questions)
	1–3	(S4)	Recent studies have begun to explore these questions at an undergraduate level.
	2–1B	(S5)	Understanding ... in the context of ..., *however*, is *as yet unexplored territory.*
Para. 5	3–1B	(S1)	*This study attempts to enter this territory by ...*
	3–1B	(S2)	*Our* focus will be on ...
	3–2	(S5)	The changes that ... *show* a skilled novice learning ...

As we might expect in an introduction of around 70 lines, a considerable amount of cycling occurs, especially with regard to gap-indications. There are, in fact, four instances of a Move 2 segment in the first four paragraphs; these are of increasing specificity and it is the *final* one that specifically establishes the niche that Berkenkotter et al. are attempting to fill. And I take it as serendipitous that the metaphor they choose is the geographic one of 'unexplored territory'! The final paragraph is given over to Move 3; it contains the only first person pronominal form in the entire introduction and concludes with a general comment about the main findings.

The second introduction poses rather more of a problem for the CARS model, but, as I shall hope to show, for rather interesting reasons. The Slater et al. introduction can be outlined as follows:

RA 2 OUTLINE STRUCTURE

Move–Step			*Signals* (my emphases)
Para. 1	1–2	(S1)	*Recently*, the relationships between ... *have been explored* by scholars from a number of disciplines.
	1–3	(S2)	
	1–2	(S3)	
Para. 2	2–1B	(S1)	*However*, the precise nature of ... has *not* been delineated.
		(S2)	... a considerable amount of research has been ... *but little* research ...
		(S3)	a considerable amount of research ..., *while a minimal amount* of this research
		(S4)	As a result, *no* comprehensive theory appears to exist.
Paras 3–8	1–3		
Para. 9	1–2	(S1)	Taken together, *these studies indicate* ...
Paras 10–12	1–3		
Para. 13	3–1A	(S1)	The *purposes* of *the present study* were two-fold:
	?	(S2)	The study thus extends the findings of previous work by examining ...

After an opening broad paragraph, the introduction proceeds (with one exception) to review previous research until it reaches the final paragraph, the review typically consisting of a series of paired statements like 'X examined the effects of ... Results indicated that ...' The main exception is the second paragraph, which is a highly elaborate Move 2 designed to establish that 'no comprehensive theory' exists. The outline shows that there are no further *closing-in* Move 2s, especially immediately prior to the onset of Move 3 – unlike in the first introduction. A close reading of the text brings out the unusual character of this introduction. The 'no comprehensive theory' argument turns out not to be establishing a niche to be filled, because the authors in fact never return to the issue of the need to start moving towards such a theory, nor do they ever claim that their present paper can be seen as making a contribution to theory. Rather, the second paragraph seems to be designed to justify the fact that it is appropriate in the circumstances to add a small further piece of empirical evidence to the puzzle. In other words, what we seem to have here is a new sub-type of Move 2–Step 1B which, by claiming that *the gap is currently unfillable*, obliquely establishes a continuing-a-tradition research space. This reading also brings the final sentence into focus, which was left unassigned in the outline. At first sight, the sentence looks as though it might be operating as an atypically-placed Move 2–Step 1D (finding extension). However, we can now see it as a typically closing Move 3–Step 1B for it *announces* the (limited) status of the present research.

Analysis of this kind will, on occasion, bring to light ambiguity and rhetorical uncertainty. If the above analysis is on the right lines, then it seems definitely odd that the authors did not take up the implication of their second paragraph in any of the ensuing 11. Indeed, one might even suggest that the introduction would have been tidier and easier to process if they had done so. Here is what might have been:

> Para. 13   The preceding review suggests that further empirical research is necessary before a comprehensive theory can be developed. In order to develop the research base, the present study was designed with the following two purposes in mind: ... The study thus extends the findings ...

The third introduction (Cordeiro) is the shortest and has the following anomalous structure:

RA 3 OUTLINE STRUCTURE

	Move–Step		*Signals* (my emphases)
Para. 1	3–1B	(S1)	*This study ... is* concerned with ...
	3–1B	(S2)	Specifically, it addresses ...
	1–3	(S3–6)	
	3–1B	(S7)	In *the present research,* ...
Para. 2	1–3		
Para. 3	1–3		
Para. 4	1–3	(S1–4)	
	2–1B	(S5)	However, the terms ... were not semantically or syntactically descriptive enough to solve ...

As the outline shows, this introduction *opens* with a Move 3. Although this option is certainly possible, it does not seem as generally common as many might suppose. It occurred, for example, just 10 times in a corpus of 110 introductions (Swales and Najjar, 1987), and on several occasions already in this section I have alluded to both the likely concerns to *create* a research space, and the perils of failing to engage the wider discourse community by too narrowly focused an opening. Something of this peril can be imagined by considering the opening sentence in full: 'This study of the writing of 22 first graders and 13 third graders is concerned with how children learn the rules of punctuation' (1988:62). The readers of this sentence are immediately faced by specifics which, while strongly appealing to a few, are likely to disengage many with no direct interest in this research topic. Apart from the promotion of Move 3, the introduction largely follows the model; for instance, it closes with the Move 2, which seems typical of the relatively few introductions of this type that have been examined.

There are, in fact, a number of interesting research questions related to introductions that begin with a Move 3. Are they processed and composed differently? Can they be associated with less experienced writers, or with those who feel, for whatever reason, less need to establish a territory? Are they more likely to occur in situations where the RA is a result of a research grant, given the widespread expectation in research grant applications that there should be *early* indications of what will be done? And if so, are they consequently on the increase?

The final introduction (Roen and Willey) is almost as long as the second but has in fact almost no cycling. The first seven of the nine paragraphs establish the territory. The final two paragraphs have the following structure:

RA 4

	Move–Step		Signals (my emphases)
Para. 8	2–1B	(S1)	Despite the announced importance of ..., *few* researchers have experimentally tested ...
	1–3	(S2–4)	Of course many studies have examined ...
	2–1B	(S5)	*No study*, however, has used an experimental design.
Para. 9	1–3	(S1)	In the light of this absence of experimental work, we conducted a pilot study (Roen, 1985) ...
	3–1A	(S2)	*We* subsequently designed the present study, an experiment to *test* ...
	3–1B	(S3)	Our two research questions were ...

The only unexpected aspect of this introduction is the character of the opening sentence in the final paragraph. Its opening phrase evinces close links with the Move 2, and it further builds up expectations of Move 3 by the switch into *we*. On the other hand, the Past Simple and an earlier dated reference disconfirm those expectations. In effect, the opening of the final paragraph communicates a somewhat mixed message. However, this is *precisely* what we might expect when authors use, as a transition, discussion of their *own* previous work which is directly and causally related to the study actually being presented.

In general, therefore, the four test introductions usefully confirm the claims made for the CARS model, particularly in terms of the linguistic exponents used to express moves and their associated steps. In outline the first and last introductions fit well, while the third appears to be a fairly typical example of the *fronted-Move 3* subtype. The fact that 25% of a very small sample opened with a Move 3 needs a little further investigation. Accordingly, I checked the 16 RAs published in *RTE* in 1987 and found that 13 used the standard placement for Move 3, two were fronted, while the remaining article was hard to categorize as it used an anecdote from the study as an attention-getting opening. If we leave this last aside, three out of 19 *RTE* RAs were *fronted*; certainly a higher proportion than found in Swales and Najjar (1987), but still under 20%. The major anomaly occurred in the second introduction, where there was no Move 2 that could be related to Move 3 in any but the most indirect of ways. It was suggested that this mismatch did not so much represent a possible weakness in the *Create a Research Space* model as a possible weakness in the introduction itself and, moreover, one that the analytic procedures themselves assisted in revealing.

7.5   Methods

In 7.2, 'The constructing of research articles', I have already presented some general findings on the language of Method sections. Here I attempt to characterize the discourse of this part of the RA genre a little more explicitly and to draw some tentative conclusions about disciplinary variation. We can begin with the opening sentences of a biochemistry Method section cited by Gilbert and Mulkay (which is very similar to the one from Knorr-Cetina discussed in 7.2):

> Heavy beef heart mitochondria were prepared by the method of Wong and stored in liquid nitrogen. Well coupled mitochondrial particles were prepared by a modification of the procedure of Madden. These particles were used to prepare inhibition-protein-depleted particles by centrifuging under energized conditions according to the method of Gale ...

(Gilbert and Mulkay, 1984:51)

We see in this fragment several of the features of Methods that have been noted by other investigators, for example Tomlin (1981) and Bruce (1983). The Past Passive is consistently chosen and the identity of the underlying agent is consistently that of the experimenters. There is also a somewhat restricted range of predicate verbs (*prepared; prepared*; and *used to prepare*). However, the most interesting feature of the above extract is the way in which the method is described – or perhaps in this case *not* described:

a) ... by the method of Wong;

b) ... by a modification of the procedure of Madden;

c) ... according to the method of Gale.

There are a number of points worth noting. First, the method is merely labeled rather than characterized. Second, in the case of (b) if not for the others, replication would appear to be impossible given the fact that the nature of the modification is not made clear. Third, the preparation processes attributable to the three researchers are, on the one hand, simply associated with their names, while, on the other, they have not apparently reached the status of being *named* methods, that is, *The Wong Method, Madden's Procedure*. It is thus unlikely that other workers could easily look up the methods themselves in a reference work. The members of this discourse community would seem to take methodological appropriacy and rigor more for granted than we will find to be the case in other communities.

The opening fragment also illustrates the important process of NP stacking discussed by Dubois (1982a) among others:

heavy beef heart mitochondria

well coupled mitochondrial particles

inhibition-protein-depleted particles

As the preparation becomes increasingly specialized it becomes increasingly complex syntactically; indeed Dubois (1982a) has argued that there may well be a coincidence of cognitive culmination and syntactic culmination. We can also note that in this particular instance, there is little NP identity across the sentence boundaries: as far as the non-specialist is concerned, 'mitochondria' have been mysteriously particulated, while the particles have been equally mysteriously transformed from 'well coupled' into ones that are 'inhibition-protein-depleted'.

Bruce (1983) makes a broadly similar point about a Method section from a medical journal:

> Urography was performed in a routine manner, the patient
> micturating immediately beforehand. Tomography was used
> to detail the caliceal pattern when necessary. Abdominal

> compression was avoided and the bladder not drained during the
> examination . . .

As he says, the text 'might appear at first sight to be incoherent –
completely lacking in the cohesive feature of anaphoric reference; but the
coherence is, of course, supplied by the shared knowledge of these
investigative procedures, and their likely sequence, that the reader brings
to the text' (1983:8). For Bruce the well-known if difficult-to-apply
Given–New paradigm (cf. Halliday, 1978) needs replacing in many
Method sections by a Known–New paradigm. Either way then, either
through the use of New Thematic Subjects (*new* on the discoursal level),
or, as we saw earlier, by a process of cognitive but not discoursal
development of the initial nominal group, ESP-related inquiries corroborate the sociologists' observations (e.g. Gilbert and Mulkay, 1984;
Myers, 1985a) that Method sections often read like checklists.

In this context, some of Weissberg's findings are particularly interesting. Weissberg (1984) classified cohesive devices in 20 Method paragraphs drawn from a range of disciplines and found only seven uses of
pronouns and three instances of superordinate expressions. On the other
hand, he noted no less than 54 occasions where 'inferential bridging' – by
relying on the readers' background knowledge or experience – was
needed for coherence. This need for 'bridging' was much more noticeable
in Methods than in Introductions and Discussions, and is thus further
evidence for the 'inconsiderate' nature of Methods texts.

One further aspect of Weissberg's paper is directly relevant. Whereas
the 20 Introduction and 20 Discussion paragraphs tended to manifest a
linear progression paragraph development (in other words, the 'classic'
Given–New paradigm), the Method paragraphs were much more variable and indeterminate in structure. Weissberg's rather patchy results,
plus the extensive reliance on inferential bridging, suggest that Method
sections, like other condensed texts such as abstracts and telexes, evince
in Hallidayan terms coherence but little cohesion, or in Functional–
Sentence–Perspective terminology are heavy on *rheme* but light on
theme. Therefore, it may well be the case that a different type of
paragraph development needs to be established for Method – one which
we might characterize as *broken linear*. In many Method paragraphs the
sentences are like islands in a string, islands which only those with
specialist knowledge and experience can easily jump across from one to
the next.

The three fields Weissberg investigated were botany, agriculture and
engineering, Gilbert and Mulkay looked at biochemistry, Bruce medicine, and Dubois zoology. These are all areas where many research
methodologies are well established, indeed protocolized, and where
scattered networks of specialists form active discourse communities.

These then are all fields that may favor the elliptical reporting of Method that we have come to expect. Indeed, Huckin (1987) has recently produced evidence to suggest that, in the biochemical area at least, the Method section is becoming increasingly de-emphasized. Method sections may be downgraded by being physically relocated towards the end of the paper. Additionally they increasingly occur in smaller print than that used for other sections, and, according to Huckin, the *Journal of Biological Chemistry* has recently begun to publish the Method section in print so small that it cannot be read without the aid of a magnifying glass.

However, it would be dangerous to suppose that such trends are equally detectable in 'softer', emerging or inter-disciplinary fields. Here, for instance, is the first paragraph from West's Method section in an article published in *TESOL Quarterly*, by no means a journal aimed at a narrow-band research readership (West, 1980:484). This paragraph has a clear Given–New character, which I have attempted to diagram informally in Figure 16. In so doing I have broken the paragraph into individual sentences.

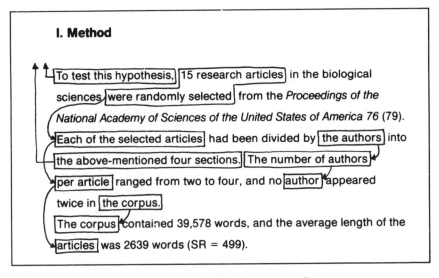

Figure 16   *Given and New in a Method paragraph*

This Method text seems to have a very different flavor to the preceding extracts from the hard sciences. The careful step-by-step description, massively supported by anaphoric reference and lexical repetition, produces the kind of explicitness that we associate with standard academic description. In contrast, Method sections in the physical and life sciences are enigmatic, swift, presumptive of background knowledge, not designed for easy replication, and with little statement of rationale or discussion of the choices made. These differences can presumably be related to a number of sociological and intellectual phenomena, such as the nature of the discourse community, the level of agreement about appropriate methodology, the extent to which a *demonstrably* adequate methodology is deemed necessary, and the role assigned to controlled experiment in the discipline. Presumably, it is parameters such as these that explain why the Method section assumes great importance in most psychological and educational research, but can be assigned scant attention and space in an area like biochemistry.

7.6   Results, Discussions and Conclusions

In the two previous sections on Introductions and Methods, various claims have been advanced which are fairly specific as to what we might expect to find in particular sets of circumstances. Our present state of knowledge about the last two elements in the IMRD pattern is, regrettably, largely restricted to an exploratory rather than hypothesis-testing stage. One initial sign of unfirm ground is the fact that we do not yet know how matters tend to be arranged even in terms of the three section labels that provide the title for this section. Even if a majority of RAs have closing Results and Discussion sections, others coalesce the two, while even others have additional or substituted sections labeled Conclusions, Implications or Applications and so on. More particularly, there is, from the discourse analyst's viewpoint, much variation in the extent to which Results sections simply describe results and the extent to which Discussion sections redescribe results.

Consider again, for example, the four articles from *RTE* 22 (1) used to validate the CARS model for introductions. In the first article Results runs to 20 pages; in the second, Results consists of three tables and 30 lines of text. Even more significant perhaps is the way results are presented in the second RA:

Para. 1   The ANOVA on ... indicated ...
          Cell means ... are shown in Table 1.
          Tukey *post hoc* tests indicated that ...
          No other effects of interest were significant.

Para. 2   The ANOVA on ... indicated ...
          Cell means ... are shown in Table 2.
          Tukey *post hoc* tests indicated that ...
          No other effects of interest were significant.

Para. 3   The ANOVA on ... indicated ...
          The cell means ... were ...

Para. 4   The ANOVA on ... indicated ...
          Cell means ... are shown in Table 3.
          Tukey *post hoc* tests indicated that ...
          No other effects of interest were significant.

Para. 5   The ANOVA on ... indicated that ...
          Students' mean rating for ... was ...

The astonishing repetitive regularity of this Results section (in paragraph organization, in grammatical structure *and* in lexical choice) is presumably deliberate, especially if we bear in mind that the authors are specialists in writing. The section's style and structure seems to be designed to deny on the authors' part any associative contamination with commentary or observation. It is not Slater and Company who are talking here, but their statistical package.

The third and fourth RAs from *RTE* also present quantitative results. The third's Results section (in fact called Findings) opens with a paragraph connecting some of the present findings with the previous literature. The ensuing paragraphs deal with the results but in a much more evaluative way than in RA 2. There are also some observational asides such as '... but it must be remembered that this study does not account directly for sentence complexity ...' (1988:68). The final article deals with statistical measures similar to those in the second, but again offers greater rhetorical intervention. ANOVAS, for instance, *reveal* rather than *indicate*, and there is some justificatory commentary – 'Given these results, we applied three a posteriori tests' (1988:81).

As even authors within a single issue of a journal can apparently distribute very differently the knowledge-claims they want to make across the Results–Discussion divide, I have decided to frame the remaining discussion within the general area of results and their discussion. Even so, the fact that I know of only a handful of studies in this area means that treatment will be brief.

Belanger (1982) analyzed 10 Discussion sections from articles in the field of neuroscience. On the basis of this data, he was able to show that 'the structure of the discussion section is closely correlated to both the number and kind of research questions posed in the introduction sections of the paper' (1982:1). Belanger proposes that after a possible general introduction and before a possible general conclusion, each research question or RQ (as identified with the help of a specialist informant) is then passed through 'a cycle':

1. *Summarizing results* and stating conclusions with references to previous research;
2. *What research suggests* with references to previous research and/or to the current work;

3. *Further questions* sometimes with possible explanations and sometimes with references.

He finds that all three elements are not always present for each RQ, but
any elements occurring follow the order given above; he also found that
sometimes the discussion of a particular RQ was iterated through the
cycle several times – an interesting parallel with Crookes' and others'
observation of 'cycling' in introductions (Crookes, 1986a). It is not clear
whether the nesting of 1–3 mini-discussions can be related to Weissberg's
(1984) finding that linear topic development was the commonest type of
Discussion paragraph. A final conclusion from Belanger's pioneering
study is that the Hill et al. diagram (1982) is over-generalized. Rather
than a broad move from specific to general, Belanger finds a series of
small-scale expansions of scope that correspond to discussion of each
research question.

Subsequent work has underlined the cyclic nature of Discussion
sections. Although Introductions may also be cyclic, they equally may not
be (as we saw in the Figure 11 text). In contrast, a 'chunked' composite
form of Discussion seems to be a rare phenomenon. The subsequent
work (McKinlay, 1984; Hopkins, 1985; Peng, 1987; Hopkins and
Dudley-Evans, 1988) has largely been concerned with elaborating and
refining the Move–Steps in the cycle and in searching for recurring
patterns in the Move–Steps. Peng (1987) and Hopkins and Dudley-Evans
(1988), for example, both offer 11–Move schemes which differ only in
minor detail. The more frequent moves are glossed as follows.

1. *Background information.* This is a somewhat free-standing move that
   can occur at any point in the cycle. As its name implies, this move is
   employed by authors when they wish to strengthen their discussion by
   recapitulating main points, by highlighting theoretical information, or
   by reminding the reader of technical information.
2. *Statement of results.* If there is a quasi-obligatory move in Discussion
   sections it is this one. Evidence suggests, as we might expect, that it is
   the starting point of a cycle – and is only likely to be preceded by a
   Move 1. Many Discussion sections will have several cycles beginning
   with a Move 2; Hopkins (1985) found that three cycles were the
   commonest pattern in his study of papers published in the proceedings
   of an irrigation and drainage conference. Additionally, we might
   expect that the stronger results will be dealt with in an early cycle and
   weaker results in a later one. On this issue, Huckin (1987) makes the
   following interesting observation:

> One of my biologists, who serves on the editorial board of a major
> journal in the field, said that the first paragraph of a discussion
> should always be reserved for the strongest claim in the study.
> Though he stated this as a prescription, my survey of papers in

both biology and physics showed it to be a description of actual practice anyway.

(Huckin, 1987:12–13)

3. *(Un)expected outcome.* Here the writer comments on whether the result is unexpected or not. This was, in fact, quite a rare move in Peng's chemical engineering texts, occurring in only four out of 52 cycles.
4. *Reference to previous research.* After Moves 1 and 2, probably the most common move. There are two main sub-types or steps: reference for purposes of *comparison* with present research and references for purposes of providing *support* for present research.
5. *Explanation.* This move is particularly common when the writer suggests reasons for a surprising result, or one at odds with those reported in the literature. At present the relationship between Moves 3 and 5 is somewhat obscure, particularly as to whether 5 is subsequent to 3 or an alternative to it.
6. *Exemplification.* Examples are most often used to support an explanation (Hopkins and Dudley-Evans, 1988).
7. *Deduction and Hypothesis.* This move is used to make a claim (however qualified) about the generalizability of some or all of the reported results.
8. *Recommendation.* The writer advocates the need for further research or makes suggestions about possible lines of future investigation. However, Huckin (personal communication) believes that the specific identification of interesting research questions at the end of a cycle or at the end of the Discussion section as a whole is a move being increasingly abandoned by US scientists because they do not wish to give advantage to others in an increasingly competitive market for research grants.

This distilled list of eight moves provides a useful provisional framework for much needed further work on the structure of RA Discussion sections. The existence of cycles seems well-established, as is the fact that complexity of the cycle can be related to the degree to which the results are 'compatible' with previous work and/or with the expected outcome to hypotheses or questions. The work reviewed here, and that of Huckin (1987) give support to the view that Discussions, in strict contrast to Introductions, move during a cycle in an 'inside-out' direction; they move from stating the results themselves, to placing them within the established literature, to reviewing their general significance.

However, we know little about disciplinary variation and little about the linguistic exponents of the moves. Indeed, on the latter point, a certain amount of obfuscation may have been caused by the heavy attention given to the famous article by Watson and Crick on DNA (e.g. Bazerman,

1981; Crombie, 1985; Fahnestock, 1986; Myers, 1989), and to the comments on its composition in *The Double Helix* (Watson, 1968). The celebrated penultimate sentence in the article, 'It has not escaped our notice that the specific pairing we have postulated immediately suggests a possible copying mechanism for the genetic material', is a Move 7 deduction–hypothesis. The double negative (*not escaped*), the choice of *postulated* as reporting verb, insertion of *possible*, and the use of *suggests*, all characterize a very modest knowledge claim not gainsaid by the more assertive *immediately*. However, as Fahnestock comments, 'Watson and Crick could afford to be coy' (1986:278); they knew that the scientific world would acknowledge their major breakthrough. The 'cause célèbre' treatment of Watson and Crick's closing statements has, I suggest, distracted attention away from what may turn out to be more normal practice. In more normal circumstances, authors may well feel a need to advance the significance of their work in more positive terms.

7.7   Review

In this chapter, the longest in the book, I have attempted to offer a depiction of what we know about research articles, especially those of a more experimental character. In many cases I have provided an overview of the main results of a particular investigation. The advantage of this approach is that the reader is provided with some content, and so does not necessarily have to follow up references in order to obtain substantive findings. The disadvantage is that the space available for investigating theoretical and procedural issues has sometimes been curtailed.

In Chapter 7 I have tried to bring together several distinct approaches to research writing (quantitative, historical, sociological, rhetorical, discoursal, linguistic) in an effort to both broaden and deepen the perceptions of those who are concerned with the genre in practical or applied ways, as teachers of research writing and critical reading, as research writers themselves, as advisors, as editors, as abstracters, as citation analysts and so on. In particular, I have tried to illustrate ways in which genre conventions may be seen to be operating, so that applied work can be grounded in whatever sense of reality the current state of knowledge permits. On the other hand, in the second half of Chapter 7, I have given prominence to work in the EAP/Applied Discourse Analysis tradition, in the hope that the careful textual studies that this tradition usually represents can offer something in return to the wider inter-disciplinary field.

As has been suggested more than once, the picture we have of the research article is far from complete. That picture suggests that there are certain characteristics of RAs which, by and large, tend to occur and recur in samples drawn from an extensive range of disciplines. It is a moot point whether the similarities are sufficiently dominant to support Widdowson's assumption of a 'macrogenre' (Widdowson, 1983a). However, it remains the case that RAs are rarely simple narratives of investigations. Instead, they are complexly distanced reconstructions of research activities, at least part of this reconstructive process deriving from a need to anticipate and discountenance negative reactions to the knowledge claims being advanced. And this need in turn explains the long-standing (Shapin, 1984) and widespread use of 'hedges' as rhetorical devices both for projecting honesty, modesty and proper caution in self-reports, and for diplomatically creating research space in areas heavily populated by other researchers.

On the other hand, the RA varies from one disciplinary sector to another in terms of degree of standardization and of the prevalence of a nominalized impersonal style (Smith, 1982). In those areas of knowledge variously described as 'hard', 'exact' or 'physical', consensus on objectives, ground-rules and points of departure has led to textual products with regularized macro-structure and with rhetorics that follow identifiable role-models. In these fields, there is a perceivable inter-relationship between the RA as a peer-group intellectual object, the abstract nominal style, and the presence of authorial intrusion mainly in contexts thought to need persuasive support, or to need some revelation of the authors' individual cognitive processes. As is well known, certain groups in the social and behavior sciences have tried, with varying degrees of success, to adopt and adapt the hard science paradigm (cf. Bazerman, 1987). Others, such as ethnographers of various persuasions, have not. These and many in the humanities tend to align their scholarly and research products to their preferred intellectual schools and scholarly traditions rather than to disciplines as such. In general, differences between the genres of articles, books, reviews, and so on are less marked in the humanities.

Finally, there are two principal corollaries of this variation – and one unexpected outcome. First, the more established the conventions, the more articulated the genre. Thus on a superficial level, the RA text becomes increasingly divided into standardized divisions (IMRD or a disciplinary variant); on a less obvious level, the more likely we will find that different sections will have different rhetorical features (e.g. Introductions in contrast to Methods). The second corollary is that as we move towards the diffuse end of the continuum the more necessary it becomes for authors to engage in acts of persuasion that will encourage the readerships to share particular visions of the research world. The surprise is that, on preliminary evidence at least, the major differences do not lie so much in Introductions and Discussions (where I believe most people would expect it) but rather in the Method and Results sections. Finally, there is perhaps an element of irony in a situation wherein social scientists are engaged in a cognitive and rhetorical upgrade of Method at a time when their mentors in the hard sciences are beginning, rhetorically at least, to downgrade its importance.

8 *Observations on other research-process genres*

As the length of Chapter 8 demonstrates, I have given in this book a lion's share of the available space to the research article. I believe this decision can be justified in a number of ways. In many scholarly or research-driven discourse communities, the RA is the key genre both quantitatively and qualitatively. There is also little doubt that, even in a state of considerable ignorance, we know much more about the RA than other research-process genres. Further, one of the aims of this book has been to show how the actual process of genre analysis might be undertaken and I have not been able to see how this aim can be achieved by simply summarizing results. An initial stage of this process involves the presenting of textual extracts. While this need soon runs up against space constraints, it has been possible to satisfy it in a small number of selected genres, of which the RA has been one and the reprint request will be another.

There is a final reason, however, for giving prominence to the RA: the RA has a dynamic relationship with all the other *public* research-process genres. Even when we leave aside private and semi-private communicative activities connected with the RA (cover letters, reviewer's reports, reprint requests, etc.), the RA still remains at the center of a spider's web (Figure 17).

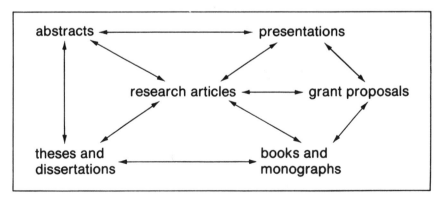

Figure 17 The RA and other research-process genres

These inter-relationships are, I believe, well enough known not to need much commentary. Most RAs these days are prefaced by homotopic abstracts, which are required by journal policy. The abstracts are, on the basis of widely-reported anecdotal evidence, written last. After publication, an abstract of the RA may appear in an abstracting journal; this abstract may be the original homotopic one, it may be specially written by an abstracter, or it may be some compromise between the two as in the *Linguistics and Language Behavior Abstracts'* 'modified author abstract'. The appearance of the abstract in the abstracting journal is, of course, designed to lead others *back* to the original RA.

Presentations at conferences (or elsewhere) and research articles are also typically in some state of dynamic tension. The presentation may report on work in progress or offer a preliminary trial of new ideas. It may be a version (from little to extensively modified to suit an oral audience) of a RA not yet published; it may even be based on an already published RA, although some academics confess to feeling uneasy about this latter scenario. A presentation may also be prepared with an eye to its appearing in the conference proceedings. Even though these possible permutations of the relationship between presentations and RAs are numerous, it is generally conceded that the effort involved in getting a presentation together typically enhances the likelihood of the presenter eventually coming up with an acceptable RA. Indeed, I am sure I am not alone in knowing people who deliberately offer to make presentations on what are for them comparatively new topics as a means of driving themselves towards published status in those topic areas.

The symbiotic relationship between RAs and successful grant applications is well known and is one of the most commonly cited instances of Merton's (1968) *Matthew effect* ('For unto every one that hath shall be given, and he shall have abundance: but from him that hath not shall be taken away even that which he hath.' (Matthew 25:29)). Published RAs increase the chances of follow-up research grants and research grants increase the chances of publishable RAs. Books and monographs may, to a lesser or greater extent, build upon or consolidate previously completed shorter and more partial studies, as indeed this particular book has done. Conversely, further technical articles may derive from the somewhat more generalist treatment generally expected of books. Chapters of theses and dissertations may already have appeared as RAs, and it is almost *de rigueur* for academic conversations with those who have just completed dissertations to turn at some stage to the new graduate's plans for article publication.

The remainder of this chapter will briefly discuss in turn five of these research-process genres: (a) abstracts, (b) research presentations, (c) grant proposals, (d) theses and dissertations and (e) reprint requests.

8.1   Abstracts

Although there exists much sound general advice on abstract writing in the leading native-speaker handbooks (e.g. O'Connor and Woodford, 1976; Day, 1979) and in the specialist literature (Cremmins, 1982), I am not aware of any published work that offers specific help for the NNS researcher and writer. One explanation for this state of affairs may be the belief that if a NNS author can write a RA he or she should have little trouble with the accompanying abstract. However, it can be the case that the abstract is the *only* piece of published writing done in English. Bloor (1984) in her Needs Analysis carried out at the University of Cordoba, southern Spain, found that Spanish academics typically wrote their RAs in Spanish but were also required to furnish the journals with abstracts in English. Many felt unequal to this task and resorted to translation services available in the city, while continuing to express anxiety about both the linguistic and substantive accuracy of these translations.

Title and abstract in published papers are at the same time both front matter and summary matter. The front matter or 'news value' element (Huckin, 1987) occurs because readers of RAs are extremely fickle: of those who will read the title, only some will read the abstract, and of those who read the abstract only some will read the article itself. Thus, abstracts function as independent discourses (Van Dijk, 1980) as well as being advance indicators of the content and structure of the following text. Bazerman (1984b) sees this detached status as a representation: 'The article's abstract serves as one further step in turning the article into an object, for the abstract considers the article as a whole and then makes a representation of it' (1984b:58).

However we might want to characterize the relationship between an abstract and what it is an abstract of, the essence of the genre is one of distillation. Essentially, it is this distilled quality that gives abstracts their particular character and makes them easy to recognize. Graetz (1985) has this to say about the language of abstracts:

> The abstract is characterized by the use of past tense, third person, passive, and the non-use of negatives. It avoids subordinate clauses, uses phrases instead of clauses, words instead of phrases. It avoids abbreviation, jargon, symbols and other language shortcuts which might lead to confusion. It is written in tightly worded sentences, which avoid repetition, meaningless expressions, superlatives, adjectives, illustrations, preliminaries, descriptive details, examples, footnotes. In short it eliminates the redundancy which the skilled reader counts on finding in written language and which usually facilitates comprehension.
>
> (Graetz, 1985:125)

Although Graetz's corpus consisted of 87 abstracts drawn from a variety
of fields, her use of the generic definite article is perhaps a little bold. Even
so, many of her conclusions would appear to be supportable. The
observation about the absence of negatives is particularly interesting, and
informal surveys do indeed suggest that the restricted length of the
abstract rarely permits the luxury of including statements of what has not
been done either by the authors or by other researchers. The point about
the elimination of redundancy can be tied in with the shortage of 'given'
information and the restricted use of anaphora that we encountered in
Method sections in areas of 'established science'.

   On the other hand, there are many abstracts – especially in abstracting
journals – that do not fit the picture. Abbreviations can be common:

> Anglo–Australian (N=48) & Greek–Australian (N=48) M & F
> high school students made personality evaluations of Standard
> Australian English & Greek–Australian–accented Eng.
>
> (*Linguistics and Language Behavior Abstracts* 8503043, sentence 1)

Complete sentences may not be used:

> A report on an ongoing project concerned with a cross-cultural
> investigation of speech act realization patterns.
>
> (*LLBA* 8503640, 'sentence' 1)

Active verbs, sometimes subjectless, may be a preferred style. *Marketing
and Distribution Abstracts*, for instance, consistently adopts this usage:

> Summarizes research which claims ... ; suggests that this
> theory ...

Additionally, there may be constructions that are unlikely to occur in
other research-process genres. One that occurs with some frequency in
LLBA is the placing of the passive participle in initial position:

> Examined are ways in which class regulation of power ...
> (8503638)
>
> Discussed are rituals & vocabulary associated with ... (8503645)

The most egregious of Graetz's claims is that abstracts are characterized
by the use of Past tense. As the immediately preceding examples show,
over a broader canvas than Graetz examined, the Present tense has
considerable popularity. The Present is likely to occur in the frequent
references to what may be found in the full text (Malcolm, 1987), for
example, 'Details of the techniques used are given'. It will tend to occur in
commentary rather than in narrative of what was done (Heslot, 1982).
We can also detect pressure on abstractors, especially if they are the
original authors, to opt for the Present tense because it intimates that the

research reported is *alive* (cf. 'the results show' v. 'the results showed') or because it reflects wider knowledge-claims. On the other hand, we can detect pressure to retreat to the Past tense whenever the 'one-off' nature of the work needs emphasizing or whenever a cautious approach to applications and extensions seems warranted (James, 1984b).

In view of Graetz's conclusions, it comes as something of a surprise to see that Rounds (1982) uncovers a considerable amount of hedging in her study of 14 abstracts from the journal *The Behavioral and Brain Sciences*. Although her texts do have phrases like 'attempt to arrive at some conclusions', 'appear to be under the influence of' and 'appears to underlie', space constraints seem in general to restrict the kind of modulation that is likely to be found in the research article itself.

Graetz claims that the most common structure for an abstract is a four-part arrangement consisting of Problem–Method–Results–Conclusions. However, review of her classification of 'introductory lines' suggests that 38 out of her 87 abstracts opened with what, in RA terms, has been called an 'establishing a territory' Move 1, while 24 more opened with a purposive or restrictive Move 3. Although further research is needed, it seems to be the case that most abstracts reflect the IMRD pattern of the RA itself, allotting a sentence or two for each section. Certainly, there is little evidence for the advice in Cremmins' *The Art of Abstracting* to place findings early in the topic sentence. On the other hand, Gopnik (1972) does provide strong and rationalized support for another recommendation to place general statements last.

Abstracts continue to remain a neglected field among discourse analysts. This is unfortunate as they are texts particularly suited to genre investigation. Moreover, study of certain types of abstracts can potentially be highly revealing of disciplinary discourse communities, particularly when the abstracts comprise the evidence on which gate-keeping decisions are made – as in the refereeing of conference abstracts. The only study I know in the area is Huckin (1988) in which he was able to show a growing devaluation of straightforward pedagogy-oriented abstracts at the Convention on College Composition and Communication.

Another under-researched aspect of abstracts is their role in the process of RA construction. Earlier I had suggested, on wide anecdotal evidence, that abstracts are *ex post facto*. However, Bazerman (1984b) in the only detailed case study of abstract–RA relationships that I know of – and that based on archival manuscripts – suggests that it may be otherwise. According to Bazerman, the famous physicist Compton in 1925 wrote a draft of the abstract (or much of it) about two-thirds of the way through the main RA draft:

> ... in order to articulate his sense of the whole and keep the parts logically and structurally consistent ... If the abstract did get

> written in stages co-ordinated with the writing of the main texts,
> that correlation would further emphasize the interaction between
> the gradual creation of the text and the growing perception and
> command of the text as an object.
>
> (Bazerman, 1984b:58–9)

It is precisely that interaction which requires further study.

8.2   Research presentations

Research into the actual characteristics of research presentations at conferences, as distinct from hortatory chapters in numerous textbooks and manuals, is, as far as I have been able to determine, extremely sparse. There is, however, one exception – and a splendid and very significant one. Throughout the eighties, Dubois in a long series of papers reported on many facets of short biomedical presentations (see below for references). The combination of scholarly treatment and pragmatic insight manifest in these studies is of a quality not found elsewhere and I have therefore decided to build this short section around Dubois' work.

For reasons connected with her involvement in US federal programs designed to assist minorities pursue graduate biomedical research careers, Dubois has for over a decade been somewhat more than a participant observer in the biomedical research community. This particular discourse community, like many others, is somewhat special with regard to its disciplinary traditions and its ensuing rhetorical opportunities and restraints. Therefore, the commentary that follows is offered as a community-specific paradigm against which conference presentations in other discourse communities need to be seen, in particular respects, either to adhere or diverge.

Dubois' main corpus consists of around 50 tape-recorded presentations made at the annual meeting of the Federation of American Societies in Experimental Biology (FASEB) in 1979. These oral accounts have a number of distinct characteristics: they are short, only 12 minutes being allowed for the presentation itself; they are typically accompanied by slides; and, as the name of the umbrella organization implies, they are largely concerned with reporting on laboratory studies.

The genre of (biomedical) presentations given at professional meetings is somewhat different to that of the research article. In the FASEB case, both the time constraint and the oral nature of the proceedings give rise to a product that has a more preliminary quality and is, in most cases, somewhat differently organized (Dubois, 1980a). There is also greater variation, as we usually expect in the spoken genre (Dubois, 1981b). While some of the speakers recorded by Dubois offered a presentation with many of the characteristics of written text, most did not. The major group 'presented more a chronicle of what happened in the laboratory than a carefully edited version such as might appear in print' (1980a:66). Presenters confess to problems, doubts and dead ends: they discuss in front of their peers unexpected results and near disasters: 'It started off normally, and then it chopped off ... I almost threw the data out, but you see it's not an artifact at all' (1980a:144). The strongly narrative character of the genre gives rise to much greater use of Past tense than in journal articles; indeed the narrative Past tense was often commonly used for stating hypotheses ('we were interested in seeing whether ... '), as well as for summary and conclusion.

In addition, there was considerable style-shifting within a presentation. A not atypical pattern is for formally written – and written out – openings and closings, more informal commentary on the slides with an occasional highly colloquial aside or supporting anecdote.

Dubois has proposed the following maximal structure for the genre she has analyzed.

I. Introduction
   A) Listener orientation
   B) Content orientation

II. Body (one or more episodes)
   A) Situation
   B) Event
   C) Commentary

III. Termination
   A) Content orientation
   B) Listener orientation

The *listener orientations*, which provide the outer frame, are a consequence of the real-time face-to-face character of the genre. They include such elements as acknowledging the chair's introduction, calling the audience to attention ('Ladies and Gentlemen') and signaling that the presentation is over and questions can be taken. The *content orientation* sets up the intellectual stage for the body of the presentation and seems to be broadly similar to RA introductions (although Dubois uses a different categorial system). The *body* consists of a background situating element – typically something about the animals – which can often serve for any further episodes. *Event-commentary* cycles then follow: what was done, then what was found. The *termination* typically offers a summary of the major results reported a few minutes previously and draws a number of conclusions (more or less tentative) from them. Although 8% of Dubois' sample ended at this juncture, allowing silence to signal that they had finished, the great majority concluded their presentations with 'thank you' or one of its variants.

Dubois (1980b) investigates the important structuring role of the slides in FASEB presentations. Indeed, she is able to show that, in some cases at least, presenters may choose their slides *first* and, on the basis of that selection, then decide what it is that they are going to say at the conference. The extent to which this type of process might be true of other discourse communities is a fascinating question. Would it be true of art, or architecture? What about geology, or botany? Conversations with colleagues in ESL suggest that documentary data can occasionally determine the shaping of the presentation, especially when video clips are involved, but it is more likely that the quality of the data principally affects the *topic* that a would-be presenter chooses to offer. Additionally Dubois (1982b) shows how language regulating the use of the slides in the presentation itself can also serve as an organizational device: when the speaker says 'And the last slide please' the audience knows where the speaker is without any need for further comment.

In a more recent paper, Dubois (1987) has addressed an aspect of research presentations that I believe to have been hitherto ignored. She investigates both the occurrence and rhetorical use of imprecise numerical expressions in her biomedical slide talk data. She finds that various kinds of imprecision are quite common: numbers are rounded up or down, approximate fractions may replace precise decimals, hedges such as 'about' recur and information is given in ranges ('from 6 to 7 grams'). Sometimes these devices are used in conjunction with each other, as in 'something on the order of about 40 to 44 beats per minute'.

As Dubois observes, a major reason for the use of approximate numerical expressions in oral presentations is that they avoid overloading the listeners with data. Precise figures, especially those involving decimal places, would create severe problems in aural processing, especially when several presentations are given each hour and the sessions may run for several hours. However, Dubois has been able to chart some very interesting strategic choices within the general processing constraints. As we might expect, background information, historical, geographic or meteorological, is usually expressed in very imprecise terms (e.g. 'about 20 years ago'). Less obvious is the finding that there were many instances of researchers using imprecision in describing their less significant results and reserving precision for what they believed to be the more significant findings. An imprecise background thus allows a precise number to become foregrounded. A final use of imprecise numbers that Dubois found was in discussion of the work of others that the presenter believed to be incorrect. For example, in one case, the presenter describes a putatively erroneous prediction as 'about 15', whilst his own counter-evidence comes in at two decimal places, 'nine point two seven' (1987:538).

The FASEB proceedings also reveal a particular rhetorical problem restricted to those discourse communities which inflict suffering on animals in the cause of improving human health care and of advancing human knowledge. Dubois (1981a) characterizes this dilemma as 'the management of pity' and is able to show that in her sample pity is regulated through a series of lexical and syntactic preferences. In a fair number of the FASEB studies, animals are put through some experimental procedure, killed and then examined. However, the verb *kill* was unattested, the preferred alternative being *sacrifice*. As Dubois points out, everyday euphemisms such as *put down* or *put to sleep* also did not occur, perhaps because they imply a concern for the comfort of the individual animal, which would go against an ethos of using animals as an unfortunately necessary means to some greater end – an ethos, of course, perfectly represented by the concept of *sacrifice*.

These kinds of lexical choice (and there are others such as dogs being *allowed* to run on treadmills and so on) are part of our general folklore on the world of biological laboratory research. The syntactic choices are less apparent. Dubois shows that a number of syntactic changes are likely to occur when the speakers reach points in their descriptions where the experimental animals are likely to be experiencing pain and suffering. She suggests, for example, that there may be moves down the following options:

a) ... we sacrificed the animals.
b) The animals were sacrificed.
c) The sacrifice of the animals ...
d) The sacrificed animals ...
e) After sacrifice ...

(Dubois, 1981a:252)

A sentence-initial subordinated nominalization like *after sacrifice* attracts much less attention to itself than would choices (a) or (b). In addition, the experimental subjects may disappear from the script being replaced by process or instrumental nouns ('ventilation was achieved by'; 'A catheter was placed'). Finally, pity is managed by switching to a higher order of term when describing violent or painful steps. For example *dogs* (as man's best friends) suddenly became *animals*.

In the preceding few pages I have attempted to provide some sort of account of Dubois' explorations into an important research-process genre. These explorations are restricted to a particular discourse community meeting at one time and place in a particular country. Clearly, generalized conclusions are inadvisable. However, the impressions that we can carry away in our efforts to understand research discourse communities which may concern us more are of an established genre separate to that of the research article. The communicative purpose is different: progress report rather than finished product. The situation is different: speech rather than writing. The main mode of discourse is different: narration rather than exposition. The constraints are different: occasional humor is here permitted but extensive use of precise numbers is dispreferred. The role of the addresser is different: the presenter is much more of a person, indeed one who can tell tales against him- or herself often to good rhetorical effect, while the writer is much more of an abstracted, calculated persona. However, it is the same discourse community that operates both genres, as it does others such as poster presentations (Dubois, 1985), abstracts, dissertations, reviews, grant proposals. These genres will share content in common, as they will ethical and technical expectations and intellectual traditions and concerns. The differences are rhetorical, but not reduced to insignificance as a consequence.

8.3   Grant proposals

Proposals that request funds in order to carry out specific research projects have become imbued with very considerable individual departmental and institutional significance in many disciplinary areas. My own university, like many others with a commitment to research, recognizes the importance of the genre in tangible terms. It has a special centrally-funded unit, one of whose main missions is to help researchers write up good fundable proposals. It joins many other groups in producing materials designed to help proposal writers. These groups include the funding agencies and foundations themselves, professional writers and successful practitioners of the art of grantmanship (Lauffer, 1983; Locke et al., 1987). Given this visibility of the genre, I shall restrict discussion to significant differences with the research article.

The typical parts of a research proposal are:

1. *Front Matter*
   a) Title or cover page
   b) Abstract
   c) Table of contents (for longer proposals)

2. *Introduction*

3. *Background* (typically a literature survey)

4. *Description of proposed research* (including methods, approaches, and evaluation instruments)

5. *Back matter*
   a) Description of relevant institutional resources
   b) References

c) Personnel
d) Budget

If we leave aside the formulation of the title, the first real rhetorical test is the one-page abstract. Indeed, it may represent the biggest hurdle of all: 'the abstract that is submitted with the full proposal bears a disproportionate share of responsibility for success or failure' (Locke et al., 1987:121). Unlike a RA abstract, it is promissory and it need not so obviously reflect proportionately the content of the full proposal. One reason for the latter freedom is that the abstract is likely to be read by a wider group than the specialists asked to evaluate the longer document. Since it needs to be written for a wider mix of discourse communities, heavy presumptions of specialized knowledge (and the associated technical vocabulary) tend to be avoided. The abstract also needs to come quickly to the proposed endeavor rather than engage in the kind of space-creating rationale that is typical of RA abstracts (which are typically straightforward condensations of the full version). As a result, abstracts to grant proposals usually begin with the objective or purpose of the study, move on to methodology (procedures and design) and close with a modest but precise statement of the project's significance.

Just as abstracts to research proposals are 'fronted', so are their introductions (Huckin and Olsen, 1983). If an extensive description of the relevant previous literature is thought to be necessary, it is usually placed in a subsequent section. Like the abstract, the introduction will often be written in such a way that administrative and program officers can easily obtain a general idea of what the proposal is about; and again like the abstract, the introduction will also typically begin with a purpose section. It is only in parts 3 (Background) and 4 (Description of proposed research) that the writers tend to assume that the reader–evaluators will be members of their discourse community.

8.4   Theses and dissertations

The thesis or dissertation – terminology does not travel easily across the oceans – can either be a *rite de passage* into the targeted discourse community, or an exit qualification that enables the holder to leave the university world and enter another one. The exigencies for meeting the requirement even in situations where the document is typically written in English vary quite widely from one country to another. The nature of 'the document' is also diversifying. In areas where books are rarely written, as in the physical sciences, there is growing challenge to requiring a student to produce a long, single and comprehensive discourse rather than an anthology of research articles (Reid, 1978; Richards, 1988). As Halstead

(1988) argues, it is the latter that certifies *relevant* practice, training and experience in today's world.

Even if we restrict discussion to the traditional culminatory text, we are still faced with the fact that nearly all of the relevant literature consists of handbooks and guides (e.g. Sternberg, 1981; Davis and Parker, 1979; Madsen, 1982). Up until now it is an area that discourse analysts have largely avoided, at least partly because of the daunting size of the typical text. However, Dudley-Evans (1986) and Hopkins and Dudley-Evans (1988) have examined the comparatively short and straightforward M.Sc. dissertations in biology from a British university. They show, in their introductions, a stronger preference for cyclic patterns which discuss various elements germane to the main topic in turn – at least in comparison to the RA. On the other hand, the discussions utilize, again cyclically, many of the moves reported for research articles.

My own preliminary findings, based on a close reading of six dissertations from The University of Michigan, suggests that the key differentiating aspect of dissertation writing is a much greater use of *metadiscourse*, or writing about the evolving text rather than referring to the subject matter (Williams, 1985). On the metadiscoursal level, we writers 'do not add propositional material but help our readers organize, classify, interpret, evaluate, and react to such material' (Vande Kopple, 1985:83). The author intrudes in order to direct the readers in some way rather than to inform them (Crismore and Farnsworth, 1988).

Although the concept of metadiscourse is easy enough to accept in principle, it is much more difficult to establish its boundaries. There is doubt, for example, as to whether sentence connectives such as *therefore* or whether lexical familiarizations or word glosses (Bramki and Williams, 1984) belong in the system as Vande Kopple and others have argued. There is less doubt that overt commentary on the text in the text is indeed metadiscoursal. Such commentary can range from Advance Labeling ('we shall need to discuss this issue in other terms in the next section') and recapitulation ('we have now discussed ... ') (Tadros, 1985) to purpose statements, advice to readers ('readers might wish to read the last section first') and various enunciations of authorial stance ('It is unfortunate that we still do not have a way of ... ').

All of these types of commentary (with one exception) are frequently used by the American authors of the six dissertations I have examined, and incidentally are somewhat less frequent in most dissertations written by non-native speakers. There is much signaling of where the authors are going, where precisely they have got to, and what they achieved so far. The one exception is obvious enough: dissertation authors never give advice to their readers since their primary and pre-designated audience is a very small group of specialists in their field who act as counsel in the process and judge of the finished product. Incorporating that kind of gentle reader steering is just *one* of the revisions that need to be done if a dissertation is to be changed into a scholarly book. And, as a Parthian shot at this topic, let me indulge myself in the higher-order meta-discoursal comment that there is a considerable amount of metadiscourse in this volume. Metadiscourse goes with extensive textual territory.

8.5   Reprint requests

Another genre related to the research article is the reprint request. A reprint request (RR) is a request for a copy, reprint or offprint of a research article mailed by a researcher (or occasionally librarian) to the author or authors of that publication. Figure 18 provides an example.

(Institutional address)

Monsieur,
Dear Sir,

Je vous serais très obligé de bien vouloir m'envoyer un tiré à part de votre article intitulé:
I would appreciate receiving a reprint of your paper:

Avec tous mes remerciements,
Sincerely yours,

Figure 18   A typical reprint request

Aspects of text role and environment

As Onuigbo observes:

> There is no doubt that preprinted request cards are part and parcel of the information traffic occurring in science today. Indeed they dominate the scene. For instance, so great is their predominance that I received only nine *letters*, in contrast to 1,014 *cards* from the United States.
>
> (Onuigbo, 1984:95)

The fact that Wilson I. Onuigbo, a medical researcher in Nigeria, has received more than 1000 cards from the United States suggests that the RR may be a comparatively large genre. Available evidence (Onuigbo, 1985; Swales, 1988a) suggests that at least 10 million RRs are dispatched each year. Thus, the genre may be relatively simple in format, but it is certainly not small.

Nor is the genre without its consequences. Whilst some authors may throw away many or most of the RRs they receive, other authors are extremely responsive. My main informant, Dr Robert Fogel (an American biologist) is happy to respond to RRs, and is not averse to including in his return package 'papers on related topics' if asked to do so and when supplies are available. Additionally, in his two main areas, Fungal Ecology and Systematics, Dr Fogel maintains mailing lists; by early 1987, the mailing list for the former consisted of 113 names and addresses. It is not surprising, therefore, that Dr Fogel may order up to 300 reprints for his ecology papers. Dr Fogel believes that responding to RRs is 'good advertising' and is therefore worth the time, trouble and cost that is incurred. More specifically, he believes that if fellow research-ers have reprints of his papers to hand, they are more likely to cite them than would be the case if they had to look up his publications in a library.

In Swales (1986b) I described the results of a questionnaire sent to people who asked for a reprint of a paper I had published in 1985. Although only 12 of the 35 questionnaires were returned, (a response rate of 34%), 11 of the 12 said that they received at least 50% of the papers they had requested. Even if the actual response rate found in a more representative sample is only 25%, this percentage would neverthe-less indicate that several million reprints are mailed out each year as a result of reprint requests. And of course this estimate excludes those mailings instigated by authors themselves.

Many (perhaps even a majority) of the RRs may finish up virtually unread or cursorily dismissed. This is because the available evidence seems to suggest that a reprint request is most often initiated by the simple scanning of authors' names, titles and/or key words. It was presumably some such scanning that led an institute concerned with rubber research to request a reprint of a paper on cohesion written by a discourse analyst colleague.

In this triggering process the role of *Current Contents* seems central. A neat illustration of its importance as a source of RRs is provided by Onuigbo (1982). In two of Onuigbo's articles indexed in *Current Contents* there occurred a printing error; in one instance a proper name was misspelled and in the other a preposition was deleted. Onuigbo found that in 26 cases there was insufficient title to indicate the source for the RR, in 52 cases the printing error was repeated (thus indicating a *Current Contents* source) and in only nine cases was the correct original title preserved (thus indicating a primary rather than secondary source). While it is not surprising that reliance on minimal information in secondary sources can lead to many disappointments, an initial and impersonal RR may have repercussive effects; it may lead to the reciprocal return of papers, a growth of correspondence, arrangements to meet at conferences and, in a few instances, to that most satisfactory outcome – collaborative research. On occasion, 'tall oaks from little acorns grow'.

The reprint request is at the same time both institutionalized and yet restricted to certain sectors of the academic world. Convincing evidence for the former claim lies in the fact that the great majority of RRs are printed by departments (and other types of research units) for the use of their members. For instance, in only six of the 127 printed RRs in the sample to be discussed below was the name of the researcher also *printed* at the top of the return address; much more typically the name of the requester is handwritten, typed or rubber-stamped. With few exceptions, therefore, RRs are produced by institutional organizations and not by individuals. On the other hand, RRs are currently restricted to certain fields, typically medicine, the life and physical sciences and engineering, with perhaps growing use in the 'harder' social sciences such as psychology. In the humanities, methods of contact and exchange tend to be much more individual and personal; in my own area I know of only one colleague who regularly uses RRs – and inevitably enough his anomalous position has required him to print his *own* cards.

The main corpus consists of 127 printed RRs generated as a result of the publication of three papers, whilst the subsidiary corpus consists of 12 further requests of a different form (four ISI Request-A-Prints and eight more personal requests). The three papers are:

1. Swales, J. M. 1985. English Language Papers and Authors' First Language: Preliminary Explorations. *Scientometrics* 8: 91–101.

2. Fogel, R. & Trappe, J. M. 1978. Fungus consumption (mycrography) by small animals. *Northwest Science* 52: 1–31.

3. Fogel, R. 1983. Root turnover and productivity of coniferous forests. *Plant and Soil* 71: 75–85.

The first journal, *Scientometrics* is published by the Hungarian Academy of Sciences, and printed by a major Dutch academic publishing house. It has an international editorship and editorial board. *Scientometrics*, as its name implies, is mainly concerned with quantitative aspects of the distribution of scientific information and with the use of quantitative methods to assess and trace the impact of certain researchers, certain research fronts and certain research institutions. The journal seems to appeal to information scientists themselves and to quite a number of other researchers who have interests in the evaluation of research and in quantitative aspects of its growth and development. The fact that I have received three times more RRs from readers of this journal than from any other suggests that by publishing in *Scientometrics* I had entered another discourse community.

Of the 33 printed RRs that I received as a result of the *Scientometrics* paper, 25 apparently emanated from those working in institutes or departments that were concerned with the medical or biological sciences, six from those in other sciences or branches of engineering, one from agriculture and one from psychology. The unexpected origins of the requests led me to poll the requesters about their RR habits and motivations. A further reason for distributing a questionnaire was my guess that only three of the 33 were native speakers of English. Nine of the 12 respondents mentioned that they selectively sent RRs for *Scientometric* articles, thus corroborating the impression given by their place of work that they have a *minor* interest in scientometric matters. Eight checked an interest in international scientific communication and a somewhat different eight checked an interest in the communication problems of non-native speakers of English. Indeed, half referred to the 'political' or 'psychological' implications of being a NNS in the anglophone world of international research, one expressing his interest in reading the paper in the following gloomy terms: 'to further define my handicaps'.

The 1978 Fogel paper was published in *Northwest Science*, which, as its name implies, is an interdisciplinary regional journal. The 1983 paper was published in a specialized international journal produced in Britain.

The profile of requesters for the two Fogel papers was, as we might expect, more predictable. The majority worked in university departments concerned with pure or applied life sciences, whilst a minority were sent by national or regional research institutions outside the university network. The 1978 paper ('Fungus consumption by small animals') drew in a number of requests from Health Institutes, and departments such as anthropology and psychology, and one from a zoo. The 1983 paper ('Root turnover and productivity of coniferous forests') naturally enough attracted many more requests from institutions concerned in some way with forestry, range science or agriculture.

The differences between the role and location of the three journals could be expected to have some effect on the provenance of the requests. Although this is undoubtedly the case with regard to Swales v. Fogel, it is much less obviously true with regard to Fogel 1978 v. Fogel 1983. The main origin of requests for the *Scientometrics* paper is clearly Europe (26 out of 36), perhaps because the journal is edited in Eastern Europe and distributed from Western Europe. However, the pattern of provenance for the two Fogel papers is perhaps less different than we might expect. North American provenance clearly predominates in both cases. Although European requests do rise in the case of the *Plant and Soil* paper, they still only amount to 13 (in contrast to 37 from North America). In the corpus as a whole, only 10 out of the 139 exemplars originated in the Third World.

The reasons for the massive quantity of RR traffic in the world today – much of it international – remain somewhat obscure. My informant Dr Fogel has explained why he responds positively to RRs, but he also knows of colleagues who are considerably less accommodating. Certainly, the system has its critics: 'I am not alone in not sending reprints to North America' (Essex-Lopresti, 1981). The final question in my questionnaire asked those who sent RRs to comment on the advantages of the RR system to them. The most common types of stated advantage were access to papers that would otherwise be difficult to get hold of (i.e. journals not carried by the institutional library etc.) and the fact that the reprints were immediately available and to hand. The latter observation, of course, gives substance to Dr Fogel's premise that if papers are to hand, they are more likely to be cited. A number of respondents also mentioned the time element (quick in contrast to inter-library loan; time needed to travel to the library; time lost by xeroxing). The Polish respondent referred to the scarcity of photocopiers. There were, in addition, a number of more individual advantages. One person emphasized the much better quality of photographs in reprints rather than photocopies, another the fact that he often lent the reprints to his students, and a third referred to 'the personal contact with colleagues' that the RR system engendered – this last an indication of the system's disguised potential for networking.

Language choice in reprint requests

An intriguing aspect of printed RRs is the language or languages chosen to express the request. If a multilingual format is chosen, the *order* of languages remains consistent in all RRs so far examined; in other words if French is the top language for the opening salutation, then it will remain the first language throughout (as can be seen in Table 7). In the following table this order is represented by 1L to 4L.

Table 7 indicates that English was used on all the RRs, and was the

TABLE 7. LANGUAGE USE PATTERNS IN THE MAIN CORPUS (n=127)

	Monolingual	Multilingual				Total
		1L	2L	3L	4L	
English	102	4	18	3	0	127
German	0	10	3	6	0	19
French	0	8	1	5	3	17
Russian	0	2	3	0	1	6
Spanish	0	1	0	0	1	2
Total	102	25	25	14	5	

only language found on monolingual cards. In fact, overall, 80% of all the RRs were monolingual English, although there was some difference between the three sub-samples (Swales 55%; Fogel 1978 90% and Fogel 1983 85%). The table also shows that four other languages occurred in addition to the ubiquitous English. These multilingual cards originated principally in Western and Eastern Europe; and, as might be expected, the francophones tended to place French first, while German speakers did the same for German. The Scandinavian cards were typically monolingual English. The six cards that carried a Russian-language request all came from Russia and Eastern Europe. Only one of the 10 cards emanating from Hispano-Portuguese speaking areas employed Spanish, suggesting that Spanish has very marginal status as a reprint request language (the other Spanish card came from a French university). Obviously enough, other potential RR languages, such as Japanese, Arabic, Italian or Chinese, did not occur.

Language choice in reprint requests is also worth examining because it provides *unusual* information about patterns of language use in international research. At present, much of the available evidence we have reflects high-order decision-making, such as the language policies adopted by journals, international associations, major conferences and abstracting and indexing services. In addition, as we have seen, there are a few studies of individual decision-making and coping strategies. However, the RR is typically produced by a *local* unit, such as a department or institute, for the convenience of its members, and thus reflects *that unit's* perceptions of the viable research languages in its field. Although the actual results in the present small corpus in fact quite closely corroborate what we know of the macro-picture, this does not mean to say that such corroboration from a different source is not useful, nor that a different kind of sample might not be instructive. For instance, a study of which languages are used on RRs produced by different departments within a single major research institution would contribute usefully to the 'linguistic scientometrics' literature, particularly if the institution were situated in a geographical area where academic language choices are complex.

A final result from this study is the disappointingly low level of RRs from the Third World, especially since the RR system is relatively low cost. If we also recognize, following Bloor (1984), that many non-native speakers, even with high-level English writing abilities, find it difficult for cultural reasons to *initiate* academic correspondence with potential colleagues in other parts of the world, then we can anticipate some advantage in encouraging more LDC researchers to adopt the system.

The structure of the reprint request

In the previous subsection I have tried to indicate something of the institutional environment within which the RR operates, and to say something about the choice of RR language in relation to international and regional scientific communication. It is, I think, clear that the reprint request has already met most of the criteria for genre status. It has a recognized name within the relevant discourse communities. Members of those communities recognize the RR as being an identifiable communicative act. Those members share an understanding of what the public purpose of a RR is, and respond to that purpose with a limited set of behaviors. The reprint request functions as a standard and typical response-type; in certain disciplines, evidence from both total numbers and from relative percentages strongly suggests that a RR is a *normal* way of obtaining a copy of a potentially interesting article. The remaining issue, therefore, is whether a RR is a sufficiently structured and standardized communicative event (with consequent constraints on allowable contributions in terms of purpose, positioning and form) to constitute a genre.

The central element of the reprint request can be expected to be the request itself (plus adequate information to indicate where the request should be sent). As we shall see, this central element is typically bounded by opening and closing salutations of types that occur throughout the range of formal correspondence genres. Given the central purpose of making a request, it also is not surprising to find that the request element is often followed by an anticipatory expression of thanks. This statement would seem to be motivated by two considerations. On the one hand, requesters may feel that a grateful acknowledgement of compliance will enhance the chances of a positive response. Secondly, the 'thanks' statement occurs on reprint requests because of the essentially 'one-shot' nature of the communicative event. *Under normal circumstances*, neither requester nor responder expects that the receipt of the requested article will call forth a simple 'thank-you' note or letter.

The data for the corpus are given in Table 8.

TABLE 8. THE STRUCTURE OF THE REPRINT REQUEST

	No. of occurrences	%	Corpus
1. Opening salutation	104	82	127
2. Request statement	127	100	127
3. Expression of thanks	89	70	127
4. Closing salutation	94	74	127

Table 8 shows that element 2 is *obligatory* (obviously enough since it carries the communicative purpose), while the three other elements are *conventional* (i.e. they occur in a majority of cases). What the table does not directly show is that the *order* of the four elements is fixed; no variations in the sequence were found. It will be remembered that the corpus consists of 127 reprint requests drawn from three sub-samples: these were responses to *Swales, Fogel I* (1978) and *Fogel II* (1983). Preliminary separate analyses of the three groups of RRs generated by the three papers suggested that variations among the groups tended to be relatively minor. I have therefore usually consolidated the results, although at times I have highlighted possibly interesting differences among the three. The analysis that follows largely concentrates on the English-language data – as might be expected in a book of this kind.

1.   OPENING SALUTATIONS

Out of the 127 RRs, 23 had no opening salutation. Of the remaining 104, 53 carried a stem-salutation inviting completion of the addressee's name and/or title. The two common forms here were 'Dear .... ' and 'Dear Dr .... '. Of the full salutations 'Dear Sir' (33 instances) and 'Dear Colleague' (11) reached double figures. There was only one instance of 'Dear Sir/Madam'. The fact that as many as 25% of the RRs used 'Dear Sir' gives cause for contemplation. At present, it doesn't seem possible to hazard whether this usage more closely reflects the extreme power of convention, (chauvinistic) expectations of the gender of the recipient, or the fact that English does not possess any obvious gender-neutral term of address that does not assume status (i.e. Dr). Dones (1989) in a follow-up study of this striking characteristic found in a larger and later corpus of RRs that even in 1987 'Dear Sir' was occurring 17% of the time and was widely distributed around the world. Equally interesting are the relatively low figures for 'Dear Colleague'. After all, this term of address is both collegial and gender-neutral (at least in English); it is also the term used on the widely-used commercial *Request-A-Print* cards produced by the Institute for Scientific Information. Finally, two requesters in Fogel II (although none elsewhere) have crossed out *Dr* and *Sir*, one writing in 'Bob' and the other writing 'Hi Bob! Send me your new loot', thus suggesting that the RR also serves as a channel of communication between known colleagues.

2.   THE REQUEST (IN ENGLISH)

The actual requests varied in length from six words to 41 words. The typical opening was the request itself, and in the corpus examined here, there is striking evidence for a *major* structure (107 instances) and a number of *minor* structures (a total of 20 instances). Of the 20 examples of the minor structures, 14 involved the lexical item *send*. The more common variants were:

> (Would you) please send me/us ... (6 cases)
>
> I would be very grateful if you could
>
> send me/us ... (4 cases)

However, the much preferred approach in the RR is not to request that a reprint *be sent*, but rather to express appreciation for a reprint *to be received*. It may not be too fanciful to speculate that the dynamic *send* is thought likely to conjure up images of work in the recipient's mind (finding, addressing, dispatching, etc.) which the static *receive* seductively and successfully avoids. The linguistic regularity in the first part of the request itself can be seen in Table 9 (letters in brackets indicate optional elements).

TABLE 9. ENGLISH REQUEST FORM: MAJOR STRUCTURE
(n = 107; 0 = missing)

A +	B +	[C] +	D +	[E]
I	would	greatly	appreciate	receiving
102	99	55	107	52
we	should	0		0
5	8	40		51
		(very much)		(others)
		12		4

The three necessary elements in the request form (A, B and D) exhibit a remarkable convergence in linguistic realization (and the very strong preference for 'I' reinforces the view that RRs are designed for individual use even though printed by units). As Column C shows, the possibility of using an intensifying adverb at C has been adapted in over 60% of the cases, by far the most popular adverbial being *greatly*. The selection of a verbal complement after *appreciate* occurs in about half the cases (+50% in Fogel I and below 50% in Swales and Fogel II).

The continuation of the request statement specifies the item being requested. The second half of the request statement consists of an obligatory element and three optional elements. The obligatory element F is realized by either *reprint* (81%), *a copy* (17%) or *the following* (2%). The request is then highly likely to be amplified by some printed statement of the document-type – with a clear preference for a personal format *of your article* or *of your paper*. At this juncture many of the printed request statements terminate, although there remain two further immediate possibilities. One is to include *entitled* (only 19%) and the other is to break up the blank spaces with an *aide-mémoire* such as *which appeared in*.

The variations on a theme that have so far been discussed are largely matters of style and specificity of information. We now need to consider four further possibilities that may add to or detract from the rhetorical effectiveness of the RR. Even though these options vary from very rare to fairly uncommon, they are, nevertheless, worth some discussion.

The first is to make the request ostensibly conditional on availability (perhaps as a device for obviating the unpleasant surprise of being charged). There were just seven of these, all from North America and all in the Fogel corpus. This option is the only sub-element in the entire corpus that exhibited positional variability, five preceding the request and two succeeding it:

Pre-request: If available for distribution ...
          If available for free distribution ...
          If the following publication is available for distribution ...
          If a reprint is available ...
          If copies are available ...

Post-request: ... if available.
          ... if copies are available for distribution.

Next, the corpus produced but four instances (all from the US) of printed statements that referred to the uses to which the RR would be put:

... for current reference and permanent files. (2)
... for use in my research program.
... for use in my teaching and research.

Third, there is one instance of a RR that attempts to both justify response and yet empathize with the recipient of the RR. The card (from the Swales corpus) is unique in the amount of 'rhetorical work' it essays and for this reason the long and complex central element is worth quoting in full:

As an institution responsible for providing scientists and oncologists throughout the German Democratic Republic with medical literature we would be exceedingly grateful if you could send us a reprint, or if it should not be available, a photocopy of your article.

Knowing that such requests can become burdensome we wish to assure you, (sic) that your assistance will be most appreciated.

These optional additions are rare enough to suggest that most producers of RRs probably believe that such embellishments have little effect on response rate. However, where they are found they are clearly designed to increase goodwill.

Any such goodwill may, of course, be diminished by requests that are considered unnecessarily onerous. It is for this reason that tagged-on requests for *other* papers present a potential problem for RR designers. Out of the 127 cards, 29 (23%) had these tagged requests, 20 of them coming from outside the US suggesting that in the USA such tags are seen as either unnecessary or unwarranted or self-defeating. Seventeen of the tags were attached to the request sentence, while 12 were following independent sentences. Most of the 17 had forms similar to one of the following:

> ... and reprints of related papers.
> ... and any other reprints on similar topics.
> ... as well as other related publications.

The use of a sentence boundary can perhaps be seen as creating a separating or distancing effect between the two requests, the use of two sentences being very common among the US cards. Even more interestingly, nine of the 12 independent sentences showed a switch into the passive, probably reinforcing by this means the separation of the requests into two classes. Typical examples are:

> Copies of other papers on this and similar subjects would be appreciated. (3)

> Copies of related articles would also be appreciated. (2)

Finally, only one of the cards made any reference to a mailing list, but this was one of the few individually-duplicated cards ('Please place me on your mailing list'). Clearly, institutionally-produced cards do not want to engage their senders in such a commitment.

3. EXPRESSION OF THANKS

In 89 out of 127 cases (70%) the request was followed by an expression of thanks. In about half the instances gratitude was expressed by a short 'thank you' statement, whereas in the other half, gratitude was somewhat more elaborated. The results are given below.

TABLE 10. FORMULATIONS OF GRATITUDE (n = 127)

Short (45)		*Elaborated (44)*	
Thank you (very much)	32	Thank you for your courtesy	22
With (many) thanks	11	Thank you for this courtesy	6
(others)	2	Thank(ing) you in advance	6
		Thank you for your kindness	3
		Thank you for your consideration	3
		Thank(ing) you in anticipation	2
		(others)	2

The percentages of gratitude statements in Swales and Fogel I and II were almost identical (69–71%), but the European-dominated Swales sub-corpus showed a very different distribution of *short* versus *elaborated* to the two Fogel samples (with their preponderance of requests from North America). The figures are as follows (Table 11).

TABLE 11. DISTRIBUTION OF SHORT AND ELABORATED FORMS

	Short	Elaborated	Total
Fogel 1978	18	9	27
Fogel 1983	23	16	39
Swales 1985	4	19	23

Thus, assumed differences in level of formality between the US and Europe are also manifest in the language of reprint requests.

4.   FORMS OF CLOSING SALUTATION (IN ENGLISH)

There was a printed closing salutation in 94 of the cards, but not in the other 33. The 94 break down as follows (Table 12).

TABLE 12. FORMS OF CLOSING SALUTATION (n = 127)

Sincerely yours	46
Yours (very) sincerely	19
Sincerely	17
Yours (very) truly	9
Yours faithfully	3

As can be expected, the greater predominance of American forms (*Sincerely yours*; *sincerely*) as opposed to British forms (*Yours sincerely*) primarily reflects the strong US provenance of the corpus and secondarily and less certainly, reflects the career experience of the individual non-native speaker researcher. The three 'yours faithfully' cards all came from Australia.

Apart from information about the return address (and very uncommon instructions such as 'cut and use stub for address') the printed RRs in the corpus essentially end at this point. Only four in fact carry additional elements. In two cases, there is reference to costs:

Please advise charges.
If costs are involved, please let me know before mailing.

The other two are designed to handle the contingency of non-availability:

If reprints are not available please return this card.
If reprints are not available please check here – and return card.

The paucity of such requests for actions other than the simple dispatch of the reprint reinforces the claim that the RR is a 'one-shot' interaction. And this is further confirmed by the existence in the corpus of three repeated cards from the same three individuals, the moral of the story being that if requesters do not succeed at first, they should send a second identical card.

PART IV APPLICATIONS

In the final part of this volume I would like to explore how a genre-based approach to research English can be turned to pedagogical account. Of course in some small ways I have already been anticipating this undertaking. 4.3 (A pedagogical illustration) offered some illustrative teaching material designed to foster both quantitative and qualitative improvement in academic correspondence, so that students can begin to participate more fully in their chosen discourse communities. Additionally, Chapter 6 (The role of English in research) concluded with task-based activities centered on a citation analysis extract – activities that start with the text itself but then require participants to investigate similarities and differences in their own specialist disciplines.

Part IV opens with a chapter entitled 'Orientations', which is designed to form a bridge between the intellectual and descriptive frameworks in Parts II and III and some sample teaching materials in Chapter 10. The first *orientation* (9.1) discusses and illustrates the value of a case-study approach to individual writers. The second *orientation* (9.2) builds upon the first by reviewing the arguments for rhetorical consciousness-raising in general and then considers how those arguments can be differently utilized in coping with classes that may, on the one hand, be composed of a single disciplinary group and, on the other, of heterogeneous specialists. The first two sections of Chapter 9 share an assumption that it is possible for the instructor to get some sort of handle on the relevant genres. 9.3, in contrast, does not make that assumption; instead it tries to show how the concept of discourse community can be invoked in order to help students, especially undergraduates, become better amateur ethnographers of their own communities. The fourth and final *orientation* relates the previous three to the important contemporary debate in both first and second language contexts about the merits and demerits of the 'process' approach to writing. In Chapter 10 I offer a small number of teaching activities which, alongside those in 4.3 and 6.2, serve in a necessarily limited way to illustrate applications of the approach advocated in this book. The volume closes with a short Epilogue, which briefly reviews the book's aims and purposes and then identifies and discusses what seems to me to be a key research question for the immediate future.

9 Orientations

9.1 Individual case work

There is a common enough view that investigative strategies are hierarchically ordered. According to this view, case studies are appropriate to the exploratory phase of an investigation, surveys appropriate to the descriptive phase, and experiments the means of making explanatory or causal links. A number of social scientists, including Yin (1984), argue that this widely-accepted hierarchical model is misguided, since each of the three main strategies can be used for all three purposes – exploration, description and explanation. However, even if the three strategies may be equal, they may also be different. Case studies and experiments may be preferred when we attempt to answer *how* and *why*, whereas surveys are better for questions of the *who, where, how many* or *how much* types. Case studies and experiments differ, of course, in that the former attempt no control over behavioral events and are therefore particularly useful when the relevant behaviors cannot easily be manipulated. Yin defines a case study as an inquiry which:

> ... investigates a contemporary phenomenon within its real life context; when the boundaries between phenomenon and context are not clearly evident; and in which multiple sources of evidence are used.

> (Yin, 1984:23)

Given such a definition, case-by-case studies of student academic writing – or for that matter of reading, listening or speaking – can have a certain contribution to make. Such writing is a real-world phenomenon in which the boundaries between the writing itself and the impinging contextual factors are rarely clear, and in which multiple sources of evidence are available. In the three cases I shall selectively discuss, all of NNS graduate students at a major US university, the sources of data include background interviews, questionnaires, the subject's behavior in a writing class, individual consultations with the instructor, a research assistant and the tutor in a writing clinic, longitudinal writing samples, and comments elicited from academic advisors.

The cases are at the same time exploratory, descriptive and explanatory. They are exploratory in the sense that they are open-ended. This open-endedness is based on the probability that academic affairs will turn out to be not what they seemed on first impression, and not to be much like what they are supposed to be according to official documentation or pronouncement. Explorers need to be ready for surprises. The cases are descriptive in the sense that they provide a partial but permanent record of relevant events in an individual's academic life over a certain period. The cases are explanatory in that they offer evidence which may verify, modify or reject hypotheses as to what really counts in the process of putting together an acceptable document *within* a broadly rhetorical universe of discourse. We may learn from a case whether any contextual factors (health, money, time, educational preparation, alienation, etc.) have strongly affected the outcome. And, after we have calibrated any such factors, we may examine residual predisposing traits for rhetorical success or failure.

Case study A: Salwa (not her real name)

Salwa is an Egyptian fish biologist who entered a doctoral program at a major US university in January 1985, having previously completed an M.Sc. at another institution in the US. She was awarded a Ph.D. in December 1988 and returned to Egypt in March 1989. Salwa's dissertation was on fish farming practices in her home country. As she says:

> There were no sufficient data recorded. Therefore I had to collect the data by myself, by interviews. It was a very hard and tough work.

On her return to the US with her data, she then encountered major problems in data analysis largely brought about by 'incompatible computer packages'. In the first half of 1988 – partly during the time when she was attending a dissertation writing course – Salwa experienced serious problems with the structure of her dissertation. She used three very different methodologies/models in her work. In introducing each she felt that she needed to give the reader some background since, as she put it, 'the reader might forget'. As a result, the draft chapters had a repetitious, recycling character that found little favor with her committee. As her advisor caustically observed to me in a later interview, 'we didn't need to read all this stuff that we'd seen a hundred times before'.

Salwa is a confident and determined person and, in consequence, the advisor and the relevant English language staff had to work hard to convince her that she should not assume that her committee comprised a bunch of inattentive loafers who needed to be continuously reminded of basic facts and principles. Eventually, a lean and tight version emerged.

She sailed through her defense, except that the committee required that her final recommendations be recast in a way that would be less abrasive to her co-nationals. It was perhaps a sign of Salwa's growing sense of her own research discourse community that two weeks after the defense she began to accept that some 'political' revision of her recommendations was both necessary and wise.

According to her advisor, Salwa entered the doctoral program as an average student but exited as a very good one. Although the advisor believes that Salwa has done exceptionally well, he is guarded and cautious about her future career. Salwa has returned to a specialized Aquaculture Institute situated some 50 miles outside Cairo, where she works with a small group of other Egyptians who also have Ph.Ds. Despite the opportunity that this select working environment provides, the advisor feels that her role may be that of a local change agent rather than an international researcher. He notes that she hasn't published much yet and 'is a bit old: in this game you need to start publishing in your late twenties'. He also believes that Salwa's biggest weakness remains her writing, and to achieve publication, writing that is 'pretty good isn't good enough'.

So let us consider Salwa's writing. Salwa stayed on after her dissertation for three to four months to give a successful paper at an international conference on Aquaculture and to try and place two or three articles based on her dissertation in good journals, her advisor being the second author. The first draft of the introduction to one of these is presented in Figure 19.

Although working with Salwa produced quite a number of changes to this draft, the major problems were identified as occurring in the opening sentence of each paragraph, labeled (a) and (b) in Figure 19. (a) has an explanatory textbook quality about it unlikely to go down well with the expert readers of a specialized journal. It is the kind of opening prone to engender among such readers comments like, 'Wow, no kidding'. The remedy, we decided, was to switch the proposition from *new* information to *old* information, from *foreground* to *background*, by inserting 'are known to be':

a1) In aquaculture, the relations among nutrients, stocking rate, water quality and weather are known to be complex.

At first sight, the change looks like a simple piece of editing. However, for Salwa to come to see the rationale for the change was for her to begin the process of moving from dissertation to research article and concomitantly, from apprentice to peer.

The opening sentence of the second paragraph in the draft (b) is not so much easy to misinterpret as hard to interpret at all. Is it a local illustration of the immediately previous literature discussion? Is it,

---

Introduction (original)

a) In aquaculture, the relation among nutrients, stocking rate, water quality and weather are complex.[1] Although nutrients are used to increase primary production, primary production may not correlate well with fish growth (Olahi, 1986). Although stocking rate is important, the stocking rate for maximum production and the best combination of species for a given farm are often determined through experience (Shang, 1981). Variation between different regions and between different farms within the same region make it difficult to predict fish yield from a given type and level of culture. Variability results from interaction between biological and physical factors. An equation has not been developed to calculate yield for different types of fish reared in different waters and even logistic curve between primary production and fish production developed by Liang et al. (1981) cannot predict for different management levels (Olahi, 1986).

b) In Egypt there is no difference in fish yield between farms that use high quantities of nutrients as supplemental feed, as organic and inorganic fertilizer, that add moderate amounts or no nutrients at all.[1] The objective of this study was to examine the relationship between different input variables and fish yield and to identify the most important input variables. In addition a comparison between farms of different investment types, culture levels, sizes, and location was done to identify the most efficient type of farm. This analysis was done using simple and multiple linear regression.

Figure 19   Draft introduction to a RA

however misplaced, a conclusion? Is it a thesis statement? Of course, Salwa meant none of these – she meant it as the problem statement that would motivate her study. The difficulty was that there were no contextual or metadiscoursal signals showing that was what it was. Again the editing work was superficially minor:

b)   In Egypt there is no great difference in fish yield between ...
b1) Recent data from Egypt apparently indicates that there is no great difference in fish yield between ...

The larger lesson concerned Salwa's approach to article preparation. Like those of many others, her draft was insufficiently 'pointed' (Williams, 1985); it lacked metadiscoursal signals (Beavais, 1989); it was characterized by 'blurred text' (James, 1984a). These were not, in fact, characteristics of the dissertation chapters themselves, but in Salwa's efforts to encapsulate findings for short journal articles, she had emphasized content and disregarded the need to keep the readership aware of what was going on. The larger lesson therefore was a new awareness of the perils of such disregard.

As we have seen, Salwa is so far a success; after all, she obtained a Ph.D. in under four years despite uncertain funding and having with her in the US a child who had a chronic illness. Although part of her success is clearly due to her advisor who, among other things, went over the drafts of her dissertation three times, much more is due to Salwa herself. Salwa's great asset is a combination of confidence, persistence, inter-personal and managerial skills. She had a clear plan and a determination to carry it out. I saw this strong sense of agenda in the data collection, in the analysis and in the write-up. Others, as was revealed in the discussion of the drafting process, have to convince *her* that the plan is wrong, for the plan is ultimately hers.

Salwa has plans for the future too. Her staying on in the US was part of the plan, as was her desire to keep contact with her advisor, and her intention to find funds to visit the US for short research visits every two years or so. A relatively new addition to the plan has been her efforts to continue to get help with her written English after she returned to Egypt. Another new part of the plan has been her recent serious reflection on how she is going to interact with her Egyptian colleagues, including such matters as joint publication. The white-hot reformist of the dissertation period has cooled into a diplomatic co-worker.

A particular reason for choosing Salwa as the first case is the fact that Salwa's return journey to the Third World is one experienced by many in the field. She, as a promising researcher, will doubtless experience the well-documented trials and tribulations of re-entry shock. Geertz (1983) comments on the 'exile from paradise' syndrome whereby graduated doctoral students in the US fan out from a smallish number of privileged research institutions to take up positions in smaller and more geo-graphically and intellectually isolated places. The move back to the Third World is, for all its re-connection with place, culture and family, an intellectual dislocation that more properly merits the term 'exile'. Is Salwa prepared? In many ways perhaps, but not as well as we might like in those areas that are most obviously our responsibility. Like many others, she *commands* (in the fullest sense) no research language. She has done very little technical writing in Arabic and now certainly prefers to write in English. She appreciates English scientific rhetoric for what she believes to be its explicitness and straightforwardness and for its attempt to take the anticipated readership into account. She is aware too that the English-language readership for her work will be larger, more inter-national, more judgmental and more important.

A second reason for discussing Salwa's case in some detail lies in the fact that it is itself open-ended. Although an important chapter in Salwa's research career closed in the spring of 1989, another important chapter has begun. If Salwa's story is going to contribute to what we know about being a non-anglophone researcher in the Third World (6.2) the case study needs to continue. Will her advisor's doubts be confirmed? Will Salwa's determination, in perhaps even more difficult circumstances, carry her through? Have those who have been concerned with Salwa's academic writing and speaking done enough?

Case study B: Hsin

Hsin comes from the People's Republic of China and entered the United States in 1982. He joined the graduate Economics program at a large US university in Fall 1984. During his second, third and fourth years there he was a teaching assistant (TA): as he was often given different TA assignments, these changes, according to Hsin, 'really slowed my pace of studies'. In his final year (1988–9) he was awarded a University Dissertation Fellowship, a highly competitive award given to those who promise outstanding dissertations. Hsin is thought to be something of a 'star', especially among more junior oriental students in the department. They say, as he does, that he is very strong in logic and has good quantitative skills. His chosen area is Comparative International Economics, where he has been attempting to develop a more comprehensive mathematical model than hitherto available.

To those of us in the English Language Institute Hsin doesn't look much like a star student, but he has become well known to us since 1987. He has taken several of our courses and is a regular at both our Speaking and Writing Clinics. Hsin's attempts to master the English language have been marked by determination but not by any obvious language aptitude, and he ascribes his disappointing progress to his age (middle thirties). An interesting aspect of Hsin's career at his present institution is the fact that he exercised an option to seek professional help with his English rather late. In his third year (when his TA assignment switched from board work on statistical problems to actually teaching Principles of Economics) he belatedly decided to make an assault on his pronunciation. As he tellingly observed, 'people do not worry about their pronunciation until they start to teach'.

Hsin participated in the same advanced writing class as Salwa in the first four months of 1988. That experience, in my view, brought two things home to Hsin. One was that many of his peers in the class were more natural writers in English than he was. The second was that if he hoped to enter the discourse community of US academic economists (as certainly was his short-term hope) his energetic activities on behalf of several organizations such as The Society for Young China Economists would have to be matched by rhetorical skills which US experts in the community would deem as appropriately focused. He recognized that he needed to understand better what those expert members were looking for (apart from being able to appreciate his pretty formalisms).

The intersection of these two perceptions persuaded Hsin that the academic letter-writing component of the course could make a particular contribution to his success. He needed to write a lot of letters in any case as he put himself on the job market; letters were relatively short; they contained genre-specific phraseologies; they tended to highlight rhetorical choices and the effects of these on the intended audience (and the instructor could serve as a sounding board for the 'real' readership). Hsin took upon himself the task of trying to master the key genres in academic letter-writing.

As the latest of Hsin's letters to hand at the time of writing appears to demonstrate, the strategy was successful:

> Dear Professor *Jones:
>
> I am pleased to accept your offer of the tenure-track assistant professor position starting from September 25, 1989.[1] I know I will enjoy working with you and other colleagues and will do my best to bring credits to our department, in terms of both research and teaching.[2]
>
> I will drive down sometime and discuss the preparation of the classes with you.[3] Meanwhile, I will start to look for an apartment or a house for lease from anytime in August.[4] Please let me know if you have some information about houses available.[5]
>
> Looking forward to meeting you again.[6]
>
> > Yours,
> >
> > Gene *Wang

* not their real names

(Sentence numbers added)

Hsin, as is now his custom, is very anxious about the impression his writing makes. But by now he is in fact usually well able to answer his own queries. In S2 he wanted to know whether 'enjoy' was appropriate and whether 'looking forward to' would be better – the tricky grammar of which he knew about – as S6 demonstrates. Should S3 be more specific? Was S5 making a reasonable request? But today he can second-guess these questions as well as I can. Genuine questions arising out of puzzlement have been replaced by pseudo-questions asking for confirmation. He didn't in fact raise a question about his use of 'our department' towards the end of S2; if asked I would have said I wouldn't have used it myself, but that I liked its heartwarming enthusiasm and spontaneity – its confident assumption of group membership. Only later did I realize that his first name, which had been 'Hsin' at least until a letter of February 3rd, had suddenly become Americanized into 'Gene'. A new life – a new name.

By the summer of 1989, Gene was writing drafts of the final two chapters of his dissertation. It is my impression that they show increasing understanding of his select group of readers. Knowledge claims themselves as well as metadiscoursal discussion of them seem better integrated into the expectations of the discourse community. It is possible that this new sense of appropriate discourse has been partly fueled by his attention to audience effects in letter-writing genres. The theoretical implications of such a possibility are taken up in Chapter 11.

Case study C: Ali (not his real name)

Ali is an Iranian who in 1988 and 1989 had become the major writer for a small research team, whose other members consisted of a senior professor in Engineering, a senior US technician, and an American graduate student, who also worked for a company. On their projects the writing gets done by Ali and the professor. In the documents I have seen, Ali's name usually comes first, then the professor and then the other two US members. Ali got to be the writer because neither of his junior colleagues wanted to do it; he also reckoned in this way he would 'learn to put (my) technical thoughts better on paper'. Ali's English is still pretty shaky; his grammar is highly erratic and his spelling directly dependent on a spelling checker. Intensive practice in a highly specific area has, however, led to a considerable narrow-band proficiency. He wrote in a questionnaire completed in February 1989:

> I am much more comfortable in research writing and it takes much less time to write than April '88. The reasons for that are: practice and reading research papers and look for writing styles as well as content.

All the evidence, including two conversations between us, indicates that the professor is one of those engineers who is very aware of the value of high-level communication skills. Ali, who clearly admires him greatly, says that the professor knows exactly what to emphasize.

The part of the case I shall deal with relates to events early in the summer of 1988. The team were planning to submit a 600-word abstract (plus drawings) to the major biennial conference on 'Sensors'. The field is technologically important and one sign of its perceived importance is the high level of Federal interest and involvement. As a result, the biennial conference constitutes a crucial opportunity for researchers to showcase their work, but competition is tough: only 64 abstracts are accepted.

The first three drafts were written by the junior members, but in each case the main author was Ali.

Draft 3 (opening paragraph)

Present measurement and automated control systems need to have sensors with higher reliability and accuracy than is practical with discrete and isolated components.[1] In addition, issues such as cost optimization of testing, packaging, and interfacing with higher level control systems have provided the motivations to change microsensors from 'isolated components' to 'integrated system elements'.[2] This paper describes the design of an addressable VLSI smart sensor capable of handling up to eight sensors with 12 bit accuracy, introduces a custom designed bus, and describes a new method for data compensation.[3]

Although we were not sure whether there was not, after all, something missing between sentences 2 and 3 (some kind of step 2 transition from the general to the particular), the deadline was approaching. The junior members submitted the full abstract – of which we have only seen the opening paragraph – to the professor. Although the professor kept much of the later material, he totally rewrote the opening paragraph:

Draft 4 (submitted copy)

As integrated transducers are combined with increasing amounts of on-chip or in-module circuitry, where to partition the electronic system and how much electronics to include with the 'sensor' become major issues. Integrated sensors, particularly those associated with automated manufacturing, are likely to evolve into smart peripherals, and the definition of appropriate sensor interface standards is currently the subject of at least three national committees. This paper describes a possible organization for such devices and appropriate interface protocols. The device described is addressable, programmable, self-testing, compatible with a bidirectional digital sensor bus, and offers 12-bit accuracy using internally-stored compensation coefficients. The design is sufficiently flexible to allow upward-compatible sensor designs to be inserted in existing equipment without reprogramming the host system and will accommodate differing sensor features.

Even a cursory comparison of drafts 3 and 4 shows that the former's narrow world of technical problem-solving in the laboratory has been replaced by a confident risk-taking sweep across the field as a whole. Draft 4 asseverates that as certain things develop so certain questions 'become major issues'. There are 'likely' evolutions and, in this rapidly moving research front, the definition of standards 'is currently the subject of at least three national committees' – the latter observation being, of course, a pretty strong *centrality claim* (see 7.4).

In this situation, the research team now offers a strongly-hedged 'possible' organization for the needed devices, but one, as the opening paragraph goes on to explain, with many attractive features. We can also see that the static frozen-in-time character of the earlier drafts has been converted into a dynamic contemporary history in which the authors, as protagonists, have a significant role to play.

As an intermittent participant–observer in this story, I remain struck by the fact that only highly 'expert' members of specialized discourse communities possess a vision that allows them to evaluate explicitly and with conviction the state of the art in their own discourse communities. So there are certain limits to what we can do and hence areas where we should fear to tread. However, these limits remain quite circumscribed, especially when we remember the size and variety of the English-language-using population of researchers and aspiring researchers spread across the world, and the range of texts, both spoken and written, that they need to produce.

Finally, the episode I have recounted has a coda. The abstract was one of the 64 accepted; in fact rather more than that, because for this particular conference it is the evaluators' custom to rank the submissions numerically. The document submitted was placed third – proof, if any is needed, of its final quality.

General comments

Despite their diversity, the three case studies broadly suggest similar kinds of conclusion. For one thing, all three reinforce the relevance of discourse communities. Salwa has begun to move away from anticipating the expectations of her doctoral committee towards those of the wider grouping of her co-specialists, while, at the same time she has been preparing to negotiate the concerns of her co-nationals. Gene has followed a different path towards recognizing subtle differences in audience. He established his credentials as an employable assistant professor in his host country and has used the insights gained in that process to renegotiate his knowledge claims for the peer research community. Ali, who only obtained his Master's degree in the summer of 1989, has further to go, but his close involvement in the work of an important mentor is beginning to provide models of communicative behavior over and above those required for in-group technical progress reports.

The case descriptions also show how all three students owe at least part of their success to the *proactive* measures they have taken. Salwa tried to commit all around her to follow her plan, Gene exploited the opportunity provided by training in academic letter-writing, and Ali pushed himself forward as the draft writer of his research group. I do not think the important role of these initiatives, not to speak of their very existence, could easily have been predicted at the outset of the studies.

Furthermore, the cases also indicate, positively in the case of Salwa and Gene, more neutrally in the case of Ali, the value of rhetorical perception in general and, more specifically, the benefit of being able to 'second-guess' how expert members of various discourse communities will react to particular writings. This issue of rhetorical awareness is the topic of the following section.

9.2   Rhetorical consciousness – course content

One tentative conclusion to be drawn from the sample of case studies in 9.1 is that there may be pedagogical value in sensitizing students to rhetorical effects, and to the rhetorical structures that tend to recur in genre-specific texts. There is, of course, nothing new in this. The following statements are representative: 'in-depth comprehension of a written academic text depends on the reader's ability to perceive the notional blocs that comprise a text and the hierarchical relationships that conceptually align them' (Blanton, 1984); 'a knowledge of the rhetorical divisions of an experimental-research paper and the function of those divisions within the paper greatly enhances ESL student reading and writing skills' (Hill et al., 1982). It would seem then that formal schemata (Chapter 5) need to be activated and developed, not so much as rigid templates against which all texts are forced to fit, but more as *caricatures* which self-evidently simplify and distort certain features in an attempt to capture general identity. At this point it may be objected that features of organization such as the IMRD pattern are too well known to be worth dealing with. Even if this is so, the concession is a small one. We can still recognize that students are helped if they can also schematize the structures of the sections themselves and so further develop an understanding of what it is that allows them to recognize a section as Method or Discussion, and what it is that allows them to argue that one section is more or less effective than another. It is likely that consciousness-raising about text-structure will turn out to be as important as it has been shown to be for grammar (e.g. Rutherford and Sharwood Smith, 1988).

Part of the reason for stressing text consciousness-raising stems from a long-standing particular experience. For several years now, I have presented various groups with the following seven sentences and title of a scientific introduction (Figure 20) on eight small slips of paper, and asked them to reassemble them into the original order (Swales, 1984b).

The task, which is usually done in pairs, has been given to NS and NNS undergraduate and graduate students in class and to numerous instructors and colleagues in workshops and presentations. Of the 250 or so pairs that have attempted the task, to date fewer than 10 have fully succeeded. How can this be? Given the composition of the groups, the consistent failure can hardly be due to low proficiency in the English language or to weakness in intellect; nor has anybody seriously argued in the ensuing discussion that the seven-sentence introduction is somehow not a properly-formed text; and very few have complained that the subject matter was too abstruse and technical that no general understanding of the argument was possible. The only remaining explanation for the unexpected difficulty of the task is that those attempting it could not call upon useful expectations as to how the introduction might be rhetorically constructed. It was not so much the case that participants in the little experiment had no schema, but that they had a *wrong* one: most strikingly, they consistently underestimated the amount of rhetorical work that the authors had done *before* they announced their own research program.

---

1. Nevertheless more experimental data are required and in particular it would seem desirable to make experiments on glassy samples whose properties can be varied slightly from one to the other.

2. The thermal conductivity has a plateau which is usually in the range 5 to 10K and below this temperature it has a temperature dependence which varies approximately as T^2.

3. Some progress has been made towards understanding the thermal behaviour by assuming that there is a cut-off in the photon spectrum at high frequencies (Zaitlin and Anderson, 1975a, b) and that there is an additional system of low-lying two-level states (Anderson et al., 1972; Phillips, 1972).

4. The specific heat below 4K is much larger than that which would be expected from the Debye theory and it often has an additional term which is proportional to T.

5. The present investigation reports attempts to do this by using various samples of the same epoxy resin which have been subjected to different curing cycles.

6. The thermal properties of glassy materials at low temperatures are still not completely understood.

7. THE THERMAL CONDUCTIVITY AND SPECIFIC HEAT OF EPOXY RESIN FROM 0.1 TO 80K.

8. Measurements of the specific heat (or the diffusivity) and the thermal conductivity have been taken in the temperature range 0.1 to 80K for a set of specimens which covered up to nine different curing cycles.

(original order: 7–6–2–4–3–1–5–8)

(from S. Kelham and H. H. Rosenburgh. 1981. *J. Phys. C : Solid State Physics* 14)

Figure 20   A scrambled introduction from a RA

In general terms, the advantages which derive from introducing rhetorical structure as a central element in a course are several:

1. The problem of heterogeneous content interests in the class (medics and economists) is partially if temporarily sidestepped.
2. Insight into rhetorical structure is useful for both the reading and the writing of research.
3. General features are examined before specific details.
4. Discussion of rhetorical structure usefully develops in participants an increasing control of the metalanguage (negotiation of knowledge claims, self-citation, metadiscourse, etc.) which, in turn, provides a perspective for critiquing their own writing and that of others.
5. Rhetorical structure may have 'novelty' value, and may thus identify the class as being different from others that participants have experienced.
6. The rhetorical element is likely to present the instructor as having something to contribute over and above methodology.

Almost inevitably, however, there will come a point in either the planning or execution of a *research-process* course when the 'problem' of content begins to loom large. Both the 'problem' and its possible solution are somewhat different according to whether the class is made up of students from a narrow or broad range of disciplines. If the class is homogeneous in disciplinary interest the instructor is now faced with having to address in some way the literature from their specialist area.

At first sight, the problem is a daunting one. Spack (1988b), for instance, presents the dilemma as follows: 'The teaching of rhetoric cannot be divorced from the teaching of content, and therefore English faculty who have little or no knowledge of a discipline cannot adequately teach or respond to discipline-specific writing' (1988:703). However, Spack's premise is open to various interpretations. Certainly if 'the teaching of rhetoric' is literally understood as, for example, 'How to write a good lab report in chemistry', she may well be right. But that is certainly not the kind of teaching advocated in this book or proposed by most supporters of the WAC and EAP movements. Rather, as the immediately preceding pages show as well as any others, the 'teaching' has been one of consciousness-raising, of discussing texts, and of offering – to the best of our abilities – prototypical examples of relevant genres. Much of our teaching then is directed to getting students to understand how and why discourse is important, to getting them to see 'that "sounding right" is the key to admittance' (Ronald, 1988: 133). Spack therefore offers us a very conservative view. Further, as Johns observes, 'It encourages us to withdraw from the academic fray at a time when the WAC movement, amongst other factors, has opened up new possibilities for joint research with faculty and creative approaches to EAP courses' (1988c: 707).

Entering the academic fray would seem to require above all an open mind; a willingness to adopt Wittgenstein's maxim of 'Don't think, but look'. A second valuable characteristic is being able to project a sense of professional purpose. There is much anecdotal evidence to suggest that colleagues from other discourse communities are both surprised and impressed when the English instructor arrives armed with lines of inquiry that show sensitivity to possible pressures on that community's central genres. In my own recent discussions with doctoral advisors, for example, I am sure something has been gained by my starting with questions about the program's views on the need either to reform the Ph.D. dissertation or to bring its changing character 'out of the closet' (Reid, 1978; Halstead, 1988). If I am right about the benefits of professionalism, then a professional approach would seem to depend, to a greater rather than lesser extent, on being able to call upon the relevant literature. Some of that literature is, I hope, contained in this volume.

While the discipline-specific class provides a *rhetorical* challenge to the instructor, the multi-disciplinary group offers more of a *managerial* problem. There would seem to be two main but complementary ways of rising to this latter challenge. One is to recognize that heterogeneity in fact offers opportunities for genuine discussion and information exchange as part of a task-based methodology; the other is to search for areas of common interest. The first approach typically relies on students supplying their own texts – for instance, short RAs from their own fields and which they have some motive for reading. An appropriate methodology is the 1–2–4–8–16 system for group discussion pioneered at the British Open University by Gibbs (1977). For a class of 16 or so graduate students coming from a wide range of schools and faculties within the university, it could work something like Figure 21.

Often the procedure works well, although of course it is not often that the numbers work out exactly right – and I dare say that the reader has already noticed that the activity itself provides a basis for the group *writing* of a short RA with some such title as 'Cross-disciplinary similarity and difference in the research article: a pilot study of rhetorical structure'.

Alternatively or additionally, the instructor may search for a common denominator. One area worth exploring is research into higher education if only because *all* participants in the course will be currently engaged in that process. Therefore, it may well be possible to find appropriate texts dealing with such topics as completion rates of Ph.Ds, the effectiveness of various lecturing styles and so on. A second area of common concern is the language and rhetoric of research-process genres themselves. Instructors, for example, may find their classes willing to work on such texts as

Step 1	A range of analytic tasks are set (section headings or not? macro-structure? relative size of main sections: reasons for this?).
Step 2	Each individual analyzes his/her own RA.
Step 3	Students in the same or very close disciplines are paired and note similarities and differences between the two papers.
Step 4	The pairs join pairs in allied disciplines, and similarities and differences among the four papers are noted.
Step 5	Groups of eight (plus or minus one or two) with broader but shared interests (e.g. the social scientist) are then aggregated and the same process gone through.
Step 6	Plenary session with representatives of each octet giving their findings; ensuing discussion.
Step 7	Summing-up by the instructor.

Figure 21   Task organization in multi-disciplinary settings

an abridged version of West (1980), which has a straightforward hypothesis, is clear in method, and applies statistical tests to the results. A third possibility is to utilize that part of the scientometric literature which examines the language variable, as I attempted to show at the end of 6.2.

9.3   Alternative uses of discourse community

The first two orientations have revealed a strong allegiance to the concept of genre, the third does so to the concept of discourse community. It recognizes that the slow process of ethnographic investigation produces more surprises than we could reasonably assume. And if that is the case, then areas that we cannot investigate through lack of time or low priority may also be, in reality, somewhat different to how they appear even to the educationally experienced eye. Ramani et al. (1988) investigated the Centre for Electronic Design Technology at the prestigious Indian Institute of Science at Bangalore. She and her co-workers found that the centre required of its students a much more elaborate series of documents than officially stated, each being 'linked to a definite stage in the R & D process' (Ramani, 1988:86). In contrast, Swales (1980) describes how a Geology Department in Africa, in its frustration with the students' inadequate command of written English, had secretly and with the connivance of the graduating students altered its grading policy so that the written field report component of the major field trip only counted for 10% of the final grade, instead of the official 50%. In both contexts, determining the real role of writing – and the reasons for that role – involved a considerable amount of work.

The surprises thrown up by such investigations cast some sort of pall over the English instructor's vision of a neat and officially-ordered academic culture. One imaginative way of avoiding such ethno-induced *angst* has been pioneered by Johns (Johns, 1988a and b; 1990). Although her work has largely been concerned with initiating ESD (English as a Second Dialect) and ESL first year students into the university world, a similar approach has been used by Ronald (1988) with advanced NS undergraduates entering more specialized discourse communities, and its value for graduates will become apparent.

Johns enjoins us to admit that, notwithstanding very considerable investigative effort, we still have difficulty in identifying those linguistic and rhetorical skills that are usefully transferable to a range of academic contexts, and separating such skills from those that are only needed in narrow disciplinary situations. She then reminds us that instructors are 'tribal chieftains' and run their classes in their own personal and often idiosyncratic ways. Even so, she argues, the consequences which follow from conceding that there may be a distinctive ethos to every class or that transferability is hard to determine can be turned around to our advantage. In particular, these consequences persuade us that we can help our students to *become* ethnographers themselves. By doing so, we can help students penetrate beyond what they may perceive as a *unidimensional* facade of institutional role and educational process. Johns' students describe and discuss the roles they and the instructors play in their content classes, the main topics and how they inter-relate, the specific writing conventions and expectations as they perceive them, the agenda of assignments (Horowitz, 1986b; Johns, 1986), and anything else that seems to them germane. In such ways, they are learning *transferable* skills of ethnographic analysis: further, in learning to analyze participant roles and sociorhetorical conventions they are preparing to survive the *rites de passage* of new discourse communities. At a more advanced level, graduate students need to learn to work within the value-systems of their target communities, or – to take a more specific example – they need to come to recognize points of contact and points of separation among the research agendas of their advisors and themselves.

Ronald (1988) stresses the importance of persuading her senior undergraduates to distance themselves from their professional discourse communities so that they create for themselves 'an opportunity to learn about the nature of language and community' (1988:147). With such students there may be less need to involve them in reflecting upon their immediately important classes. In my own case I encourage the juniors and seniors taking a writing-intensive discourse analysis course to 'drop in out of the blue' on some ongoing class and write up what they see and hear as a *mini-ethnography*. As preparation we read and discuss certain papers on university lecture discourse such as Rounds (1987) on pronoun use, McKenna (1987) on student questions, or Bailey (1984) on teaching assistant profiles. The first extract shows a student being aware of the first of these topics:

> At 1:54, the fourth and final episode began. This was the conclusion. First he summarized the material *talked about* in lecture. Next, he previewed the rest of the week. During this segment of the conclusion, I noticed that three different pronouns were used. He first stated 'Next time we're going to ... ' This soon changed into 'I will teach ... ' Finally, 'You will use ... ' This shift seemed to work effectively in his explanation of the next class. It was precise and to the point, telling exactly what would be done by the class (including the instructor), by the instructor, and by the class (excluding the instructor). Finally, he answered any final questions the students had. At 1.59 the instructor finished his conclusion. The students gathered up their books.

The second fragment is from a 'drop-in' description of a Mathematics class being given by an oriental teaching assistant. It shows demonstrable acuity of observation:

> Now he began to focus on the new material. Through diagrams and example problems, he tried to direct the class on the new material. At this point, he noticed a puzzled look on a student's face and went over the just introduced information again. It was here, in the third episode, that he first noticed I was taking notes on his performance, not the mathematics. I was surprised that it took him twenty five minutes to realize I didn't belong in this class. Obviously, this TA did not develop a personal relationship with his students. He did not call on any by name throughout the entire class period. After noticing what I was doing, he spoke louder and tried to keep his English more clear.

The final extract relates to a previous class discussion as to whether peripatetic instructors consistently deliver *main* discourse from 'center-stage' and *subsidiary* discourse from 'the wings'.

> With about ten minutes left to go in the class, Professor .... takes several steps to his left to leave his post of authority. He goes on to explain that he gave a wrong formula during last week's lecture. The subject was brought up because he was using the same formula in today's lecture. It is interesting to note that the only time he left his symbolic power post was to explain his mistake.

These three very short extracts, perhaps especially the last, would seem to reveal two things. One is that many students are, with a little prompting as to what to look for, very good at this kind of mini-ethnography. The second follows from the first: the actual findings can be valuable for the instructors and, on occasion at least, are worth incorporating in the public record. The last student's commentary on mistake-explaining behavior is worth some sort of follow-up.

9.4   Reflections on the 'process' approach to writing

As the importance of *process* in writing is now well established in both the L1 and L2 fields, it is no longer necessary to review the basic arguments, except perhaps to reiterate that nearly all writing in research-process genres is recursive (as 7.2 was at pains to establish) and also heuristic (i.e. the process itself leads to further insights and connections over and above those previously residing in notes or in thoughts). However, at this juncture I would like to inject a certain note of caution. Certainly, it would be unwise to neglect the internal aspects of composing such as developing pre-writing and invention strategies, fostering apprentices' awareness of their own writing processes, inculcating the value of redrafting and encouraging selection of topics of personal interest (Raimes, 1983; Spack, 1984; Zamel, 1983; Hamp-Lyons, 1986). And yet, as I have earlier argued, the increased self-confidence and sensitivity that may accrue are not themselves sufficient for the acquisition of genre skills. Davies (1988) is surely right when she observes that a crucial condition for success in writing courses is that the students 'will need a working environment in which they can be confident that their efforts will be respected' (1988:16–17). It does not follow, however, that such respect is only possible in strongly humanistic environments or when the students are protected from the exigencies of external criteria for evaluating their written products (i.e. in 'soft' process). And if that is so, a process orientation towards genre acquisition needs to pay at least equal attention to the external determinants of composing (Horowitz, 1986b; Widdowson, 1983a and b), for here the emphasis is less on the cognitive relationship between the writer and the writer's internal world and more on the relationship between the writer and on his or her ways of anticipating and countenancing the reactions of the intended readership (i.e. 'hard' process).

An interesting issue for what I might advocate as a 'hard' process orientation is the use of 'reformulation' (Cohen, 1983; Allwright et al., 1988). According to Allwright et al. it works like this: a class is set a common writing task; one student product is passed to a native-speaker colleague who rewrites it in such a way that the reformulation tries to be faithful to the original writer's probable intentions; typed versions of the original and the reformulation are then distributed and form the basis of a class discussion focusing on the likely reasons for and effects of the alterations that the NS academic has made. As Allwright et al. maintain, the main value of the technique lies in the discussion rather than in the reformulation *per se*. However, in a genre-based approach it is possible to conceive of useful modifications of the technique. One is to relax the constraint that the reformulator should be someone other than the writing instructor; indeed, it can be particularly valuable to have more than one reformulation of a particular piece. While it is true that the presence of the instructor's reformulation may cause it to become (at least audibly) over-privileged in the minds of the class, it also provides an opportunity for the class to extract from the instructor something of the *processes* that led to the changes. Secondly, there is merit in searching for reformulators who are experts in the field. In this way, a class can compare apprentice texts (both NS or NNS), writing instructor texts and those reworked by full members of the relevant discourse communities. Although, of course, under certain WAC arrangements, the latter two may be constituted by the same individual.

10 *Exhibits*

The purpose of this penultimate chapter is essentially two-fold. It deals with certain aspects of academic genres which have so far been little considered: titles, suggestions for further research, and course descriptions. In that sense, I have tried to offer something new on the descriptive level. However, I have also endeavored to deal with the topics in such a way that they represent pedagogical activities. For want of a bolder term, I have simply called the sections 'Exhibits'. The exhibits vary somewhat in the amount of accompanying commentary, in their concern for the non-native speaker of English, and in the degree to which they offer material that could be directly used in class.

Exhibit A: Titles

We know from studies such as Bazerman (1985) that academics use article titles as an early decision point in deciding to read no further. Partly for that reason, it comes as little surprise that composing the few words of a title can take up an inordinate amount of time, discussion and mental effort. And even then things can go wrong. I have a biologist acquaintance who now languishes in unsatisfactory semi-employment principally because, or so he believes, he failed to recognize the humorous effects of the titles of his first two publications: 'Some British Pansies' followed by 'An irruption of tits in Norfolk'. And what are we to make of the following?

> J. Hartley and R. L. Mills. 1973. Unjustified experiments in typological research and instructional design. *British Journal of Educational Technology* 2: 120–31.

One class activity therefore could be the repair of unfortunate titles. Another is to rework titles so that their implied research space is either expanded or contracted by the subtraction or addition of 'hedges' (cf. Skelton, 1988). We could take an original title such as, 'On the structure of scientific texts' (Hutchins, 1977). What, we may ask, will be the effects of the following variations:

1. On the structure of scientific text;
2. The structure of scientific texts;
3. Aspects of the structure of scientific text;
4. A preliminary analysis of aspects of scientific text structure.

We can make use of Dudley-Evans (1984:44) in which he describes the processes whereby Master's theses titles become finalized in a team-taught Plant Genetics class. Here is an example:

Student – first attempt: *Evaluation of beet collected in Algeria.*

First comment from subject lecturer:	*Evaluation* is a vague term. It means different things to different people. The external examiner is an agronomist and might see the 'evaluation' as being from the point of view of agronomy. So we need to know which aspects you are dealing with.
Student:	The taxonomic aspects.
Language teacher:	I suggest adding *with special reference to its taxonomy.*
Subject lecturer:	The method also needs to be stated.
Final suggestion:	*Characterization and principal components analysis of beet collected from Algeria.*

This kind of prompt (and videotape is even better) can encourage class participants to reflect on their own processes of title formation, to discuss what they consider to have been their successes and failures, and to exchange ideas about what they consider to be 'typical' titles for their own fields. (Parodies are always another possibility.)

Finally, we might also recognize that there may be *national* rather than disciplinary propensities operating in this area. The following light-hearted fancy is adapted from James (1980):

> A famous university decided to establish an endowed professorship in Elephantology. It carried out an international search and invited the five finalists to visit the university and each give a scholarly presentation. As it happened the five finalists were all of different nationalities: American, British, French, German and Spanish. Who gave which paper?
>
> 1. The Elephanticity of the elephant.
>
> 2. A regression analysis of patterns of elephant feeding behavior under two controlled experimental conditions.
>
> 3. Ecological implications of troop movements among the Elephants of South Somalia: Findings from three case studies.

4. Structural Semantics and the Love-Making of Elephants: a dialectical approach.

5. A Prolegomena to a taxonomy of types of Elephant tusks.

Titles consist of only a few words, but they are serious stuff. They can also be fun. Getting students to work with titles, including their reactions to them, is under-recognized as an entertaining and enlightening set of rhetorical tasks.

Exhibit B: Suggestions for further research

The next exhibit is somewhat more elaborated as the NNS class is cast first in the role of informants, then as discussants of a research presentation and finally as researchers themselves. After a simple explanation of *inanimate subject* (e.g. 'this paper') and *animate verb* (e.g. 'examines'), Figure 22 is distributed.

The results of the questionnaire are then used (a) to generate prepared class discussion and (b) to give participants an opportunity for writing a

---

It would help us in our research if you could complete the following task. Read carefully the sentences below. Note that each has an inanimate subject followed by an animate verb. Ask yourself in each case whether that subject–verb combination is possible in your own first language. If it is possible (and natural) mark the sentence with a Y; if it is impossible (or unnatural) mark the sentence with an N. If it is somewhere in between mark it with a ?

1. This paper analyzes the results of ....
2. This paper describes the interactions of ....
3. This paper proposes a new analysis of ....
4. This paper takes the view that ....
5. This paper defends the use of ....
6. The results confirm the hypothesis ....
7. The data support Boyle's Law ....
8. The experiment involves the determination of ....
9. This method can identify the differing factors ....
10. The Periodic Table arranges the elements in order of increasing atomic number ....

Name ....
First language ....

Thank you for your assistance.

Figure 22   Student questionnaire

paragraph or two dealing with 'suggestions for further research'. The instructor collects the questionnaires, analyzes the results and constructs an appropriate write-up of the Results and Discussion sections. My own version follows as Figure 23: blanks have been left for preposition completion as a minor enabling task.

Results

The task illustrated .... page 45 of the course pack was administered .... ELI 320 in Fall 1987 and to ELI 313 in Fall 1988. The number of subjects amounted .... 49; 11 different first languages were represented. The results are as follows:

Language	Number of informants	% judged impossible	Range (0–10)
Farsi	1	60	n/a
Korean	8	54	1–7
Turkish	2	45	3–6
Punjabi	1	40	n/a
Chinese (Mandarin?)	29	28	0–7
Japanese	2	25	2–3
Thai	2	10	0–2
Gujarati	1	10	n/a
Arabic	1	0	n/a
Hebrew	1	0	n/a
Portuguese	1	0	n/a

Discussion

These results need to be treated .... considerable caution. In only two cases were there more than two representatives of a particular language. Moreover, the extensive use of question marks and the wide range of responses .... a particular language group both suggest much uncertainty .... carrying out the task. A third problem is that responses .... individual sentences have not yet been analyzed. As the table shows, only overall scores are reported.

One surprise is the relatively low percentages .... Japanese; this finding apparently does not fit very well .... arguments raised .... Kojima and Kojima (1978). Indeed, the figures show that structure tested is less acceptable in the Korean language. As it happens, one Chinese-speaking student completed the task in both 1987 and in 1988; in 1987 she accepted all 10 structures as being possible in Chinese, whereas in 1988 she questioned two of them. The implications of this are obscure.

Figure 23 Inanimate subject and animate verb

The text is distributed, completed – and assimilated via whatever teacher intervention is needed. The class is then told that they are going to hear shortly an oral version of the research paper as if it were given at a departmental seminar or conference. They must assume that the instructor is an 'outside speaker' not known to them. They (as audience) are told that they are expected to take part in a formal discussion at the end of the paper. Preparation for the formal discussion then follows (Figure 24).

One important aspect of academic discussion is the making of suggestions – suggestions about further work, about a change of direction, or about doing something again differently. Among friends, in small groups, or in informal situations, the language used is often quite simple and straightforward:

How about checking it out in the library?
Why don't you do a statistical test?
(etc.)

However, academic suggestions in *formal settings*, especially to unknown people are more complicated. The message has to be *softened*. Suggesters want to appear impressed, helpful and sympathetic, but at the same time the messages may not be entirely welcome. As a result, many academic suggestions use *elaborate* forms of language. Below are some of the main sub-types.

a) *Yes–Buts*

Yes   While   I think what you're doing is very
      Even though   interesting . . .
                   I can appreciate the strength of
                      your arguments . . .
                   I'm sure your analysis is generally
                      on the right lines . . .

Buts   I'm not quite sure . . .
       I think it's also possible . . .
       I'm still a little unconvinced . . .

b) *I may be wrong–buts*

I may be wrong, but . . .
I may be mistaken, but . . .
Please correct me if I am wrong, but . . .
Please let me know if I have misunderstood your position,
   but . . .
I know this isn't really my area, but . . .
I'm not an expert in this, but . . .

c) *If I were you*

If I were you,	I might want to ...
If I were in your position,	I might try to ...
	I might ask myself
	whether ...
	I think I might be interested
	in seeing whether ...

d) *Polite questions*

Do you think there might be a case for ...?
Do you see any merit in the argument that ...?
Wouldn't you say that a possible alternative ...?
I wonder whether there isn't another possible
   explanation ...?
Wouldn't it also be possible ...?

Sometimes, of course, these elaborate suggestions are not
understood, or not responded to for other reasons. The most
common follow-up structures are:

Let me try and make myself clear ...
What I'm trying to say is ...
The point I'm trying to get across is ...
The point I'm trying to make is ...

Task   In groups, rehearse and prepare your suggestions for the
presenter of the 'inanimate Subject' research. You have 15 minutes.

Figure 24   Academic suggestions (spoken)

After the preparation time is over, a cassette or video recorder is turned
on, the instructor leaves the room momentarily and returns as the
visiting speaker. He or she provides an oral version of the results and
discussion and closes with some remarks like the following:

> As I made clear at the outset, I have today reported on a
> preliminary study. I'm therefore very interested in hearing your
> comments and suggestions.

My limited experience with this activity (two opportunities to date) has
been encouraging. On both occasions the atmosphere for the actual
presentation shifted dramatically to the formal. There was a strange
tenseness in the room as the students crouched on the edge of their seats
poised to make their formal comments. *They* had uncovered flaws in the
research; indeed, after the second occasion, one student wrote me a note
reiterating why I really ought to take her criticisms seriously.

Following review of the taped discussion, both for language and for content – which will give rise to further discussion – the instructor then turns affairs to what the *presenter* now might write in a concluding paragraph about future research. The key issue that the class needs to appreciate at this juncture is that the situation has changed, not so much in the switch to written medium, but in the *role* of the person making the suggestions. Presenters/writers are now in control of their own material and their own texts. While they need to acknowledge the limitations of the present study (in order to create further research space?) they equally need to avoid undermining it totally. Furthermore, they no longer need to engage in quite the tentativeness that characterized the oral discussion. These are now their *own* suggestions and can therefore be used to demonstrate, in a fairly straightforward way, their *new* awareness and acuity. Overall, a fairly subtle balancing act is required. The cycle ends, therefore, with the class, either individually or in small groups, completing the writer's task largely based on group and plenary discussion.

Exhibit B is more detailed than any of the others in the chapter. This has been partly due to the fact that the preparation phase is directly aimed at a non-native speaker clientele. In addition, however, Exhibit B has illustrated a relationship between *genre* and *task*. The genre skills are those of communicating afterthoughts – and thereby mitigating criticism – at the close of research papers. The activities are doubly differentiated between speech and writing and between self-criticism and criticism of others. They are sequenced in terms of the different roles students play, and yet those roles are more than token simulations, because of their cognitive involvement in both their native languages and in research design (areas where they are likely to command expertise). And in the end, the tasks are goal-directed in that they are designed to promote success in the final written outcome.

Exhibit C: Course descriptions

Exhibit C is somewhat different to the previous ones since it constitutes the first writing assignment from a writing intensive linguistics course ('Discourse and Discipline') designed for undergraduates in their third or fourth year (cf. Hamp-Lyons and McKenna, forthcoming). The course in fact uses as its main reading materials extracts from the writings of many of the people who have figured prominently in this book. The opening section is entitled 'Maps of the Territory' and uses material from Geertz, Becher and Bazerman among others. The second section is concerned with techniques of genre analysis itself, while the third presents a series of case studies – Knorr-Cetina, Dubois, Adams

Smith, Bazerman and so on. The final reading section contains three papers which discuss student writing experiences (McCarthy, Maimon, Herrington), and closes (deliberately) with the difficulties professors can experience in their endeavors to shape an acceptable written product (Myers).

The course description summarizes an orientation which by now will have become familiar:

> The aims of this course are: (1) to provide a structured opportunity for participants to reflect upon similarities and differences among the disciplinary and departmental cultures they have experienced; (2) to relate those experiences to the work of scholars who have examined such cultures from differing perspectives; (3) to investigate, via various techniques of discourse analysis, primary data in the university environment (textbooks, classes, course descriptions, faculty research and citational practices, assignments; and (4) to discuss findings in a range of written formats. Thus the course hopes to demonstrate the value of linguistics as an inter-disciplinary inquiry and to provide perceptions that will assist participants in becoming members of future discourse communities. There are no Linguistics prerequisites, and those from other concentrations are especially welcome. The course can be elected as certification for the Junior/Senior Writing Requirement.

Apart from Lenze (1988), a student in the course, the only people known to me who have referred in print to course descriptions from a discoursal viewpoint are Benson and Greaves (1980). They say:

> A reader consults the course description with the expectation that he will discover what he needs to know. He predicts that the field of discourse will be from a particular discipline, that the mode of discourse will be written to be read, that the personal tenor will be relatively formal, and that the function will be summary exposition.

(Benson and Greaves, 1980:45–6)

There is, I would suggest, something rather unfinished about this commentary, for it does not quite reach the real communicative purpose of the course description: course descriptions (CDs) surely exist not so much as summary expositions but as traffic control mechanisms designed to steer the right kinds of students in the right kinds of numbers towards certain courses and away from those that are inappropriate or over-populated. Course descriptions, at least in US contexts, nicely meet the criteria for genre status. They have a recognized role, allow a limited range of responses, possess a recognized name within the discourse community, invoke both formal and content schemata among the initiates, and have constraints on allowable elements in terms of their content, positioning and form. And, as Benson and Greaves observe, they have also been exposed to parody by no less a person than Woody Allen (Allen, 1973).

The class activity turns into a collaborative effort designed to throw light on a variety of questions, such as the following:

a) What are the processes whereby CDs get written? Are they written by individuals or by committee groups? Does the department play some editing role? Does the individual versus committee question tend to be answered differently in different areas (e.g. science and the humanities)? Does the kind of authorship seem to affect the textual product?

b) To what extent does a department's popularity (too many students, about right, not enough) affect the CDs? Will we expect to find more 'enticing' CDs from units who are anxious to recruit?

c) What differences can we expect to find between introductory and advanced courses, or between those without prerequisites and those with them, or among those emanating from the different divisions or faculties? And how can we account for any emerging differences?

d) What are the preferred uses of personal pronouns? Why are there preferences for *we* as opposed to *I* or *you*? How do students respond to such choices?

e) Is the primary orientation of the CD towards the *course* ('The aim of this course is to ... ') or towards the participants ('In this course we will be studying ... ')? How does this pattern vary – and why?

f) What about verb choices, such as active versus passive? What about lexical choices, as between verbs that describe the administration of the course and those that refer to content? Why is it that rhetorical questions are unlikely to occur in natural science CDs but may be quite common in the humanities? Why is it that chemistry CDs tend to be very short?

g) What can we discover about student-customer response to CDs? Under what circumstances does the discourse of a CD sufficiently attract or repel to affect a decision?

In my experience a class project such as the above has considerable merits – and there are useful alternatives like *assignments* and *examinations*. First, it provides a useful training ground for both textual and ethnographic analysis. Secondly, it can be sold as genuine research since we do not, in fact, have very good answers to the questions. Third, it draws genuinely and valuably upon the different disciplinary experiences of the participants. Fourth, the CD project can lead to collaborative discussion and collaborative writing: in 1988, two undergraduates presented the work of *all* the class, with suitable acknowledgements, at a conference later in the semester (Lenze and Naylor, 1988). Finally, and perhaps most importantly, it initiates a process whereby intelligent young people, often without any prior linguistic training, can be brought to see how linguistic and rhetorical decisions can affect the way even the most mundane texts are perceived and reacted to, and further, that those decisions and those reactions are already moderated by disciplinary experience and expectation.

11 *Epilogue*

Genre Analysis has depicted, despite its serious and abiding attention to the work of others, one individual's attempt to come to terms with a professional environment. In the narrowest sense, it represents my efforts to become a more informed and more alert, if not better, teacher of the English language to university students. More broadly, the book reflects a deep concern to upgrade the status of that teaching so that it can rightfully enjoy a settled and respected place in academic affairs. I know of course that many, perhaps most, of my colleagues in post-secondary ESL, Composition and Business and Technical Communication share that concern and are at least equally committed to defending their activities against the simplistic stigma of remediation. Even so, the tactics offered in this book are perhaps somewhat unusual. Throughout I have stressed the advantage of capturing and occupying the higher ground of advanced English. I have also assumed that if we are going to defend that ground successfully, one of the things we need to do is examine the terrain with as much care and continuing attention as our talents and resources permit. In our present partial and fragmented state of knowledge, teaching research English requires its own research agenda. Hence, the book also represents one individual's attempt to depict (as a basis for that agenda) what is in fact known, and to indicate via illustration of techniques and approaches how our understanding may be further broadened and deepened.

Even more widely, the book reflects a long-standing interest in helping those who need to develop further their communicative competence in academic English to achieve that goal. For many years, this clientele consisted largely of NNS undergraduates and beginning graduates. More recently it has expanded to include NS undergraduates and NNS doctoral students and post-doctoral researchers and academics. The cause of the former group already has, especially in the US, a number of powerful champions (Bizzell, 1986b; Brooke, 1987; Rose, 1988); I have, in the last decade, argued that the communicative difficulties of the latter deserve more attention.

The book itself has been arranged in four parts. Part I brought together the key players in the arena, the EAP and WAC practitioners, and tried to relate their activities to broader developments in such fields as composition, ESL and applied linguistics. Part II delineated a concerted effort to provide some intellectual justification for a genre-based approach by developing and inter-relating the three key concepts of discourse community, genre itself and language-learning task. Part III opened with a discussion of the current status of English as the main language of research and scholarship and of what it may be like to be a non-native speaker of English in that anglophone world. It then went on to describe and discuss present knowledge of English language research-process genres. Finally, Part IV has been concerned with ways and means of utilizing the theoretical and descriptive work for good pedagogical effect.

Despite a fairly impressive array of observational and anecdotal evidence, there remain of course several underlying questions about the validity of the genre-based approach. Only the most important of these will be considered in this Epilogue, and that is whether, to what extent and under what conditions skills acquired within one genre are transferable to another. Selinker and Douglas (forthcoming), in a paper dealing with contextual SLA research and Interlanguage (IL), suggest that such skills may transfer more easily across activity types (chatting, teaching, being interviewed) than across genres or 'discourse domains' (content-related verbal activities). They write:

> We also hypothesize that the problem of SLA is in large part the ability to transfer forms learned in one context to another i.e. success in internal-1L transfer. Furthermore we hypothesize that there will be 'harder' and 'softer' contextual boundaries, over which the learner will have a harder or easier time respectively transferring 1L forms. Our current conclusion is that knowledge/genre/domain contexts provide harder internal 1L boundaries than do various activity types.
>
> (Selinker and Douglas, forthcoming)

If this hypothesis should be verified on a broad scale, it would indeed undermine the approach presented here. It happens, however, there is one directly relevant piece of evidence about genre transfer contained in 9.1. We may recall the case of Hsin/Gene (Case study B), who was apparently able to transfer his newly acquired skill in academic letter-writing genres to job interviews and dissertation writing. Based on this case – and to some lesser extent on other cases and other experiences – it is possible to hypothesize that there can indeed be relatively *soft* boundaries between genres, but only under certain conditions. It is likely that those conditions are at least threefold:

1. All the communicative activity (in the different genres) is directed to the same discourse community or to discourse communities with overlapping characteristics.

2. The direction is from the more rhetorically-accessible (e.g. application letters) to the less rhetorically-accessible (e.g. job interviews).

3. The acquired genre skill involves not only competence with the product but also a raised rhetorical consciousness; in other words, there is a perceived rationale for the communicative behavior.

We can further note the essentially logical point (with which Selinker and Douglas would surely concur) that for transfer to take place at all there must be some higher competence to generalize. All transfer – indeed including heat transfer – travels downhill. There is independent value, therefore, in the small-scale rhetorical mastery effects that a genre approach is particularly and peculiarly able to foster. The conditions under which these gains can optimally be transferred to other contexts thus emerges, as Selinker and Douglas importantly note, as a highly significant investigative issue.

References

Adams Smith, Diana E. 1984. Medical discourse: aspects of author's comment. *The ESP Journal* 3:25–36.
  1987. Variation in field-related genres. *ELR Journal* 1:10–32.
Al-Shabbab, Omar S. 1986. Organizational and textual structuring of radio news discourse in English and Arabic. Unpublished Ph.D. dissertation, Aston University, Birmingham, U.K.
Allen, Woody. 1973. *Getting even*. New York: W. H. Allen.
Allwright, R. L., M-P Woodley and J. M. Allwright. 1988. Investigating reformulation as a practical strategy for the teaching of academic writing. *Applied Linguistics* 9:236–56.
Anderson, P. V., R. J. Brockman and C. R. Miller (eds.) 1983. *New essays in technical and scientific communication*. Farmingdale, NY: Baywood.
Ard, Josh. 1982. The semantics of tense and aspect in scientific discourse. Paper given at Ohio State University Conference on the Semantics of Tense and Aspect, May, 1982.
  1983. The role of the author in scientific discourse. Paper given at the annual American Applied Linguistics Meeting, Minneapolis, Minn, December, 1983.
  1985. Vantage points for the analysis of scientific discourse. *English for Specific Purposes* 4:3–20.
Armstrong, S. L., L. R. Gleitman and H. Gleitman. 1983. What some concepts might not be. *Cognition* 13:263–308.
Arrington, Phillip and Shirley K. Rose. 1987. Prologues to what is possible: introductions as metadiscourse. *College Composition and Communication* 38:306–18.
Arvanitis, Rigas and Yvon Chatelin. 1988. National scientific strategies in tropical soil sciences. *Social Studies of Science* 18:113–46.
Atkinson, J. M. and P. Drew. 1979. *Order in court: the organization of verbal behaviour in judicial settings*. London: Macmillan.
Atkinson, Max. 1982. Understanding formality: the categorization and production of formal interaction. *British Journal of Sociology* 33:86–117.
  1984. *Our masters' voices*. London: Methuen.
Bailey, K. M. 1984. A typology of teaching assistants. In Bailey, Pialorski and Zukowski/Faust (eds.): 110–25.
Bailey, K. M., F. Pialorski and J. Zukowski/Faust (eds.) 1984. *Foreign teaching assistants in U.S. universities*. Washington: National Association for Foreign Student Affairs.
Baldauf, Richard B. 1986. Linguistic constraints on participation in psychology. *The American Psychologist* 41:220–4.

Baldauf, R. B. and B. H. Jernudd. 1983a. Language of publications as a variable in scientific communication. *Australian Review of Applied Linguistics* 6:97–108.

1983b. Language use patterns in the fisheries periodical literature. *Scientometrics* 5:245–55.

1986. Aspects of language use in cross-cultural psychology. *Australian Journal of Psychology* 38:381–92.

Ballard, Brigid. 1984. Improving student writing: an integrated approach to cultural adjustment. In Williams, Swales and Kirkman (eds.): 43–54.

Ballard, Brigid and John Clanchy. 1984. *Study abroad – a manual for Asian students*. Kuala Lumpur: Longman.

Barber, C. L. 1962. Some measurable characteristics of modern scientific prose. In *Contributions to English syntax and phonology*: 1–23. Stockholm: Almquist & Wiksell.

Barthes, Roland. 1975. *The pleasure of the text*. (translated by R. Miller) New York: Hill.

Bartlett, F. C. 1932. *Remembering*. Cambridge: Cambridge University Press.

Bates, Martin. 1976. Writing 'Nucleus'. In Mackay and Mountford (eds.): 78–96.

Bavelas, Janet B. 1978. The social psychology of citations. *Canadian Psychological Review* 19:158–63.

Bazerman, Charles. 1980. Laboratory life: the social construction of scientific facts (review). *Social Studies of Science Newsletter* 5:14–19.

1981. What written knowledge does: three examples of academic discourse. *Philosophy of the Social Sciences* 11:361–82.

1983. Reporting the experiment: the changing account of scientific doings in the *Philosophical Transactions of the Royal Society, 1665–1800* (mimeo).

1984a. Modern evolution of the experimental report in physics: spectroscopic articles in *Physical Review, 1893–1980*. *Social Studies in Science* 14:163–96.

1984b. The writing of scientific non-fiction: contexts, choices, constraints. *PRE/TEXT* 5:39–74.

1985. Physicists reading physics: Schema-laden purposes and purpose-laden schema. *Written Communication* 2:3–24.

1987. Codifying the social scientific style: the APA publication manual as a behaviorist rhetoric. In Nelson, Megill and McCloskey (eds.): 125–44.

1989. *Shaping written knowledge*. Madison, Wis: The University of Wisconsin Press.

Beavais, Paul J. 1989. A speech act theory of metadiscourse. *Written Communication* 6:11–31.

Becher, Tony. 1981. Towards a definition of disciplinary cultures. *Studies in Higher Education* 6:109–22.

1987. Disciplinary discourse. *Studies in Higher Education* 12:261–74.

Becker, A. L. 1983. Correspondences: an essay on iconicity and philology (mimeo).

Becker, J. H. 1984. German-language psychological journals: an overview. *The German Journal of Psychology* 8:323–44.

Belanger, M. 1982. A preliminary analysis of the structure of the discussion sections in ten neuroscience journal articles (mimeo).

Ben-Amos, Dan. 1976. Introduction. In D. Ben-Amos, (ed.) *Folklore Genres*, ix–xv. Austin: University of Texas Press.

Benson, James D. and William S. Greaves. 1980. Field of discourse: theory and application. *Applied Linguistics* 1:45–55.

(eds.) 1985. *Systemic perspectives on discourse*, Vol. 1. Norwood, NJ: Ablex.

Berkenkotter, Carol, Thomas N. Huckin and John Ackerman. 1988. Conventions, conversations and the writer: case study of a student in a rhetoric Ph.D. program. *Research in the Teaching of English* 22:9–44.

Bhatia, V. K. 1983. *An applied discourse analysis of English legislative writing*. Birmingham, UK: The University of Aston Language Studies Unit.

1987. Language of the law. *Language Teaching* 20:227–34.

Bizzell, Patricia. 1982. Cognition, convention, and certainty: what we need to know about writing. *PRE/TEXT* 3:213–41.

1986a. Foundationalism and anti-foundationalism in composition studies. *PRE/TEXT* 7:37–58.

1986b. What happens when basic writers come to college? *College Composition and Communication* 37:294–301.

1987. Some uses of the concept of 'discourse community.' Paper presented at the Penn State Conference on Composition, July, 1987.

(forthcoming). What is a discourse community?

Blair, Catharine P. 1988. Only one of the voices: dialogic writing across the curriculum. *College English* 50:383–9.

Blanton, Linda L. 1984. Using a hierarchical model to teach academic reading to advanced ESL students: how to make a long story short. *English for Specific Purposes* 3:37–46.

Bley-Vroman, R. and L. Selinker. 1984. Research design in rhetorical/grammatical studies: a proposed optimal research strategy. *English for Specific Purposes* 82–83:1–4 and 84:1–6.

Blickenstaff, J. and M. J. Moravcsik. 1982. Scientific output in the third world. *Scientometrics* 4:135–69.

Bloomfield, L. 1933. *Language*. New York: Holt & Company.

Bloor, D. 1983. *Wittgenstein – a social theory of knowledge*. London: Macmillan.

Bloor, Meriel. 1984. English language needs in the University of Cordoba: the report of a survey. Birmingham, UK: The University of Aston Language Studies Unit (mimeo).

Braithwaite, Charles A. 1984. Towards a conceptualization of 'speech community'. In *Papers from the Minnesota Regional Conference on Language and Linguistics*: 13–29.

Bramki, Doudja and Ray Williams. 1984. Lexical familiarization in economics texts and its pedagogical implications in reading comprehension. *Reading in a Foreign Language* 2:169–81.

Breen, M. P. 1987. Learners' contributions to task design. In Candlin and Murphy (eds.): 23–46.

Bridwell-Bowles, Lillian. 1988. The politics of change in writing instruction: sources of the mandate. Paper presented at the College Composition and Communication Convention, St. Louis, Mo, March, 1988.

Brooke, Robert. 1987. Underlife and writing instruction. *College Composition and Communication*: 141–53.

Bruce, N. J. 1983. Rhetorical constraints on information structure in medical research report writing. Paper presented at the ESP in the Arab World Conference, University of Aston, UK, August, 1983.

Bruffee, K. A. 1986. Social construction, language, and the authority of knowledge: a bibliography. *College English* 48:773–90.

Byrne, A. 1983. How to lose a nation's literature: database coverage of Australian research. *Database* 6:10–17.

Campbell, Karlyn Kohrs and Kathleen Hall Jamieson. 1978. Form and genre in rhetorical criticism: an introduction. In Campbell and Jamieson (eds.): 9–32.

  (eds.) 1978. *Form and genre: shaping rhetorical action*. Falls Church, Va: The Speech Communication Association.

Candlin, C. N. 1981. Discoursal patterning and the equalizing of interpretive opportunity. In Smith (ed.): 166–99.

  1987. Towards task-based language learning. In Candlin and Murphy (eds.): 5–22.

Candlin, C. N., J. Bruton and J. M. Leather. 1976. Doctors in casualty: specialist course design from a database. *IRAL* 14:245–72.

Candlin, C. N. and D. F. Murphy (eds.) 1987. *Language-learning tasks*. Englewood Cliffs, NJ: Prentice-Hall International.

Carrell, Patricia L. 1983. Some issues in studying the role of schemata, or background knowledge, in second language comprehension. *Reading in a Foreign Language* 1:81–92.

  1987. Content and formal schemata in ESL reading. *TESOL Quarterly* 21:461–82.

Carrell, Patricia, Joanne Devine and David Eskey (eds.) 1988. *Interactive approaches to second language reading*. Cambridge: Cambridge University Press.

Carroll, John B. (ed.) 1956. *Language, thought and reality: selected writings of Benjamin Lee Whorf*. New York: John Wiley.

Celce-Murcia, Marianne and Diane Larsen-Freeman. 1983. *The grammar book: an ESL/EFL teaching course*. Rowley, Mass: Newbury House.

Chaudron, Craig. 1988. *Second language classrooms: research on teaching and learning*. Cambridge: Cambridge University Press.

Clark, H. H. and E. V. Clark. 1977. *Psychology and language*. New York: Harcourt Brace.

Clyne, Michael. 1987. Cultural differences in the organization of academic texts. *Journal of Pragmatics* 11:211–47.

Cohen, Andrew D. 1983. Reformulating compositions. *TESOL Newsletter* XVII(6):1–5.

Cole, P. and J. L. Morgan (eds.) 1975. *Syntax and semantics 3: speech and acts*. New York: Academic Press.

Coleman, Hywel. 1987. Little tasks make large returns: task-based language learning in large crowds. In Candlin and Murphy (eds.): 121–46.

  1988. Analysing language needs in large organizations. *English for Specific Purposes* 7:155–70.

Comrie, Bernard. 1985. *Tense*. Cambridge: Cambridge University Press.

Connor, Ulla and Robert B. Kaplan (eds.) 1987. *Writing across languages: analysis of L2 text*. Reading, Mass: Addison-Wesley.

Connor, Ulla and Ann M. Johns (eds.) 1990. *Coherence: research and pedagogical perspectives*. Washington, D.C.: TESOL.

Cooper, Catherine. 1985. Aspects of article introductions in IEEE publications. Unpublished M.Sc. dissertation, University of Aston, UK.

Cooper, C. A. and S. Greenbaum (eds.) 1986. *Studying writing: linguistic approaches*. Beverly Hills, Cal: Sage Publications.

Copeland, J. E. and P. W. Davis (eds.) *The Seventh LACUS FORUM 1980*: 249–57. Columbia, SC: Hornbeam.

Coulthard, M. (ed.). *Talking about text*. Birmingham, UK: English Language Research, Birmingham University.

Coupland, Nikolas. 1983. Patterns of encounter management. *Language in Society* 12:459–76.

1984. Aims and attitudes in teaching communication studies and English for specific purposes: the challenge of sociolinguistics. *ELT Documents* 117:9–14.

Couture, Barbara (ed.) 1986. *Functional approaches to writing: research perspectives*. Norwood, NJ: Ablex.

1986. Effective ideation in written text: a functional approach to clarity and exigence. In Couture (ed.): 69–92.

Cremmins, Edward T. 1982. *The art of abstracting*. Philadelphia: ISI Press.

Crismore, Avon and Rodney Farnsworth. 1988. Metadiscourse in popular and professional science discourse. Paper presented at The Society for Literature and Science Conference, Albany, NY, October, 1988.

Crombie, Winifred. 1985. *Discourse and language learning: a relational approach to syllabus design*. Oxford: Oxford University Press.

Cronin, Blaise. 1981. The need for a theory of citing. *Journal of Documentation* 37:16–24.

Crookes, Graham. 1986a. Towards a validated analysis of scientific text structure. *Applied Linguistics* 7:57–70.

1986b. Task classification: a cross-disciplinary review. Technical Report No. 4, Center for Second Language Classroom Research, University of Hawaii.

Cukor-Avila, Patricia and John Swales. 1989. Investigating the needs of research students: building case law. Paper presented at the TESOL Convention, San Antonio, March, 1989.

Danet, B., K. B. Hoffman, N. W. Kermish and W. J. Rafu. 1980. An ethnography of questioning in the courtroom. In Shuy and Shnukal (eds.): 222–34.

Darian, S. 1982. The role of definitions in scientific and technical writing: forms, functions and properties. In Hoedt et al. (eds.).

Das, B. K. (ed.) 1985. *Communicative language teaching*. Singapore: Singapore University Press.

(ed.) 1987. *Language education in human resource development*. Singapore: RELC.

Davies, Florence. 1988. Designing a writing syllabus in English for academic purposes: process and product. In Robinson (ed.).

Davis, G. B. and C. A. Parker. 1979. *Writing the doctoral dissertation: a systematic approach*. Baron's Educational Series.

Day, R. A. 1979. *How to write and publish a scientific paper*. Philadelphia: ISI Press.

de Bolivar, Adriana C. 1985. Interaction through written text: a discourse analysis of newspaper editorials. Unpublished Ph.D. dissertation, University of Birmingham, UK.

Devine, J., P. L. Carrell and D. E. Eskey (eds.) 1987. *Research in reading in English as a second language*. Washington D.C.: TESOL Publications.

Doheny-Farina, Stephen. 1986. Writing in an emerging organization: an ethnographic study. *Written Communication* 3:158–85.

Dones, Leigh. 1989. Gender assumptions: a study of the addressee (mimeo). The University of Michigan, Ann Arbor.

Douglas, Dan. 1977. *From school to university*. Khartoum, Sudan: Khartoum University Press.

Downes, William. 1984. *Language and society*. London: Fontana Paperbacks.

Dubois, B. L. 1980a. Genre and structure of biomedical speeches. *Forum Linguisticum* 5:140–69.

1980b. The use of slides in biomedical speeches. *English for Specific Purposes* 1:45–50.

1981a. The management of pity in biomedical speeches. In Copeland and Davis (eds.): 249–57.

1981b. Nontechnical arguments in biomedical speeches. *Perspectives in Biology and Medicine* 24:399–410.

1982a. The construction of noun phrases in biomedical journal articles. In Hoedt et al. (eds.): 49–67.

1982b. And the last slide please. Regulatory language function at biomedical meetings. *World Language English* 1:263–8.

1985. Popularization at the highest level. Poster sessions at biomedical meetings. *International Journal of the Sociology of Language* 56:67–85.

1986. From *New England Journal of Medicine* and *Journal of the American Medical Association* through the Associated Press to the local newspaper: scientific translation for the laity. In T. Bungarten (ed.) *Wissenschaftssprachen und Gesellschaft: Aspekte der Kommunikation und des Wissenstransfers in der heutigen Zeit*: 243–53. Hamburg: Akademion.

1987. Something on the order of around forty to forty-four: imprecise numerical expressions in biomedical slide talks. *Language in Society* 16:527–41.

1988. Citation in biomedical journal articles. *English for Specific Purposes* 7:181–94.

Dudley-Evans, Tony. 1984. A preliminary investigation of the writing of dissertation titles. In James (ed.): 40–6.

1986. Genre analysis: an investigation of the introduction and discussion sections of M.Sc. dissertations. In Coulthard (ed.).

(ed.) 1987. Genre analysis and E.S.P. *ELR Journal* 1.

Dudley-Evans, Tony and John Swales. 1980. Study modes and students from the Middle East. In Greenall and Price (eds.): 91–103.

Dundes, Alan. 1980. *Interpreting folklore*. Bloomington, IN: Indiana University Press.

Edge, Julian and Virginia Samuda. 1983. Methodials: the role and design of materials and method. In Richards (ed.): 50–67.

Een, John A. 1982. Tense usage in reporting research in geotechnical writing. In *Working papers in ESL(2)*: 72–91. Minneapolis: University of Minnesota.

Eggington, William A. 1987. Written academic discourse in Korean: implications for effective communication. In Connor and Kaplan (eds.): 153–68.

Elbow, Peter. 1988. Closing my eyes as I speak: an argument for ignoring audience. *College English* 49:50–69.

El-Hassan, S. A. 1977. Educated spoken Arabic and the Levant: a critical review of diglossia and related concepts. *Archivum Linguisticum* 8:112–32.

Ellis, Donald E. and William A. Donohue (eds.) 1986. *Contemporary issues in language and discourse processes*. Hillsdale, NJ: Lawrence Erlbaum.

Erickson, F. and J. Schultz. 1982. *The counselor as gatekeeper*. New York: Academic Press.

Essex-Lopresti, M. 1981. Why request reprints? *British Medical Journal* 283:790.

Ewer, J. R. 1979. *The modals in formal scientific discourse: function, meaning and use*. Santiago, Chile: Research Report, Department of English.

Fahnestock, Jeanne. 1986. Accommodating science: the rhetorical life of scientific facts. *Written Communication* 3:275–96.

Faigley, Lester. 1986. Competing theories of process: a critique and a proposal. *College English* 48:527–42.

Faigley, Lester and K. Hansen. 1985. Learning to write in the social sciences. *College Composition and Communication* 136:140–9.

Fennell, Barbara, Carl Herndl, and Carolyn Miller. 1987. Mapping discourse communities. Paper presented at the CCC Convention, Atlanta, Ga, March, 1987.

Fish, Stanley. 1980. *Is there a text in this class?* Harvard, Mass: Harvard University Press.

Fishman, Joshua (ed.) 1971. *Sociolinguistics: a brief introduction*. Rowley, Mass: Newbury House.

Flavell, J. and E. M. Markman (eds.) *Cognitive development* (Vol. III) of P. H. Mussen (gen. ed.) *Handbook of child psychology* (fourth edition). New York: John Wiley.

Flower, Linda. 1979. Writer-based prose: a cognitive basis for problems in writing. *College English* 41:19–37.

Flower, Linda and John R. Hayes. 1981. A cognitive theory of writing. *College Composition and Communication* 32:365–7.

Flowerdew, John. 1986. Cognitive style and specific-purpose course design. *English for Specific Purposes* 5:121–30.

Ford, Boris (ed.) 1983. *The new pelican guide to English literature*. Harmondsworth, UK: Penguin Books.

Foucault, Michel. 1972. *The archaeology of knowledge*. New York: Harper & Row.

Fowler, Alastair. 1982. *Kinds of literature*. Oxford: Oxford University Press.

Frankel, R. 1984. From sentence to sequence: understanding the medical encounter through microinteractional analysis. *Discourse Processes* 7:135–70.

Freed, Richard C. and Glenn J. Broadhead. 1987. Discourse communities, sacred texts, and institutional norms. *College Composition and Communication* 38:154–65.

Friedman, A., I. Pringle and J. Yalden (eds.) 1983. *Learning to write: first language/second language.* Harlow, UK: Longman.

Frow, John. 1980. Discourse genres. *The Journal of Literary Semantics* 9:73–9.

Fulwiler, T. and A. Young (eds.) (forthcoming). *Writing across the curriculum: programs, practices, problems.* Upper Montclair, NJ: Boynton/Cook.

Gardner, Roderick. 1984. Discourse analysis: implications for language teaching, with particular reference to casual conversation. *Language Teaching* 17:102–17.

Garfield, Eugene. 1978. The Science Citation Index as a quality information filter. In Warren (ed.): 68–77.

    1983. Talking science (review). *Nature* 303:354.

Geertz, Clifford. 1973. *The interpretation of cultures.* New York: Basic Books.

    1983. *Local knowledge: further essays in interpretive anthropology.* New York: Basic Books.

Gibbs, Graham. 1977. *Learning to study: a guide to running group sessions.* Milton Keynes, UK: The Open University.

Gilbert, G. Nigel. 1977. Referencing as persuasion. *Social Studies of Science* 7:113–22.

Gilbert, G. N. and M. Mulkay. 1984. *Opening Pandora's box: a sociological analysis of scientific discourse.* Cambridge: Cambridge University Press.

Goffman, Erving. 1981. *Forms of talk.* Oxford: Basil Blackwell.

Gopnik, Myrna. 1972. *Linguistic structures in scientific texts.* The Hague: Mouton.

Grabe, William. 1988a. Reassessing the term 'interactive'. In Carrell, Devine and Eskey (eds.): 56–70.

    1988b. English, information access and technology transfer: a rationale for English as an international language. *World Englishes* 7:63–72.

Graetz, Naomi. 1985. Teaching EFL students to extract structural information from abstracts. In Ulijn and Pugh (eds.): 123–35.

Greenall, G. M. and J. E. Price (eds.) 1980. *ELT Documents 109.* London: The British Council.

Gregory, Michael. 1967. Aspects of varieties of differentiation. *Journal of Linguistics* 3:177–98.

Gregory, M. and S. Carroll. 1978. *Language and situation: language varieties and their social contexts.* London: Routledge & Kegan Paul.

Grice, H. P. 1975. Logic and conversation. In Cole and Morgan (eds.): 41–58.

Grimes, J. E. 1975. *The thread of discourse.* The Hague: Mouton.

Gumperz, John J. 1962. Types of linguistic communities. *Anthropological Linguistics* 4:28–40.

Halfpenny, Peter. 1988. Talking of talking, writing of writing: some reflections on Gilbert and Mulkay's *Discourse Analysis* (review). *Social Studies of Science* 18:169–82.

Halliday, M. A. K. 1978. *Language as a social semiotic.* London: Edward Arnold.

Halliday, M. A. K. and R. Hasan. 1976. *Cohesion in English.* London: Longman.

Halliday, M. A. K., A. McIntosh and P. D. Strevens. 1964. *The linguistic sciences and language teaching*. London: Longman.

Halstead, Beverly. 1988. The thesis that won't go away. *Nature* 331:497–8.

Hamp-Lyons, Liz. 1986. No new lamps for old yet, please. *TESOL Quarterly* 20:790–6.

Hamp-Lyons, Liz and Eleanor McKenna. (forthcoming). Ten years of writing across the curriculum at The University of Michigan. In Fulwiler and Young (eds.).

Harris, Joseph. 1989. The idea of community in the study of writing. *College Composition and Communication* 40:11–22.

Hawkes, Terence. 1977. *Structuralism and semiotics*. Los Angeles: University of California Press.

Hawkey, R. and C. Nakornchai. 1980. Thai students studying. In Greenall and Price (eds.): 70–8.

Hepburn, Ronald. 1983. Literature and the recent study of language. In Ford (ed.): Vol. 8, 494–508.

Hepworth, G. R. 1979. Rhetorical competence and EST discourse. In Yorio et al. (eds.): 148–59.

Herrington, Anne. 1985. Writing in academic settings: a study of the context for writing in two college chemical engineering courses. *Research in the Teaching of English* 19:331–61.

   1989. The first twenty years of *Research in the Teaching of English* and the growth of a research community in composition studies. *Research in the Teaching of English* 23:117–38.

Herzberg, Bruce. 1986. The politics of discourse communities. Paper presented at the CCC Convention, New Orleans, La, March, 1986.

Heslot, J. 1982. Tense and other indexical markers in the typology of scientific texts in English. In Hoedt et al. (eds.): 83–103.

Hewings, Ann and Willie Henderson. 1987. A link between genre and schemata: a case study of economics text. *ELR Journal* 1:156–75.

Hill, S. S., B. F. Soppelsa, and G. K. West. 1982. Teaching ESL students to read and write experimental research papers. *TESOL Quarterly* 16:333–47.

Himley, Margaret. 1986. Genre as generative: one perspective on one child's early learning growth. In Nystrand (ed.): 137–58.

Hinds, John. 1987. Reader versus writer responsibility: a new typology. In Connor and Kaplan (eds.): 141–52.

Hoedt, J. et al. (eds.) 1982. *Pragmatics and LSP*. Copenhagen: Copenhagen School of Economics.

Hoey, Michael. 1979. *Signalling in discourse*. Birmingham University, UK: ELR Monographs No. 6.

   1983. *On the surface of discourse*. London: George Allen & Unwin.

Holes, Clive. 1984. Textual approximation in the teaching of academic writing to Arab students: a contrastive approach. In Swales and Mustafa (eds.): 228–42.

Holliday, Adrian. 1984. Research into classroom culture as necessary input into syllabus design. In Swales and Mustafa (eds.): 29–51.

Holliday, Adrian and Terence Cooke. 1982. An ecological approach to ESP. In Waters (ed.): 123–43.

Holmes, Janet. 1988. Doubt and certainty in ESL textbooks. *Applied Linguistics* 9:29–44.

Hopkins, A. 1985. An investigation into the organizing and organizational features of published conference papers. Unpublished M.A. dissertation, University of Birmingham, UK.

Hopkins, Andy and Tony Dudley-Evans. 1988. A genre-based investigation of the discussion sections in articles and dissertations. *English for Specific Purposes* 7:113–22.

Horowitz, Daniel M. 1986a. What professors actually require: academic tasks for the ESL classroom. *TESOL Quarterly* 20:445–62.

  1986b. Process not product: less than meets the eye. *TESOL Quarterly* 20:141–4.

Houghton, D. 1980. Writing problems of Iranian students. In Greenall and Price (eds.): 79–90.

Houghton, D. and M. Hoey. 1983. Linguistics and written discourse: contrastive rhetoric. In Kaplan (ed.) ARAL III:2–22.

Huckin, Thomas N. 1986. Prescriptive linguistics and plain English: the case of 'whiz-deletions.' *Visible Language* 20:174–87.

  1987. Surprise value in scientific discourse. Paper presented at the CCC Convention, Atlanta, Ga, March, 1987.

  1988. 4C's proposals and what they tell us about field. Paper presented at the CCC Convention, St. Louis, Mo, March, 1988.

Huckin, Thomas N. and Leslie A. Olsen. 1983. *English for science and technology: a handbook for non-native speakers.* New York: McGraw-Hill.

  1984. On the use of informants in LSP discourse analysis. In Ulijn and Pugh (eds.): 120–9.

Huddleston, R. D. 1971. *The sentence in written English.* Cambridge: Cambridge University Press.

Hudson, Liam. 1967. *Contrary imaginations.* Harmondsworth, UK: Penguin.

Hudson, R. A. 1980. *Sociolinguistics.* Cambridge: Cambridge University Press.

Hutchins, John. 1977. On the structure of scientific texts. In *UEA Papers in Linguistics* 5:18–39. Norwich, UK: University of East Anglia.

Hutchinson, Tom and Alan Waters. 1987. *English for specific purposes: a learning-centered approach.* Cambridge: Cambridge University Press.

Hyltenstam, K. and M. Pieneman (eds.) 1985. *Modelling and assessing second language acquisition.* London: Multilingual Matters.

Hymes, Dell. 1974. *Foundations in sociolinguistics: an ethnographic approach.* Philadelphia: University of Pennsylvania Press.

Inman, M. 1978. Lexical analysis of scientific and technical prose. In Trimble, Trimble and Drobnic (eds.): 242–56.

Jablin, F. M. and K. Krone. 1984. Characteristics of rejection letters and their effects on job applicants. *Written Communication* 1:387–406.

Jacoby, Sally. 1986. The inevitable forked tongue: an analysis of references to other researchers in literary research articles. Unpublished M.A. thesis, The University of Birmingham, UK.

  1987. References to other researchers in literary research articles. *ELR Journal* 1:33–78.

James, G. (ed.) 1984. *The ESP Classroom*. Exeter, UK: Exeter Linguistic Studies.

James, Kenneth. 1980. Seminar overview. In Greenall and Price (eds.): 7–21.

1984a. The writing of theses by speakers of English as a foreign language: the results of a case study. In Williams et al. (eds.): 99–113.

1984b. Mr. Sulaiman, the buttoning of cauliflowers and how I learnt to love the abstract. In James (ed.): 58–66.

Jamieson, Kathleen M. 1975. Antecedent genre as rhetorical constraint. *Quarterly Journal of Speech* 61:406–15.

Jarvis, Jennifer. 1983. An ESP teacher's guide to functional analyses. *The ESP Journal* 2:101–12.

Jernudd, B. H. and R. B. Baldauf, Jr. 1987. Planning science communication for human resource development. In Das (ed.): 144–89.

Johns, Ann M. 1986. Coherence and academic writing: some definitions and suggestions for teaching. *TESOL Quarterly* 20:247–65.

1988a. The discourse communities dilemma: identifying transferable skills for the academic milieu. *English for Specific Purposes* 7:55–60.

1988b. ESP and the future: less innocence abroad. In Tickoo (ed.): 21–6.

1988c. Another reader reacts ... *TESOL Quarterly* 22:705–7.

1990. Coherence as a cultural phenomenon: employing ethnographic principles in the academic milieu. In Connor and Johns (eds.): 209–26.

Johns, T. F. and A. Dudley-Evans. 1980. An experiment in team-teaching of overseas postgraduate students of transportation and plant biology. In Greenall and Price (eds.): 6–23.

Johnson, R. K. (ed.) 1989. *The second language curriculum*. Cambridge: Cambridge University Press.

Jones, Priscilla. 1982. A stylistic analysis of minutes and its implications in preparing a business English course. M.Sc. Dissertation, The University of Aston, Birmingham, UK.

Kageyama, M., K. Nakamura, T. Oshima and T. Uchida (eds.) 1981. *Science and scientists*. Tokyo: Japan Scientific Societies Press.

Kamil, M. L. and A. J. Moe (eds.) 1979. *Reading research: studies and applications*. Clemson, SC: National Reading Conference.

Kaplan, R. B. 1966. Cultural thought patterns in intercultural education. *Language Learning* 16:1–20.

1987. Cultural thought patterns revisited. In Connor and Kaplan (eds.): 9–22.

Kaplan, R. B. and S. Ostler. 1982. Contrastive rhetoric revisited. Paper read at the 1982 TESOL Convention, Honolulu, Hawaii.

Katz, J. J. and J. A. Fodor. 1963. The structure of a semantic theory. *Language* 39:170–210.

Kinay, A. N., L. P. Muloshi, M. R. Musakabantu and J. M. Swales. 1983. Pre-announcing results in article introductions (mimeo). Birmingham, UK: The University of Aston, Language Studies Unit.

Kinneavy, James L. 1971. *A theory of discourse: the aims of discourse*. Englewood Cliffs, NJ: Prentice-Hall International.

Knorr-Cetina, K. D. 1981. *The manufacture of knowledge*. Oxford: Pergamon.

Kojima, S. and K. Kojima. 1978. S(inanimate subject) + V + O – a syntactical problem in EST writing for Japanese. In Trimble, Trimble and Drobnic (eds.): 198–226.

Kress, Gunther. 1982. *Learning to write.* London: Routledge & Kegan Paul.

Kuhn, Thomas S. 1970. *The structure of scientific revolutions* (second edition). Chicago: University of Chicago Press.

Kumaravadivelu, B. 1988. Designing materials for task-based approaches: some theoretical and practical issues. Paper presented at the annual RELC Seminar, Singapore, April, 1988.

Labov, William. 1966. *The social stratification of English in New York City.* Washington, D.C.: Center for Applied Linguistics.

Lackstrom, J. 1978. Teaching modals in EST discourse. In Trimble, Trimble and Drobnic (eds.): 53–73.

Lackstrom, J., L. Selinker and L. Trimble. 1972. Grammar and technical English. *English Teaching Forum* X(5):3–14.

1973. Technical rhetorical principles and grammatical choice. *TESOL Quarterly* 7:127–36.

Lakoff, G. 1972. Hedges: a study in meaning criteria and the logic of fuzzy concepts. In *Papers from the Eighth Regional Meeting, Chicago Linguistic Society*, 183–228.

Latour, Bruno and Stephen Woolgar. 1979. *Laboratory life: the social construction of scientific facts.* Beverly Hills, Cal: Sage Publications.

Lauffer, A. 1983. *Grantsmanship.* Newbury Park, Cal: Sage Publications.

Lemke, J. L. 1985. Ideology, intertextuality, and the notion of register. In Benson and Greaves (eds.): Vol. 1, 275–94.

Lenze, James. 1988. Course descriptions across the disciplines. *Papers in Applied Linguistics – Michigan* 3(2):53–72.

Lenze, James and Kelly Naylor. 1988. Towards a typology of course descriptions. Paper presented at the Second Annual Conference on Pragmatics and Language Learning, Urbana-Champaign, Ill, April, 1988.

Levinson, S. C. 1979. Activity types and language. *Linguistics* 17:356–99.

1983. *Pragmatics.* Cambridge: Cambridge University Press.

Lewin, R. A. and D. K. Jordan. 1981. The predominance of English and the potential use of Esperanto for abstracts of scientific articles. In Kageyama, Nakamura, Oshima and Uchida (eds.): 433–41.

Locke, L., F. W. Wyrick Spirduso and S. J. Silverman. 1987. *Proposals that work* (second edition). Newbury Park, Cal: Sage Publications.

Lodge, D. 1981. *Working with structuralism.* Boston: Routledge & Kegan Paul.

Long, M. H. 1985. A role for instruction in second language acquisition: task-based language learning. In Hyltenstam and Pieneman (eds.): 77–99.

Longacre, Robert E. 1983. *The grammar of discourse.* New York: Plenum.

Lopez, G. S. 1982. Article Introductions in Spanish: a study in comparative rhetoric. Unpublished Master's Thesis, Aston University.

Lury, C. 1982. An ethnography of an ethnography: reading sociology. Occasional Paper No. 9. Manchester, UK: Department of Sociology.

McCarthy, Lucille P. 1987. A stranger in strange lands: a college student writing across the curriculum. *Research in the Teaching of English* 21:233–65.

MacDonald, D. 1960. *Parodies.* London: Faber & Faber.

MacKay, R. and A. Mountford (eds.) 1976. *English for Specific Purposes.* London: Methuen.

McKenna, Eleanor. 1987. Preparing foreign students to enter discourse communities in the US. *English for Specific Purposes* 6:187–202.

McKinlay, K. 1984. An analysis of discussion sections in medical journal articles. Unpublished M.A. dissertation, University of Birmingham, UK.

McQuade, D. A. (ed.) 1986. *The territory of language.* Carbondale: Southern Illinois University Press.

Madsen, D. 1982. *Successful dissertations and theses: a guide to graduate student research from proposals to completion.* San Francisco: Josey-Bass.

Maher, John. 1986a. English for medical purposes. *Language Teaching* 19:112–45.

1986b. The development of English as the international language of medicine. *Applied Linguistics* 7:206–18.

Maimon, Elaine P. 1986. Knowledge, acknowledgement, and writing across the curriculum: toward an educated community. In McQuade (ed.): 89–102.

Malcolm, Lois. 1987. What rules govern tense usage in scientific articles? *English for Specific Purposes* 6:31–44.

Malinowski, Bronislaw. 1960. *A scientific theory of culture and other essays* (second edition). New York: Oxford University Press.

Marshall, Hazel. 1987. Quantity surveying reports. In Dudley-Evans (ed.): 117–55.

Martin, J. R. 1985. Process and text: two aspects of human semiosis. In Benson and Greaves (eds.): 248–74.

Martin, James R. and Joan Rothery. 1986. What a functional approach to the writing task can show teachers about 'good writing'. In Couture (ed.): 241–65.

Merton, R. K. 1968. The Matthew Effect in Science. *Science* 159:56–63.

1973. *The sociology of science.* Chicago: University of Chicago Press.

Mervis, C. B. and E. Rosch. 1981. Categorization of natural objects. *Annual Review*, Psychology 32:89–115.

Meyer, Bonnie J. F. 1975. *The organization of prose and its effects on recall.* New York: North Holland.

1979. Organizational patterns in prose and their use in reading. In Kamil and Moe (eds.): 109–17.

Miller, Carolyn R. 1984. Genre as social action. *Quarterly Journal of Speech* 70:151–67.

Mohan, Bernard A. and Winnie A-Y Lo. 1985. Academic writing and Chinese students: transfer and development factors. *TESOL Quarterly* 19:515–34.

Moravcsik, M. J. 1985. *Strengthening the coverage of third world science.* Eugene, OR: Institute of Theoretical Science.

Mulkay, Michael. 1985. *The word and the world: explorations in the form of sociological analysis.* London: George Allen & Unwin.

Murphy, Herta A. and Herbert W. Hildebrandt. 1984. *Effective business communications* (fourth edition). New York: McGraw-Hill.

Murray, D. 1982. *Learning by teaching.* Montclair, NJ: Boynton/Cook.

Myers, Greg. 1985a. Texts as knowledge claims: the social construction of two biology articles. *Social Studies of Science* 15:593–630.

1985b. The social construction of two biologists' proposals. *Written Communication* 2:219–45.

1989. The pragmatics of politeness in scientific articles. *Applied Linguistics* 10:1–35.

(forthcoming). The social construction of popular science: the narrative of science and the narrative of nature.

Najjar, Hazem Y. 1988. The research article in English and Arabic (mimeo).

1989. Scientific Arabic: The agricultural research article. Unpublished Ph.D. dissertation, The University of Michigan, Ann Arbor.

Neale, Stephen. 1980. *Genre.* London: British Film Institute.

Nelson, J. S., A. Megill and D. N. McCloskey (eds.) 1987. *The rhetoric of the human sciences.* Madison, Wis: Wisconsin University Press.

Nelson, Katherine and Leslie Gruendel. 1979. At morning it's lunchtime: a scriptal view of children's dialogues. *Discourse Processes* 2:73–94.

North, Stephen M. 1986. Writing in a philosophy class: three case studies. *Research in the Teaching of English* 20:225–62.

Nystrand, Martin. 1986. *The structure of written communication – studies in reciprocity between writers and readers.* Orlando, FL: Academic Press, Inc.

O'Connor, M. and F. P. Woodford. 1976. *Writing scientific papers in English.* Amsterdam: North-Holland.

Onuigbo, W. I. B. 1982. Printer's devil and reprint requests. *Journal of the American Society for Information Sciences* 33:58–9.

1984. The utilization of request-a-print. *Social Studies of Science* 14:94–6.

1985. Reprint requests – a tool for documentation. *International Forum on Information and Documentation* 10:7–9.

Oring, Elliott. 1986. Folk narratives. In E. Oring (ed.), *Folk groups and folklore genres*, 121–46. Logan: Utah State University Press.

Osbiston, R. (ed.) 1987. *Communication for the public sector for southern Africa.* Lusaka, Zambia: NIPA.

Osman, Neile. 1959. *Situational English.* London: Longman.

Oster, Sandra. 1981. The use of tenses in reporting past literature. In Selinker, Tarone and Hanzeli (eds.): 76–90.

Ostler, Shirley E. 1987. English in parallels: a comparison of English and Arabic prose. In Connor and Kaplan (eds.): 169–85.

Owen, M. L. 1981. Conversation units and the use of 'well' ... In Werth (ed.): 99–116.

Painter, Claire. 1986. The role of interaction in learning to speak and learning to write. In Painter and Martin (eds.): 62–97.

Painter, C. and J. R. Martin (eds.) 1986. *Writing to mean: teaching genres across the curriculum.* ALAA Occasional Papers 9.

Peck MacDonald, Susan. 1987. Problem definition in academic writing. *College English* 49:315–31.

Peng, Jingfu. 1987. Organizational features in chemical engineering research articles. *ELR Journal* 1:79–116.

Perelman, Chaim and L. Olbrechts-Tyteca. 1969. *The new rhetoric: a treatise on argumentation.* Notre Dame, IN: Notre Dame University Press.

Perrin, M. (ed.) 1985. *Pratique d'aujourd'hui et besoins de demain*. Bordeaux: Université de Bordeaux II.

Peters, Douglas P. and Stephen J. Ceci. 1982. Peer-review practices of psychological journals: the fate of published articles, submitted again. *The Behavioral and Brain Sciences* 5:187–255.

Pettinari, C. 1982. The function of a governmental alternative in fourteen surgical reports. *Applied Linguistics* 4:55–76.

Piaget, Jean. 1962. *Language and thought of the child* (third edition). Atlantic Highlands, NJ: Humanities Press.

Popken, Randall L. 1987. A study of topic sentence use in academic writing. *Written Communication* 4:209–28.

Porter, James E. 1988. The problem of defining discourse communities. Paper presented at the CCC Convention, St. Louis, March, 1988.

Potter, Jonathan and Margaret Wetherell. 1987. *Discourse and social psychology*. London: Sage Publications.

Poulsen, D., E. Kintsch, W. Kintsch and D. Premack. 1979. Children's comprehension and memory for stories. *Journal of Experimental Child Psychology* 28:379–403.

Prabhu, N. S. 1985. Communicative teaching: communicative in what sense? In Das (ed.): 32–40.

Preston, Dennis R. 1986. The fifty some-odd categories of language variation. *International Journal of the Sociology of Language* 57:9–47.
    1989. *Sociolinguistics and second language acquisition*. Oxford: Basil Blackwell.

Prince, G. 1982. *Narratology: the form and function of narrative*. Berlin: Mouton.

Psathos, G. (ed.) 1979. *Everyday language: studies in ethnomethodology*. New York: Irvington.

Quirk, R. and H. G. Widdowson (eds.) 1985. *English in the world*. Cambridge: Cambridge University Press.

Rabkin, Y. M. and H. Inhaber, 1979. Science on the periphery: a citation study of three less developed countries. *Scientometrics* 1:261–74.

Raimes, Ann. 1983. Tradition and revolution in ESL teaching. *TESOL Quarterly* 17:535–52.

Ramani, Esther, Thomas Chacko, S. J. Singh and Eric H. Glendinning. 1988. An ethnographic approach to syllabus design: a case study of the Indian Institute of Science, Bangalore. *English for Specific Purposes* 7:81–90.

Ravetz, J. R. 1971. *Scientific knowledge and social problems*. Oxford: Oxford University Press.

Reid, W. Malcolm. 1978. Will the future generations of biologists write a dissertation? *Bioscience* 28:651–4.

Relman, Arnold S. 1978. Are journals really quality filters? In Warren (ed.): 54–60.

Richards, E. (ed.) 1983. *Concepts and functions in current syllabuses*. Singapore: RELC.

Richards, J. C. and R. W. Schmidt (eds.) 1983. *Language and communication*. Harlow, UK: Longman.

Richards, Rebecca T. 1988. Thesis/dissertation writing for ESL students: an ESP course design. *English for Specific Purposes* 7:171–80.

Robertson, F. 1985. Teaching radiotelephony to pilots. In Perrin (ed.): 295–314.

1988. *Airspeak: radiotelephony communication for pilots.* New York: Prentice-Hall.

Robinson, P. (ed.) 1988. *Academic writing: process and product.* London: MEP.

Ronald, Kate. 1988. On the outside looking in: students' analyses of professional discourse communities. *Rhetoric Review* 7:130–49.

Rorty, Richard. 1979. *Philosophy and the mirror of nature.* Princeton, NJ: Princeton University Press.

Rosch, E. 1975. Cognitive representations of semantic categories. *Journal of Experimental Psychology (General)* 104:192–233.

1978. Principles of categorization. In Rosch and Lloyd (eds.): 27–48.

Rosch E. and B. Lloyd (eds.) 1978. *Cognition and categorization.* Hillsdale, NJ: Lawrence Erlbaum.

Rose, Mike. 1988. Narrowing the mind and page: remedial writers and cognitive reductionism. *College Composition and Communication* 39:267–302.

Rounds, P. L. 1982. Hedging in written academic discourse: precision and flexibility (mimeo). Ann Arbor: The University of Michigan.

1987. Multifunctional personal pronoun use in the educational setting. *English for Specific Purposes* 6:13–29.

Rutherford, William and Michael Sharwood Smith (eds.) 1988. *Grammar and second language teaching.* New York: Newbury House.

Sacks, H., E. A. Schegloff and G. Jefferson. 1974. A simplest systematics for the organization of turn-taking in conversation. *Language* 50:696–735.

Salager, F. 1983. The lexis of fundamental medical English: classificatory framework and rhetorical function (a statistical approach). *Reading in a Foreign Language* 1:54–64.

Samuda, Virginia and Carolyn Madden. 1985. Task-based test design: testing as a reflection of classroom methodology. *Papers in Applied Linguistics Michigan* 1:84–94.

Sanford, Anthony J. and Simon C. Garrod. 1981. *Understanding written language.* Chichester, UK: John Wiley & Sons.

Sarig, Gissi. 1987. High-level reading in the first and in the foreign language: some comparative process data. In Devine, Carrell and Eskey (eds.): 105–120.

Saville-Troike, Muriel. 1982. *The ethnography of communication.* Oxford: Basil Blackwell.

Scarcella, Robin. 1984. How writers orient their readers in expository essays: a comparative study of native and non-native English writers. *TESOL Quarterly* 18:671–88.

Schank, R. and R. Abelson. 1977. *Scripts, plans, goals and understanding.* Hillsdale, NJ: Lawrence Erlbaum.

Schauber, Ellen and Ellen Spolsky. 1986. *The bounds of interpretation.* Stanford, Cal: Stanford University Press.

Schegloff, E. A. 1979. Identification and recognition in telephone conversation openings. In Psathos (ed.): 23–78.

Schiffren, D. (ed.) 1984. *Meaning, form and use in context: linguistics applications.* Washington, D.C.: Georgetown University Press.

Scotton, Carol Myers and Janice Bernsten. 1988. Natural conversations as a model for textbook dialogue. *Applied Linguistics* 9:372–84.

Searle, J. R. 1969. *Speech acts: an essay in the philosophy of language.* Cambridge: Cambridge University Press.

Selinker, Larry. 1979. On the use of informants in discourse analysis and language for specialized purposes. *IRAL* 17:189–215.

Selinker, Larry and Dan Douglas. (forthcoming). Research methodology in contextually-based second language research. *Second Language Research* 5:1–34.

Selinker, Larry, B. Kumaravadivelu and D. Miller. 1985. Second language composition teaching and research: towards a 'safe-rule' perspective. *Papers in Applied Linguistics Michigan* 1(1):53–83.

Selinker, L., E. Tarone and V. Hanzeli (eds.) 1981. *English for academic and technical purposes: studies in honor of Louis Trimble.* Rowley, Mass: Newburg House.

Selinker, L., R. M. Todd Trimble and L. Trimble. 1976. Presuppositional rhetorical information in EST discourse. *TESOL Quarterly* 10:281–90.

Shapin, Steven. 1984. Pump and circumstance: Robert Boyle's literary technology. *Social Studies of Science* 14:481–520.

Shatz, Marilyn. 1983. Communication. In Flavell and Markman (eds.): 841–89.

    1984. A song without music and other stories: how cognitive process constraints influence children's oral and written narrative. In Schiffren (ed.): 313–24.

Shih, M. 1986. Content-based approaches to teaching academic writing. *TESOL Quarterly* 20:617–48.

Shuy, R. and A. Shnukal (eds.) 1980. *Language use and the uses of language.* Washington D.C.: Georgetown University Press.

Skelton, John. 1988. The care and maintenance of hedges. *ELTJ* 42:37–44.

Smith, E. E. and D. L. Medin. 1981. *Categories and concepts.* Cambridge, Mass: Harvard University Press.

Smith, Edward L. 1982. Writer–reader interactiveness in four genres of scientific English. Unpublished Ph.D. dissertation, The University of Michigan, Ann Arbor.

Smith, L. E. (ed.) 1984. *English for cross-cultural communication.* London: Macmillan.

Smith, Louise Z. 1988. Why English departments should 'house' writing across the curriculum. *College English* 50:390–5.

Smith, Raoul. 1982. A statistical syntactic study of four English genres. Ph.D. dissertation, The University of Michigan, Ann Arbor.

Spack, Ruth. 1984. Invention strategies and the ESL college composition student. *TESOL Quarterly* 18:649–70.

    1988a. Initiating ESL students into the academic discourse community: how far should we go? *TESOL Quarterly* 22:29–52.

    1988b. The author responds to Braine ... *TESOL Quarterly* 22:703–5.

Spolsky, Bernard. 1966. A psycholinguistic critique of programmed foreign language instruction. *IRAL* 4: 119–29.

St John, Maggie Jo. 1987. Writing processes of Spanish scientists publishing in English. *English for Specific Purposes* 6:113–20.

Stanley, R. M. 1984. The recognition of macrostructure: a pilot study. *Reading in a Foreign Language* 2:156–68.
Sternberg, David. 1981. *How to complete and survive a dissertation*. New York: St Martin's Press.
Strevens, Peter. 1988. ESP after twenty years: a re-appraisal. In Tickoo (ed.): 1–13.
Swaffar, J. K., K. Arens and M. Morgan. 1982. Teacher classroom practices: refining method as task hierarchy. *Modern Language Journal* 66:24–33.
Swales, John. 1980. The educational environment and its relevance to ESP programme design. *ELT documents special – projects in materials design*: 61–70.
    1981a. Definitions in science and law: a case for subject-specific ESP materials. *Fachsprache* 81(3):106–12.
    1981b. *Aspects of article introductions*. Birmingham, UK: The University of Aston, Language Studies Unit.
    1984a. A review of ESP in the Arab world 1977–1983 – trends, developments and retrenchments. In Swales and Mustafa (eds.): 9–20.
    1984b. Research into the structure of introductions to journal articles and its application to the teaching of academic writing. In Williams, Swales and Kirkman (eds.): 77–86.
    1985a. *Episodes in ESP*. Hemel Hempstead, UK: Prentice-Hall International.
    1985b. English language papers and authors' first language: preliminary explorations. *Scientometrics* 8:91–101.
    1985c. ESP – the heart of the matter or the end of the affair? In Quirk and Widdowson (eds.): 212–23.
    1986a. A genre-based approach to language across the curriculum. In Tickoo (ed.): 10–22.
    1986b. ESP in the big world of reprint requests. *English for Specific Purposes* 5:81–5.
    1987a. Communication in the public sector: a discourse community approach to skills. In Osbiston (ed.): 4–15.
    1987b. Utilizing the literatures in teaching the research paper. *TESOL Quarterly* 21:41–67.
    1988a. Language and scientific communication: the case of the reprint request. *Scientometrics* 13:93–101.
    1988b. 20 years of the *TESOL Quarterly*. *TESOL Quarterly* 22:151–63.
    1989. Service English course design and opportunity cost. In Johnson (ed.): 79–90.
    1990. Non-native speaker graduate engineering students and their introductions: global coherence and local management. In Connor and Johns (eds.): 187–207.
Swales, J. and H. Mustafa (eds.) 1984. *English for specific purposes in the Arab world*. Birmingham, UK: The University of Aston.
Swales, John and Hazem Najjar. 1987. The writing of research article introductions. *Written Communication* 4:175–92.
Swan, M. and C. Walter. 1982. The use of sensory deprivation in foreign language teaching. *ELTJ* 36:183–5.
Tadros, A. 1985. *Prediction in text*. Birmingham, UK: The University of Birmingham, English Language Research.

Tarone, E., S. Dwyer, S. Gillette and V. Icke. 1981. On the use of the passive in two astrophysics journal papers. *The ESP Journal* 1:123–40.

Thomas, J. A. 1983. Cross-cultural pragmatic failure. *Applied Linguistics* 4:91–112.

1984. Cross-cultural discourse as unequal encounter: towards a pragmatic analysis. *Applied Linguistics* 5:226–35.

Throgmartin, C. 1980. Which language for students in social sciences? A survey to help academic advisors. *Anthropological Newsletter* 21:6.

Tickoo, M. L. (ed.) 1986. *Language across the curriculum*. Singapore: RELC.

(ed.) 1988. *ESP – state of the art*. Singapore: RELC.

Tinberg, R. Jon. 1988. The pH of a volatile genre. *English for Specific Purposes* 7:205–12.

Todorov, Tzvetan. 1976. The origin of genres. *New Literary History* 8:159–70.

Tomlin, R. S. 1981. Clause-level syntax and information types in EST discourse (mimeo).

Toulmin, Stephen. 1972. *Human understanding: the collective use and evolution of concepts*. Princeton, NJ: Princeton University Press.

Trimble, M. T. and L. Trimble. 1982. Rhetorical-grammatical features of scientific and technical texts as a major factor in written ESP communication. In Hoedt et al. (eds.): 199–216.

Trimble, Mary Todd, Louis Trimble and Karl Drobnic (eds.) 1978. *English for specific purposes: science and technology*. Corvallis: Oregon State University.

Ulijn, J. M. and A. K. Pugh (eds.) 1985. *Reading for professional purposes*. Leuven, Belgium: ACCO.

Van Dijk, T. A. 1972. *Some aspects of text grammars*. The Hague: Mouton.

1977. *Text and context*. London: Longman.

1980. *Macrostructures*. Hillsdale, NJ: Lawrence Erlbaum.

1986. News Schemata. In Cooper and Greenbaum (eds.): 155–86.

Vande Kopple, W. J. 1985. Some exploratory discourse on metadiscourse. *College Composition and Communication* 36:82–93.

Velho, L. and J. Krige. 1984. Publication and citation practices of Brazilian agricultural scientists. *Social Studies of Science* 14:45–62.

Ventola, Eija. 1983. Contrasting schematic structures in service encounters. *Applied Linguistics* 4:242–58.

1984. Orientation to social semiotics in foreign language teaching. *Applied Linguistics* 5:275–86.

Vygotsky, L. A. 1962. *Thought and language*. (translated by E. Haufmann and G. Vakov) Cambridge, Mass: M.I.T. Press.

Warren, Kenneth S. (ed.) 1978. *Coping with the biomedical literature explosion: a qualitative approach*. New York: Rockefeller Foundation.

Warren, Kenneth S. and William Goffmann. 1978. Analysis of a medical literature: a case study. In Warren (ed.): 31–53.

Warren, K. S. and V. S. Newill. 1967. *Schistosomiasis: bibliography of the world's literature from 1852 to 1962*. Cleveland, OH: The Press of Case Western Reserve University.

Waters, A. (ed.) 1982. *Issues in ESP*. Oxford: Pergamon.

Watson, James D. 1968. *The double helix*. London: Weidenfeld & Nicolson.

254   *References*

Weissberg, Robert. 1984. Given and new: paragraph development models for scientific English. *TESOL Quarterly* 18:485–500.

Werth, P. (ed.) 1981. *Conversation and discourse*. London: Croom Helm.

West, G. K. 1980. That-nominal constructions in traditional rhetorical divisions of scientific research papers. *TESOL Quarterly* 14:483–9.

Widdowson, H. G. 1979. *Explorations in applied linguistics*. Oxford: Oxford University Press.

   1981. Criteria for course design. In Selinker, Tarone and Hanzeli (eds.): 1–11.

   1983a. *Learning purpose and language use*. Oxford: Oxford University Press.

   1983b. New starts and different kinds of failure. In Friedman, Pringle and Yalden (eds.): 34–47.

   1984. *Explorations in applied linguistics* 2. Oxford: Oxford University Press.

Wilkins, David. 1973. Grammatical, situational and national syllabuses. *ELT Documents* 73(6):2–8.

Williams, J. M. 1985. *Style: ten lessons in clarity and grace*. Glenview, Ill: Scott, Foresman.

Williams, Marion. 1988. Language taught for meetings and language used in meetings: is there anything in common? *Applied Linguistics* 9:45–58.

Williams, Ray, John Swales and John Kirkman (eds.) 1984. *Common ground: shared interests in ESP and communication studies*. Oxford: Pergamon.

Wingard, P. 1981. Some verb forms and functions in six medical texts. In Selinker, Tarone and Hanzeli (eds.): 53–64.

Winter, Eugene. 1986. Clause relations as information structure: two basic text structures in English. In Coulthard (ed.): 88–108.

Wittgenstein, Ludwig. 1958. *Philosophical investigations*. Oxford: Basil Blackwell.

Wood, A. S. 1982. An examination of the rhetorical structures of authentic chemistry texts. *Applied Linguistics* 3:121–43.

Wood, D. N. 1967. The foreign-language problem facing scientists and technologists in the United Kingdom – report of a recent survey. *Journal of Documentation* 23:117–30.

Yin, Robert E. 1984. *Case study research: design and methods*. Beverly Hills, Cal: Sage Publications.

Yorio, C. et al. (eds.) 1979. *On TESOL '79*. Washington, D.C.: TESOL.

Young, Art and Toby Fulwiler (eds.) 1986. *Writing across the disciplines: research into practice*. Upper Montclair, NJ: Boynton/Cook.

Zamel, Vivian. 1983. The composing processes of advanced ESL students: six case studies. *TESOL Quarterly* 17:165–87.

Zappen, J. P. 1983. A rhetoric for research in sciences and technologies. In Anderson, Brockman and Miller (eds.): 123–38.

Ziman, J. M. 1968. *Public knowledge*. Cambridge: Cambridge University Press.

Zuck, Joyce G. and Louis V. Zuck. 1984. Scripts: an example from newspaper texts. *Reading in a Foreign Language* 2:147–55.

Zumrawi, Fatma. 1984. Using the specialized educational informant – some implications for course design and content. *ESPMENA Bulletin* 18:7–13.

Index

Author index

Abelson, R., 84
Ackerman, J., 161–3
Adams Smith, D., 3, 131, 133, 136, 137, 140, 228–9
Al-Shabbab, O., 63
Allen, W., 230
Allwright, J. and R., 220–1
Ard, J., 110, 114, 128–9, 131, 151, 154
Arens, K., 73
Armstrong, S., 49, 51, 52
Arrington, P., 137
Arvanitis, R., 97, 98, 99, 100–1, 108
Atkinson, J., 46
Atkinson, M., 47, 58

Bailey, K., 219
Baldauf, R., 10, 78, 96–7, 98, 99, 100, 102–3, 104–6
Ballard, B., 66
Barber, C., 2, 115, 130, 137
Barthes, R., 112
Bartlett, F., 83
Bates, M., 107
Bavelas, J., 7
Bazerman, C., 5, 14–15, 18, 93, 95, 107, 110–11, 112–13, 114–16, 123, 133, 151, 173–4, 175, 179, 181–2, 222, 228, 229
Beavais, P., 206
Becher, T., 5, 28, 228
Becker, A., 86
Becker, J., 99
Belanger, M., 132, 171–2
Ben-Amos, D., 34
Benson, J., 40, 229, 230
Berkenkotter, C., 8, 30, 161–3
Bernsten, J., 13
Bhatia, V., 1, 3, 63, 130

Bizzell, P., 4 , 9, 25, 27, 29–30, 32, 162, 232
Blair, C., 6, 69
Blanton, L., 213
Bley-Vroman, R., 128–9, 140
Blickenstaff, J., 95
Bloomfield, L., 23
Bloor, D., 51
Bloor, M., 179, 194
Braithwaite, C., 23
Bramki, D., 188
Breen, M., 74, 75
Bridwell-Bowles, L., 69
Broadhead, G., 23
Brooke, R., 232
Bruce, N., 15, 132, 133, 167–8
Bruffee, K., 21
Bruton, J., 54
Byrne, A., 97

Campbell, K., 43
Candlin, C., 17, 54, 59, 74–6
Carrell, P., 83, 85, 87–8, 89
Carroll, J., 29, 40
Ceci, S., 103
Celce-Murcia, M., 153
Chatelin, Y., 97, 98, 99, 100–1, 108
Chaudron, C., 13, 72
Clanchy, J., 66
Clark, E. and H., 51
Clyne, M., 65
Cohen, A., 220
Coleman, H., 74
Comrie, B., 153
Connor, U., 64
Cooke, T., 69
Cooper, C., 132, 140, 148, 158, 161
Coupland, N., 11, 17
Couture, B., 41

Cremmins, E., 179
Crismore, A., 188
Crombie, W., 18, 174
Cronin, B., 7
Crookes, G., 73, 75, 128, 132, 140,
    158, 172
Cukor-Avila, P., 10

Danet, B., 46
Darian, S., 131, 137
Davies, F., 220
Davis, G., 188
Day, R., 179
de Bolivar, A., 3
Devine, J., 83
Doheny-Farina, S., 7
Dones, L., 196
Donohue, W., 128
Douglas, D., 8, 233, 234
Downes, W., 64
Drew, P., 46
Dubois, B., 62, 125–6, 131, 133, 167,
    168, 182–6, 228
Dudley-Evans, T., 3, 8, 17, 66, 76, 132,
    158, 172–3, 188, 223
Dundes, A., 34
Dwyer, S., 3, 129, 131, 135

Edge, J., 74
Een, J., 131, 151, 153, 154
Eggington, W., 66–7
El-Hassan, S., 104
Elbows, P., 63
Ellis, D., 128
Erickson, F., 54
Eskey, D., 83
Essex-Lopresti, M., 193
Ewer, J., 131

Fahnestock, J., 126, 127, 174
Faigley, L., 4, 21
Farnsworth, R., 188
Fennell, B., 22
Fish, S., 21
Fishman, J., 23
Flower, L., 4, 64
Flowerdew, J., 14
Fodor, J., 49, 50
Foucault, M., 21
Fowler, A., 37–8
Frankel, R., 54
Freed, R., 23
Frow, J., 40

Fulwiler, T., 4

Gardner, R., 58
Garfield, E., 95, 97
Garrod, S., 83, 85
Geertz, C., 4, 19, 21, 35, 207, 228
Gibbs, G., 216
Gilbert, G., 7, 48, 118, 123–5, 129,
    166, 168
Gillette, S., 3, 129, 131, 133, 135
Gleitman, H. and L., 49, 51, 52
Goffman, E., 62, 99
Goffmann, W., 58
Gopnik, M., 181
Grabe, W., 86, 100
Graetz, N., 179–81
Greaves, W., 40, 229, 230
Gregory, M., 40, 62
Grice, H., 58
Grimes, J., 61
Gruendel, L., 90
Gumperz, J., 18

Halfpenny, P., 124
Halliday, M., 2, 5, 18, 40, 168
Halstead, B., 71, 187–8, 216
Hamp-Lyons, L., 220, 228
Hansen, K., 4
Hanzeli, V., 129
Harris, J., 32
Hasan, R., 5
Hawkes, T., 38
Hawkey, R., 66
Hayes, J., 4
Henderson, W., 89
Hepburn, R., 37
Hepworth, G., 132
Herndl, C., 22
Herrington, A., 5, 8, 28, 31–2, 229
Herzberg, B., 21–2, 29
Heslot, J., 3, 131, 133, 135, 137, 180
Hewings, A., 89
Hildebrandt, H., 53
Hill, S., 131, 133, 134, 137, 172, 213
Himley, M., 92
Hinds, J., 66
Hoey, M. 18, 65, 89, 119
Hoffman, K., 46
Holes, C., 66
Holliday, A., 66, 69
Holmes, J., 70
Hopkins, A., 3, 132, 158, 172–3, 188
Horowitz, D., 31, 47, 218, 220

Houghton, D., 65, 66
Huckin, T., 8, 15, 30, 31, 70, 116,
    129–30, 133, 161–3, 169, 172–3,
    179, 181, 187
Huddleston, R., 2, 115, 130, 136
Hudson, L., 14
Hudson, R., 23
Hutchins, J., 133, 222
Hutchinson, T., 72, 73, 74, 75, 108
Hymes, D., 18, 23, 38, 39

Icke, V., 3, 129, 131, 133, 135
Inhaber, H., 101
Inman, M., 131

Jablin, F., 70–1
Jacoby, S., 131, 133, 140, 148–50, 151
James, G., 181
James, K., 31, 65, 66, 206, 223
Jamieson, K., 42–3
Jarvis, J., 130
Jefferson, G., 60
Jernudd, B., 10, 96, 98, 99, 100,
    102–3, 104–6
Johns, A., 8, 12, 30, 76, 215–6, 218
Johns, T., 76
Jones, P., 54
Jordan, D., 103

Kaplan, R., 64, 65
Katz, J., 49, 50
Kermish, N., 46
Kinay, A., 132
Kinneavy, J., 42, 133
Knorr-Cetina, K., 11, 95, 118–21,
    123–4, 136, 166, 228
Kojima, K. and S., 160, 225
Kress, G., 91
Krige, J., 101
Krone, K., 70–1
Kuhn, T., 21, 31
Kumaravadivelu, B., 75, 82, 153

Labov, W., 23
Lackstrom, J., 131, 133, 151, 152
Lakoff, G., 112
Larsen-Freeman, D., 153
Latour, B., 118, 122–3, 125, 158
Lauffer, A., 186
Leather, J., 54
Lemke, J., 91
Lenze, J., 229, 230
Levinson, S., 38, 45, 58

Lewin, R., 103
Lo, W., 66
Locke, L., 186, 187
Lodge, D., 50
Long, M., 74, 75
Longacre, R., 61
Lopez, G., 140
Lury, C., 125

McCarthy, L., 8, 229
MacDonald, D., 47
McIntosh, A., 2
McKenna, E., 32, 219, 229
McKinlay, K., 132, 172
Madden, C., 74, 75
Madsen, D., 188
Maher, J., 1, 96, 100
Maimon, E., 79, 229
Malcolm, L., 131, 151, 153–4, 180
Malinowski, B., 35
Marshall, H., 89
Martin, J., 17, 26, 40, 41, 46, 53, 91
Medin, D., 51
Merton, R., 178
Mervis, C., 51
Meyer, B., 87
Miller, C., 18, 22, 43, 44, 46, 47
Mohan, B., 66
Moravcsik, M., 95, 97
Morgan, M., 73
Mulkay, M., 48, 118, 123–5, 129, 166,
    168
Murphy, H., 53
Murray, D., 127
Myers, G., 5, 94, 117, 120, 126, 127,
    168, 174, 229

Najjar, H., 25, 65, 70, 97, 99, 101,
    104, 105, 132, 144, 145, 161, 165,
    166
Nakornchai, C., 66
Naylor, K., 230
Neale, S., 34
Nelson, K., 90
Newill, V., 98–9
North, S., 8
Nystrand, M., 62, 88–9

O'Connor, M., 179
Olbrechts-Tyteca, L., 21
Olsen, L., 129–30, 187
Onuigbo, W., 189, 190
Oring, E., 35

Osman, N., 16
Oster, S., 132, 133, 151, 152–3
Ostler, S., 64–5
Owen, M., 60

Painter, C., 90–1
Parker, C., 188
Peck MacDonald, S., 5
Peng, J., 132, 172
Perelman, C., 21
Peters, D., 103
Pettinari, C., 130
Piaget, J., 90
Popken, R., 131
Porter, J., 21, 22
Potter, J., 128
Poulsen, D., 90
Prabhu, N., 75
Preston, D., 33, 39, 58, 64
Prince, G., 61

Rabkin, Y., 101
Rafu, W., 46
Raimes, A., 220
Ramani, E., 217
Ravetz, J., 7
Reid, W., 187, 216
Relman, A., 94
Richards, J., 58, 60
Richards, R., 187
Robertson, F., 60
Ronald, K., 215, 218
Rorty, R., 21
Rosch, E., 51–2
Rose, M., 232
Rose, S., 137
Rothery, J., 41, 91
Rounds, P., 181, 219
Rutherford, W., 213

Sacks, H., 60
Salager, F., 130
Samuda, V., 74, 75
Sanford, A., 83, 85
Sarig, G., 14
Saville-Troike, M., 23, 39–40, 64
Scarcella, R., 157
Schank, R., 84
Schauber, E., 38
Schegloff, E., 18, 60
Schmidt, R., 58, 60
Schultz, J., 54
Scotton, C., 13

Searle, J., 47
Selinker, L., 72, 128–9, 130, 131, 133, 140, 151, 152, 153, 233, 234
Shapin, S., 11, 112, 175
Sharwood Smith, M., 213
Shatz, M., 90
Shih, M., 76
Skelton, J., 222
Smith, E., 175
Smith, E. E., 51
Smith, L. E., 6
Soppelsa, B., 131, 133, 134, 137, 172, 213
Spack, R., 215, 220
Spolsky, B., 16, 38
St John, M., 102
Stanley, R., 89, 131, 133
Sternberg, D., 188
Strevens, P., 2
Swaffar, J., 73
Swales, J., 6, 7, 10, 12–13, 18, 57, 66, 69, 70, 72, 89, 100, 107, 116, 127, 132, 137, 140, 144, 145, 147, 148, 151, 152, 157, 159, 161, 165, 166, 189, 190, 213, 217
Swan, M., 48

Tadros, A., 148, 188
Tarone, E., 3, 129, 131, 133, 135
Thomas, J., 85
Throgmartin, C., 98
Tinberg, R., 9, 131
Todorov, T., 36, 38
Tomlin, R., 131, 167
Toulmin, S., 138, 140
Trimble, L., 131, 132, 133, 151, 152
Trimble, M., 132, 151

Van Dijk, T., 15, 61, 85, 179
Vande Kopple, W., 188
Velho, L., 101
Ventola, E., 17, 40
Vygotsky, L. A., 51, 90

Walter, C., 48
Warren, K., 98–9
Waters, A., 72, 73, 74, 75, 108
Watson, J., 174
Weissberg, R., 131, 133, 168, 172
West, G., 131, 133–5, 137, 169, 172, 213, 217
Wetherell, M., 128

Widdowson, H., 3, 14, 16, 62–3, 65, 83–5, 130, 175, 220
Wilkins, D., 16
Williams, J., 188, 206
Williams, M., 69, 70
Williams, R., 188
Wingard, P., 131, 137
Winter, E., 133
Wittgenstein, L., 21, 49–50, 51, 216
Wood, A., 132, 133
Wood, D., 96
Woodley, M-P., 220–1

Woodford, F., 179
Woolgar, S., 118, 122–3, 125, 158

Yin, R., 203
Young, A., 4

Zamel, V., 220
Zappen, J., 132, 138–40, 142
Ziman, J., 94
Zuck, J., 84, 89
Zuck, L., 84, 89
Zumrawi, F., 130

Subject index

abstracts, 178, 179–82, 210–12
academic counseling, 54
academic correspondence, 77–82, 209
agentives, 120, 167

business communication, 4, 11, 232

case studies, 203–13
citations and references, 6, 7, 114–15, 116, 148–51
classes
  adjunct, 76
  as discourse communities, 32
  discourse analysis, 218–20, 228–31
  dissertation writing, 12, 77, 204, 208
  engineering, 31–2
cohesion and coherence, 168, 169
communicative event, 45–6
communicative purpose, 10, 46–8, 53, 185
competence
  native-speaker, 10, 11
  non-native speaker, 10
composition, 2, 5, 232
connectives, 154
course descriptions, 228–31

deictics, 159–60
disciplinary discourse, 5, 181, 230
discourse analysis, 18, 71–2, 174
discourse community
  and speech community, 23–4
  and student ethnographers, 217–20
  and world view, 29–31
  as cluster of ideas, 21–2
  as owner of genres, 9
  defining characteristics, 24–7

  as sociorhetorical network, 9
  illustrated, 27–9
dissertations, 178, 187–9, 216

English
  business, 69–70
  journalistic, 3, 63
  legal, 1, 3, 63
  medical, 1, 3, 17, 53–4, 136
  scientific, 2, 3, 182–6
ethnography, 7, 38, 68–9, 217–18, 230

family resemblance, 49–50
further research,
  language of, 226–7

genre
  acquisition of, 83, 90–2, 233–4
  and communicative purpose, 46–8, 53
  and discourse community, 26
  and parody, 47–9
  and schemata, 86–9, 214
  and task, 228
  and text-role, 6
  as communicative event, 9, 45–6
  defined, 58
  in dictionaries, 33
  in folklore studies, 34–6
  in linguistics, 38–42
  in literary studies, 36–8
  in rhetoric, 42–4
  nomenclatures, 39–40, 54–8
  shifts, 126
  variation, 49, 52, 61–4
grant proposals, 178, 186–7

groups,
  sociolinguistic, 24
  sociorhetorical, 24
  special interest, 24

hedges, 112, 119, 174, 175, 181, 211

knowledge claims, 117

lexis, 115, 155, 179, 185, 197, 200

metadiscourse, 188–9, 206
modals, 136
move analysis, 140–8, 154–66,
  171–4, 181, 183, 195

negation, 155–6, 179–80
noun phrases, 167, 175

parody, 47–9
pedagogical illustrations, 77–82,
  107–9, 213–14, 216–17, 222–7
personal pronouns, 4, 135, 137, 179,
  219
pre-genres
  conversation, 58–60
  narrative, 61
problem–solution analysis, 138–40
prose
  reader-based, 62–3
  writer-based, 63–4
prototype
  texts, 49
  analysis, 51–2

radiotelephony, 60
reading strategies, 13–15
reformulations, 220–1
register, 2, 3, 40, 41–2
remediation, 2
repertoires, 123–4
reporting verbs, 115, 150, 151,
  152–3, 224–5
reprint requests
  language choice in, 193–4
  structure, 196–201
research article, 10, 11, 15
  and non-native speakers, 102–6
  and related genres, 99–102
  and Third World, 99–102
  annual production, 93
  composing process, 117–27
  history, 110–17

macrostructure, 133–4
methods of analysis, 128–30
role of English in, 96–102
research article sections
  introductions, 118–19, 137–66, 175
  methods, 120–1, 133, 137, 166–70,
    175–6
  results and discussions, 121, 133,
    170–4, 175
research presentations, 178, 182–6
rhetoric
  as subject, 3, 5, 42–4
  contrastive, 64–7
rhetorical consciousness, 213–15

schemata
  content, 10, 83, 86–7
  formal, 10, 84–5, 87–9, 213–14
service encounters, 17
science popularizations, 125–7
specialist informants, 129–30, 140, 172–3
speech community, 23–4
speech event, 38–9
student ethnographers, 30, 218–20
syllabus
  skills, 13
  situational, 16
  notional, 16, 17–18

task
  and language-learning approach, 82
  and methodology, 72–3
  and text-processing, 9
  and pedagogy, 77, 222–8
  definitions of, 73–6
technical communication, 3, 4, 11, 232
team-teaching, 8, 76
tense, 119, 120, 135, 151, 153–4,
  160–1, 179, 180–1
text typology, 39
that-nominals, 133–5
titles, 222–4

validation of teaching materials, 13,
  69–71
voice, 4, 133, 167, 179

writing across the curriculum, 2, 4–6,
  11, 215
writing process
  cognitive models, 4
  social models, 21–2
  'soft' and 'hard', 220–1